ON THE FRONT COVER

The Cleveland Indians were in the midst of their championship run in the summer of 1948 when the aerial view
of Cleveland's lakefront west of the E. Ninth Street pier was taken.

PUBLISHED BY:

INSTANT CONCEPTS, INC.
CLEVELAND OFFICE
440 Beeler Dr.
Berea, OH 44017
•
Columbus
4856 Sawmill Rd. #341
Columbus, OH 43235

(440)-891-1964 • FAX (440)-826-1920

NATIONWIDE: 1-800-644-7769

e-mail: calendar@infinet.com

•

First Printing • November, 1997
Second Edition, First Printing • May, 1998
Third Edition • February, 1999

Electronic Pre-Press:
Camelot Typesetting
Cleveland, Ohio

ISBN 1882171-21-7

About the Editor

George E. Cormack is a 1971 graduate of Berea High School in Berea, Ohio and a 1977 graduate of Ohio State University. Mr. Cormack is a member of the Western Reserve Historical Society, the Berea Historical Society and the Society for American Baseball Research.

About Municipal Stadium- Memories on the Lakefront

Sources used for verifying information in this publication include The Cleveland Press; The Cleveland Plain Dealer; The Cleveland Leader; The Cleveland News; Sports Illustrated; The New York Times; The Cleveland Press Collection at Cleveland State University; The Columbus Dispatch; Total Baseball, 2nd edition; The Baseball Encyclopedia, 8th edition; The Football Encyclopedia; "Cleveland-The Making of a City" by William Ganson Rose; and "The Encyclopedia of Cleveland History" by Van Tassel and Grabowski. The Cleveland Press Collection at Cleveland State University is the source for all photographs found in this edition.

Every attempt has been made to ensure the accuracy of the information found in this publication. Unfortunately, we regret that errors and omissions do occur. Should you have any questions about the material or information contained within, or have information or photographs that can be used in further editions, please do not hesitate to call our office.

About Instant Concepts, Inc.

Instant Concepts, Inc. is a historical research and marketing company specializing in the publication of historical products including books and calendars. Instant Concepts has published collector edition History of Cleveland and Cleveland Sports History calendars since 1993. Back issues of these publications can be obtained by contacting the publisher.

Instant Concepts actively collects historical information and photographs on regional, national and international events and personalities. Instant Concepts also maintains an ever-growing electronic database of over 12,000 historical entries.

MUNICIPAL STADIUM

(Above) Gate E / November 1, 1965

Memories on the Lakefront

A 50-YEAR PICTORIAL HISTORY
1931 TO 1981

Featuring over 420 images from the Cleveland Press Collection.

VOLUME 1

My first memories of Municipal Stadium date back to the late 1950's and early 1960's when my father and I sat among the thousands who came to watch the Mickey Mantle-led New York Yankees play the Cleveland Indians with players like Vic Power, Woody Held, Jim Perry, Tito Francona, Herb Score, Mudcat Grant, Sam McDowell and Jimmy Piersall in the starting lineup. I remember too, watching the Indians battle their American League opponents on Little League and Safety Patrol days, banging our seats with anticipation as Rocky Colavito came up to bat. Today I wish I still had the bats I "earned" on Bat Days or had gotten more autographs. I also wish I could say "I was there," more than I can. I feel truly privileged however, to have been among the thousands of Browns backers who watched Jim Brown, Leroy Kelly, Bill Nelsen, Bernie Kosar and Lou "The Toe" Groza star among the best at the Stadium. I missed seeing the Beatles, Pink Floyd and the Rolling Stones, but I can say I saw the Beach Boys and experienced the Rock and Roll Hall of Fame concert, Municipal Stadium's last rock hurrah. I can also say that I was among the over 70,000 who watched the Indians and the New York Yankees battle in the last Stadium home opener.

I dedicate this book to everyone who has a Municipal Stadium story to tell and hope the photographs and stories inside allow these memories to be shared with their friends and families.

My thanks goes out to the many people who have made this unique publication possible including William Becker, University Archivist, Cleveland State University, who has been an immense help in putting this project together; Tom Poole, Bryan Rapp, Rick Colby, Joe Mengel, Marilyn & Paul Wieber, my mother, and the thousands of wonderful folks who have shared their personal recollections with me throughout the years. I look forward to hearing many more of these wonderful stories in the future!

Sincerely,

George Cormack
Editor
Municipal Stadium- Memories on the Lakefront

A special dedication: This book is also dedicated to Jeff Farmer, a friend of many years who recently passed away at age 43. Jeff helped me get my first major job, which in turn, helped me cover my tuition at Ohio State. He will be missed.

Table of Contents

(About the Above Photograph)

The photograph of Chief Wahoo with the upcoming Cleveland Indians schedule appeared in The Cleveland Press on Tuesday, July 20, 1954. The newspaper caption beneath the photograph began, "Seems Like Old Times," referring to the Monday, July 26th date with St. Louis. For years, Cleveland competed against the St. Louis Browns for the American League title. However, after the 1953 season, Browns owner Bill Veeck, Jr. sold the St. Louis franchise to an investor group that moved the team to Baltimore, beginning play in 1954 as the Baltimore Orioles. The July 26th date was actually promoting an exhibition match between the Cleveland Indians, who were leading the American League, and the National League St. Louis Cardinals, not the Browns. The Cardinals-Indians game was scheduled to be the featured attraction of the annual Cleveland Baseball Federation Amateur Day program. St. Louis beat the Indians, 2-1, before 33,375 at the Stadium. In the Class A contest, the J. Schrader Co. beat Telco Tool, Inc., 3-1, as southpaw Bill Bonness (10-2), got the win over Telco starter George Newman. The event raised $34,000 for the CBF.

Opening the City's New Municipal Stadium

Respected Cleveland Press sports columnist Franklin Lewis wrote in his Saturday, September 18, 1943 column, "It was just twenty years ago today that a wiry, ambitious prospecting newcomer named Floyd A. Rowe walked into the office of Mayor Fred Kohler and told him the city ought to have a fine athletic plant along the Lakefront where then was a dump against which Lake Erie lapped cadaverously." Lewis went on to explain that Rowe, as the new director of physical welfare for the Cleveland public schools in 1923,was trying to stimulate interest in a downtown stadium of

20,000 to 25,000 seats for use by local high school football teams. Lewis wrote, "There was a shortage of gridirons so acute that Glenville High School, the district's top eleven, didn't have a field on which it could play West." Though talk of a downtown facility had actually surfaced in November of 1917, it wasn't until local businessman Alva Bradley purchased the city's major league baseball franchise, the Cleveland Indians, from the estate of Chicagoan James C. Dunn in November of 1927, that discussions began to move the baseball team from aging League Park at E. 66th and

Breaking Ground
June 24, 1930

On June 24 1930, four days before the city's massive new Union Terminal complex on Public Square was dedicated, ground was broken for the city's new stadium on the lakefront. The photographs above show the first dirt being moved by the "giant steam scoop" operated by W. J. Stark of the Fifth City Excavation Company. The steam scoop was one of two placed at the excavation site to begin moving dirt at the bottom of W. 3rd Street. When asked why work was beginning on the long delayed project without fanfare, City Manager Daniel E. Morgan responded unceremoniously, "why celebrate?" Morgan stated that the administration thought it made more sense to hold a public ceremony when the cornerstone was laid and not hold up the project while the grading and excavation work was getting underway. The $29,000 project was expected to take sixty days. The following week, bids were received for $1 million in steel and foundation work. Nearly 4,600 tons of structural steel was used to complete the Stadium infrastructure, about a quarter of the steel used to erect the Terminal Tower Building on Public Square. Five hundred tons of reinforcing steel, 3,300,000 bricks, 130,000 pounds of aluminum sheets, 70 miles of electrical wiring and twenty miles of electrical conduit were used in building the outdoor arena. The main Stadium deck housed 37,896 seats set in 51 rows. 29,380 seats were contained in the upper deck, arranged in 34 rows. Nighttime lighting was provided at the Stadium by 250 1,000 watt Novalux flood light projectors providing 50 million candlepower, enough to light a town of 3,000. Twenty-four wash rooms for men and twenty-four wash rooms for women were distributed throughout the complex.

(Right) William J. Stark of 4505 Liberty Ave., South Euclid, at work on the 12-acre stadium project.

Lexington Avenue, to a new downtown structure. On Tuesday, November 6, 1928, as Americans voted Herbert Hoover into the White House, among the local issues passed by city voters was a $2.5 million levy for the erection of a "fireproof stadium on the Lakefront." The bond issue passed by a healthy 60% margin- 112,448 to 76,975- 8,000 votes more than the 55% needed for passage. Only one other local bond issue received stronger support. After a lengthy series of legal, financial and structural delays, dedication ceremonies were held at the 78,189-seat facility on Thursday, July 2, 1931. While most seats were offered free to the public, twenty thousand 25¢ "choice" seats were reserved for paying patrons, with box seat tickets priced at 50¢. Though preparations were made to host up to 75,000 spectators, an estimated 8,000 showed up

The photograph above appeared in The Cleveland Press on Wednesday, June 24, 1931. It was used to show ticket holders where to enter the massive egg-shaped arena for the upcoming championship fight on Friday, July 3, 1931.

for the inaugural celebration. As the ceremonies began at 8 P.M. with music provided by Walter Logan's WTAM orchestra, a bouquet of flowers from the National Air Race Corporation was dropped into the bowl from an autogyro flying overhead. Local dignitaries delivered speeches from a boxing ring erected for the Stadium's first major event the following night, a seven-bout evening of fisticuffs featuring as its main event, a heavyweight championship fight between Max Schmeling and challenger William L. (Young) Stribling. During the presentations, City Manager Daniel E. Morgan declared to the crowd, "The ancient world never saw a structure like this," as the city's seventh unit in its Mall Plan was christened. A bank of 250 floodlights along the Stadium's upper deck illuminated the presenters who were, "plainly visible to those in the upper tier of the grandstand." Between speeches, musical presentations were delivered by two choruses of 1,000 voices seated in the bleachers under the direction of Harper Garcia Smyth. A 100-piece band accompanied the massed chorus. Smyth also led the crowd over the Stadium's new $10,000 public address system in such traditional favorites as "America," and "Let Me Call You Sweetheart;" during a special session of "community singing." A 15-minute fireworks display ended the opening night festivities in grand fashion. On July 4th and 5th, the American Legion sponsored "Family Party" open houses, ending each evening with an hour-long fireworks display billed as "the biggest pyrotechnic display ever seen in Cleveland." Over 20,000 paid either 25¢, 50¢ or $1 to attend the fireworks display offered at the Stadium on Saturday, July 4th.

January 30, 1931
The Concrete Tower Collapse

On the afternoon of Friday, January 30, 1931, two W. J. Schirmer Co. iron workers, John Last, 35, 1192 E. 114th St., and Thomas E. Kelly, 36, 1446 E. 92nd St., lost their lives while they were securing the newly-erected top section of a 120-foot elevator tower to the Stadium's steelwork. As Last worked on a lower section of the tower, Kelly was hauling a section of tubing to the 120-foot level, when quarter-inch steel cables holding the tower erect snapped. It was believed that a strong gust of wind rocked the tubular steel structure (on the ground below and at right), forcing the support cables to tear away from their anchors. Two other workers narrowly missed being struck by the tower as it crashed to the ground. Immediately following the accident, investigations were launched by Coroner A. J. Pearse and Building Commissioner William D. Gulon. Pearse later stated he found no evidence to suggest negligence on the part of the workers or the construction company. It was the first accident of a such a serious nature at the construction site. The tower was being erected to pour a portion of the 15,000 cubic yards of reinforced concrete used on the Stadium project. The two men were survived by their widows.

January, 1931 / The Stadium Bleachers

When the Stadium bleachers under construction below were completed, the benches were arranged in 52 rows, offering eighteen inches of seating space for 10,913 spectators on planks seven inches in width. The 330-foot bleacher section was separated from the main grandstand by two entrance ways at either end described as "each large enough for two automobiles to enter abreast." Eight of the Stadium's 48 turnstiles were located in the bleacher section. There were a total of 2,521 composite piles of wood and concrete driven to a depth of 65 feet under the grandstand sections of the Stadium, but none under the free-standing bleachers. One of the concrete delivery towers similar to the one involved in the accident on the opposite page, is visible beyond the section of Stadium bleachers under construction. The photograph was taken in January of 1931, only days before the tragic accident occurred.

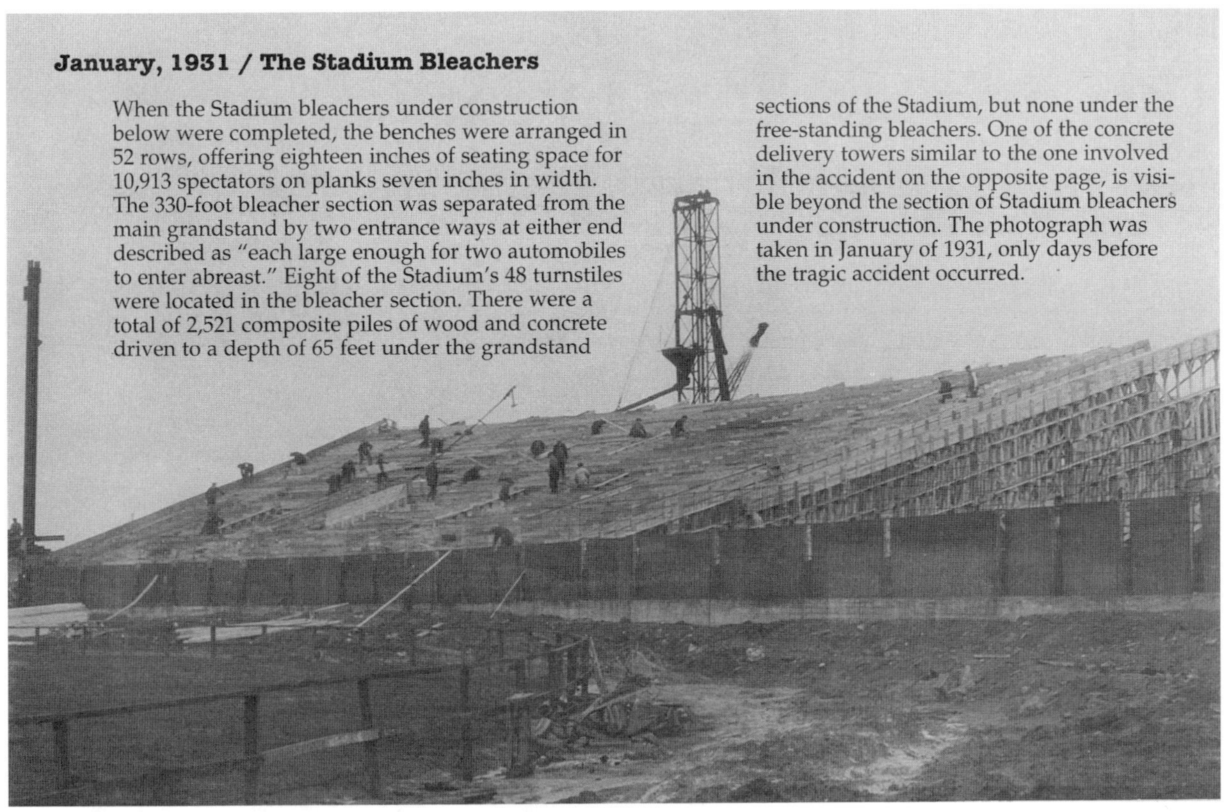

(Below) March 17, 1933 / The New Stadium Trees

In the fall of 1932, the city of Cleveland, short of money, agreed to plant a number of trees around the city if local home owners and businesses would cover the cost of the trees and top soil. On Tuesday, March 17, 1933, Cleveland Press landscape consultant Donald Gray published in his column, "Today Cleveland was to take its first step toward reclaiming its former title, the Forest City," as workers from the civic reforestation committee chaired by Mrs. Kenmode Gill began sending out letters to some 250 good samaritans describing what type of tree they would either be donating or receiving and the purchase price. With Gray's story that day was the photograph at left showing Associated Charities workers planting one of 200 sycamore and poplar trees being placed around the Stadium. The new Stadium trees were donated to the city and being planted under the direction of the Parks Department.

The First Stadium Event

Heavyweight Champion Max Schmeling vs. Wm. L. (Young) Stribling

"Never will a championship fight have been held under more ideal arena conditions than here," declared fight promoter R. G. Dunn, when Municipal Stadium was chosen over Chicago's Soldier Field to host the 15-round heavyweight championship fight between Max Schmeling and William L. (Young) Stribling on Friday evening, July 3, 1931. Before the main event, a series of five-round preliminary matches were held. Local fighter George Pavlik recorded the first knockdown at the Stadium in his win over Frank Morris, dropping Morris eight seconds into the fight's second round. The first knockout was recorded two bouts later, when young local heavyweight Frankie Simms dropped Joe Vincha of Boston at 2:04 in the opening round. Though the paid attendance fell far short of original estimates, many celebrities were on hand to witness the fisticuffs. Among the fighters introduced that night were heavyweight champs Gene Tunney and Gentleman Jim Corbett; Johnny Kilbane, Cleveland's first world champion and heavyweight challenger Primo Carnera, considered to be a contestant at a future Stadium bout, possibly against the Schmeling-Stribling winner. The loudest crowd ovation came when golfer Bobby Jones was introduced. Also among the attendees were retailers Bernard Gimble and Gus Nordstrom, RCA president David Sarnoff, Coca Cola president R. W. Woodruff, fighter Fidel La Barba, auto executives Walter P. Chrysler and Edsel Ford, who had flown in for the fight, and U. S. Senator Robert LaFollette of Wisconsin, who arrived on a yacht. Among the celebrities at ringside were new Chicago mayor Anton Cermak, baseball commissioner Judge Kenesaw Mountain Landis and former champ James J. Jeffries. One notable "miss-

(Above) On Tuesday, May 5, 1931, heavyweight champion Max Schmeling was in Cleveland to choose between Conneaut Lake Park and Cedar Point as the site for his training camp. On the morning of the 5th, Max (second from left), visited the Stadium construction site. Schmeling, his manager Joe (Yussel the Muscle) Jacobs (far left), Max Machon, his trainer (second from right), and Joe Jacob's partner, Will McCarney (far right), were given a personal tour of the stunning facility by Stadium manager George H. Bender (center, pointing).

ing" at the title fight was Chicago gangster "Scarface" Al Capone, who was "barred" by Safety Director Edwin D. Barry from attending the event. Reports surfaced here that Capone, who was scheduled to be sentenced for violating Federal tax laws, had his sentencing postponed until later in the month so he could buy a ringside seat for the fight. It was also learned that New York gang leader "Half Pint" Joe Genosa was reportedly arranging a reception for Capone in Cleveland. "We'll throw him in jail if he comes here for the fight or for any other purpose," declared Barry, who stated he could use the city's suspicious persons ordinance to arrest Capone. Following the championship fight, 185-pound local heavyweight Johnny Risko, who had fought both Schmeling and Stribling, won an eight-round decision over 226-pound "Two-Ton" Tony Galento in what was billed as a semi-final bout.

(Right) Fans and construction workers greet Schmeling during his Stadium visit on May 5th. In addition to exploring the new structure, Max climbed ladders, laid bricks, mixed cement, painted and "did everything else a horde of photographers asked him to do." Later that evening, Schmeling and his manager travelled to Public Hall were they watched Cleveland heavyweight Johnny Risko win a 10-round decision over promising Californian Max Baer. It was Risko's fourth fight in five weeks. Schmeling knocked out Risko in a fight two years earlier.

(Below) Schmeling (right), his manager Joe Jacobs, and Stadium manager George Bender (far left), stroll up the Stadium stands under construction on May 5th. Max returned to the area on Tuesday, May 19th to begin training at Conneaut Lake Park. Jacobs was the one who pushed for the prize fight to be held at new Municipal Stadium over Chicago's Soldier Field. When the contract was signed after nearly seven months of negotiation, it called for the promoters to pay the city $20,000 in rental fees and cover all event expenses including lighting, payroll and temporary seating.

(Left) Cleveland Press sports columnist Franklin Lewis (left), joins Schmeling during his Stadium tour on May 5th. The photograph was published in The Press on Thursday May 29, 1941, for a column Lewis wrote about the fighter's life as the paper ran an United Press story on its front page reporting that Schmeling had been killed in Crete by British gunfire. The next day, The Press published a second wire service story on its front page quoting German sources who stated British reports of Schmeling's death were inaccurate and that he was indeed alive and well.

Fight Night / July 3rd
FIVE-ROUND PRELIMINARY BOUTS

Frank Cawley (185), Pittston, Pa.; decision over George Panka (195), Pittsburgh, Pa.

George Pavlik (173), Cleveland; decision over Frank Morris (181), New York, New York

Battling Bozo (182), Birmingham, Alabama; decision over Natie Brown (187), Oakland, California

Frankie Simms (206), Cleveland; first round knockout (2:04) over Joe Vincha (187), Boston, Massachusetts

Charley Retzlaff (195), Duluth, Minn.; fifth round knockout over Marty Gallagher (207), Washington

EIGHT ROUND SEMI-FINAL BOUT

Johnny Risko (185), Cleveland; decision over Tony Galento (229), Orange, N. J.

(Right) Young Stribling poses at Geauga Lake with Al Koran potentate John B. Shaub. While Schmeling chose to train at Conneaut Lake Park, Stribling picked Geauga Lake Park for his pre-fight training. Stribling conducted his first formal workout at Geauga Lake on May 24, 1931, as more than 300 spectators paid 50¢ each on the cold and rainy Sunday, to watch Stribling jump rope for two rounds, shadow box for another round and then spar two rounds with "Battling Mimms." According to Cleveland Plain Dealer reporter Alex Zirin, "Mimms concentrated on taking Stribling's punches on his head, where they would do no damage."

(Left) "Pa" Stribling (left), Young Stribling's father and manager, measures his son's chest at their Geauga Lake Park training camp. If Stribling had won the fight, he would have been the first heavyweight champion with more than one hundred fights to claim the title. Stribling entered the Stadium contest with 295 fights to his credit. Pa said he picked the Geauga Lake site on the hunch it might be good luck for his Bainbridge, Georgia-born son since nearby was the Bainbridge race track.

(Left) Cleveland Press sports editor Stuart Bell (left), chats with Schmeling (second from right), Joe Jacobs and trainer Max Machon at Max's training camp cottage on the lakefront at Conneaut Lake Park. As Stribling opened his training camp at Geauga Lake Park on Sunday, May 24th, over at Conneaut Lake Park, more than 1,000 curious fans tried to catch a glimpse of Schmeling, who tried a little golfing in the morning, a bit of rowing and fishing in the afternoon and then spent the rest of the day posing for "moving picture men." Joe Jacobs, Schmeling's manager, was forced to hire four special policemen to keep onlookers away from the champion's cottage that day. On Monday, June 1st, 2,000 Germans visited Schmeling during his daily workout, but the light in the indoor arena was so poor, that he had trouble even seeing his sparring partners. Before the workout, Schmeling took in a nearby soccer match.

(Right) Heavyweight champion Max Schmeling (left), poses with challenger Young Stribling before their July 3rd fight as E. J. Kulas, president of Madison Square Garden of Ohio, looks on. Though early estimates by Madison Square Garden's R. G. Dunn predicted gross receipts of $1 million, based on 100,000 tickets sold at $25, $12.50, $5.49 and $3 for bleacher seats, the gate was actually much smaller, when only 36,936 paid to see the prize fight. Cleveland Press reporter Joe Williams, who called the Stadium too big for a prize fight, wrote, "At 7:30 P.M. the big Stadium was almost as deserted as a Mayfield road speakeasy after an unannounced social visit by the federals." The final gate was set at $349,416 against expenses of well over $400,000. Dunn said it was, "Laid strictly to the unpopularity of both Schmeling and Stribling before the battle on the lake by intimate followers of boxing." Schmeling was scheduled to receive 40% of the gate receipts. Stribling's take was 12.5%. On July 6th, a local paper reported that Schmeling owed the U. S. government $17,546 of the $106,138.36 he won for the fight. Stribling owed $3,116 on his take of $33,168.24.

Max Schmeling Germany		W. L. (Young) Stribling Macon, Ga.
25	-Age-	26
189	-Weight-	186 1/2
6' 1"	-Height-	6' 1/4"
75"	-Reach-	74"
42"	-Chest (normal)-	38"
43 1/4"	-Chest (expanded)-	42 1/4"
17 1/8"	-Neck-	16 1/2"
15"	-Biceps-	14 3/4"
12 1/2"	-Forearm-	13 1/2"
7 3/4"	-Wrist-	7 1/4"
33"	-Waist-	33"
23"	-Thigh-	22"
15"	-Calf-	14 1/2"
9 1/2"	-Ankle-	9"

Local Odds- Stribling 10-9 favorite

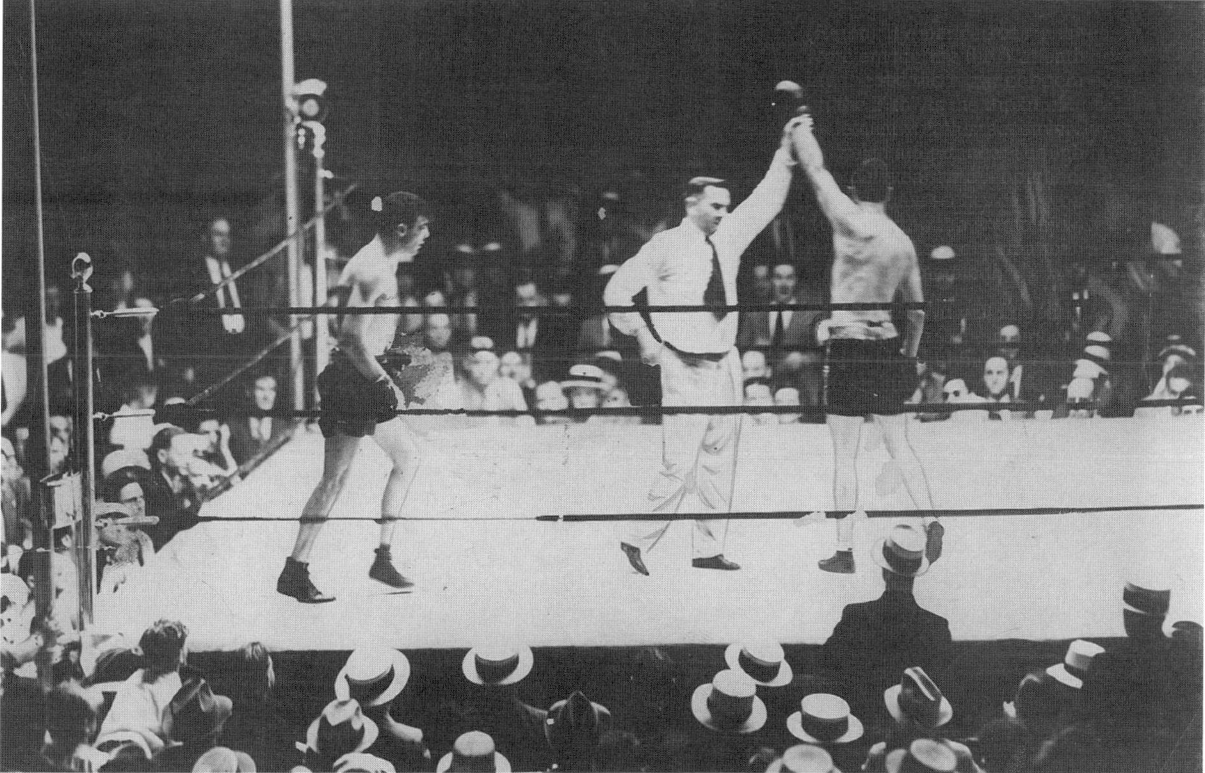

(Above) The fight began after 11 P.M. with Stribling fighting to bring the heavyweight title back to the U. S. for the first time since 1930. The Georgia fighter suffered a bloody beating at the hands of the powerful German, laying claim to only two rounds, the second and the eighth. Schmeling drew the first blood in the fourth round, when he scored with three left hooks to Stribling's nose. The most intense action came in the sixth round, when both fighters released a number of rights to each other's head and body. By the tenth round, Stribling, nursing a cut over his right eye, could only hope to avoid being knocked out. After driving Stribling (getting up at left), to the canvas with 2 minutes and 45 seconds gone in the 15th round, referee George Blake declared "Mighty Max" the winner by TKO. Though the fight lost money, the promoters said they were pleased with the outcome, claiming that more money might have been lost in another city. The prize fight was aired coast-to-coast over the NBC radio network with noted sportscaster Graham McNamee joining Floyd Gibbons behind the microphones.

The Shriners Come to Town

The week of July 12-18, 1931 was billed as "Hospitality Week," in Cleveland, as the city welcomed the arrival of over 100,000 visitors coming to town for the 57th Annual International Shrine Convention of the Ancient Arabic Order of Nobles of the Mystic Shrine. Sponsored locally by the Al Koran Temple at an estimated cost of $250,000, the four-day convention opened on Monday, July 13th, with band concerts and a festive nighttime Mardi Gras party. On the morning of the 14th, Municipal Stadium served as the endpoint of a parade that involved over 10,000 marchers representing 33 Temples from across the nation and Canada. When they reached the Stadium, the parade participants were welcomed to the city by Governor George White and Cleveland Mayor John D. Marshall. That night, the first of two lavish "A Night in the Orient," spectacles was presented at the Stadium. A grand parade, circus acts, a 200-meter race and the Stadium's first baseball game, were all part of a day-long Shrine festival at the Stadium on Wednesday, July 15th. That evening, an "illuminated" parade was held with over 10,000 Shriners marching with torches in hand along downtown streets to the Stadium. An encore performance of "A Night In The Orient" was presented at the Stadium on the 16th, as the convention came to a close.

(Left) The Al Sirat Grotto Drum and Bugle Corps enters Municipal Stadium on Tuesday, July 14th. The Al Sirat group was part of one of the city's most colorful spectacles in years, as over 10,000 Shriners and twenty bands marched in full regalia along Euclid Avenue from E. 30th to the Stadium. The parade began at 9 A.M., with Police Chief George J. Matowitz, who rode in a city police car, leading the way. Following Matowitz were twenty of the city's mounted policemen, riding the "department's finest horses." More than 20,000 waited for the parade groups to enter the Stadium.

(Left) The official escort of the Imperial Potentate of the Shrine circles the Stadium infield under the hot summer sun on July 14th. The Shrine parade, assembled in seven different divisions, took over three hours to complete. Crowd estimates along the parade route varied from 100,000 to 200,000, making the Shrine parade one of the most watched downtown events in recent police memory. As the first parade groups passed the Shriner's reviewing stand at the Stadium, the tail of the parade was just getting underway on Euclid Avenue. Fire Chief James E. Granger, a member of the Al Koran Temple, served as the parade's grand marshall. When the Shrine festivities concluded at the Stadium, much of the crowd shifted its attention to the circus carnival quartered on land east of the Stadium, featuring menageries from the Hagenbach-Wallace and John Robinson circuses.

July 14, 1931
"A Night In The Orient"

Described in the newspaper advertisement as "America's Greatest Spectacle," the Shriners presented the first of two "A Night In The Orient," extravaganzas at the Stadium on Tuesday, July 14, 1931. Produced at a cost of over $100,000, the lavish two-hour event featured twenty different acts and involved over 600 entertainers and hundreds of animals including camels, zebras, Arabian horses and twenty trained elephants. Oriental dancers, forty-two models painted in bronze and silver, and a full circus with clowns, tumblers and tight rope walkers, further enhanced the grand theme. Cleveland Plain Dealer reporter Roelif Loveland described the pageantry as, "A combination of a three-ring circus, the Last Days of Pompeii, and a Russian ballet." As the presentation came to a close, the village set was "destroyed" by an impressive fireworks designed to represent an erupting volcano provoked by the wrath of Allah.

(Upper left) Professionally trained singers and ballet dancers were joined by a number of locally-recruited amateur cast members.

(Upper right) Over 40,000 turned out on July 14th for the first performance of "A Night In The Orient," setting a new high in Stadium attendance. The program was presented again on Thursday, July 16th, the final night of the Shrine convention.

(Above right) Much of the "A Night in the Orient" action centered around an elaborate village built in the Stadium outfield, seen as the village caliph poses with his harem. In his Plain Dealer article, Loveland lamented, "It's really too bad that the first chance a fellow gets to see a real genuine caliph's harem he's so far away that opera glasses don't help much."

(Right) An intense pyrotechnic display "destroys" the caliph's village during the final scenes of "A Night In The Orient," on July 14th.

The First Baseball Game

"Batter Up" first echoed through Municipal Stadium on Wednesday, July 15, 1931, when a game between area sandlot stars representing the Al Koran Shrine and Al Sirat Grotto marked the debut of organized baseball at the outdoor arena. Over 30,000 watched the 3 P.M. contest, which climaxed a daylong Shrine festival that included a parade with marching bands, circus acts and a 200-meter race featuring local track star Stella Walsh. "Stadium Proves Ideally Suited to Diamond Sport," proclaimed the next morning's Cleveland Plain Dealer headline, after the Al Koran team, led by former National League spitballer Bill Doak, beat the Al Sirat squad, 6-1. The win was clinched by a three-run Shrine rally in the eighth inning. The final runs were scored by Boone and Kress off Al Sirat reliever Rube Marquardt.

(Above left) Charlie Dunkel (left), captain of the Al Sirat Grotto team, shakes hands with Al Koran captain Bill Able during pre-game ceremonies on July 15th. In 1923, Dunkel, playing for the Favorite Knits, became only the second sandlotter to hit a home run over the right field fence at League Park, home of the Cleveland Indians.

(Left) Al Sirat right fielder Bill Arndt (at bat in the first inning,) was the first player to officially bat at the Stadium. The lead-off hitter collected two of the team's 10 hits, all singles. Catching is Kress for the Koran side. The next inning, Al Koran first baseman Lefty Krause hit the first Stadium home run, an inside the park smash that rolled to the right field wall.

Stella Walsh

The first track event held at the Stadium was a special 200-meter race before the Shrine game on July, 15th. Cleveland's incomparable world record holder Stanislawa Walasiewicz (Stella Walsh), right, at left, set a new American record of 26.1 seconds in beating a field of five Canadian and American competitors, including her chief rival, Margaret Coles of Toronto, Canada. After the race, Walsh, who bettered her rivals by a 15-yard margin, complained that the new track was "too heavy," causing her to pull a tendon in her left leg, but ruled out medical treatment, instead telling reporters that the injury would be treated with "home remedies." It was Walsh's first competition on an oval track. On the same date a year later, Walsh was preparing to run for her native Poland at the Los Angeles Olympic Games. The Cleveland sprinter won Olympic gold by finishing first in the 100-meter dash.

(Right) Al Sirat manager Petie Johns (kneeling at left), and Al Koran manager George R. Williams pose with the Ralph K. Rex trophy. Standing behind the two men are Al Koran potentate John B. Shaub (left), D. Charles Sterling of Al Sirat Grotto, Ralph K. Rex and Charles D. White (right), chairman of the Shrine baseball committee. Valued at $1,000, the Rex trophy was awarded to the winner of a best two out of three series between the two teams. The Stadium victory gave the Al Koran side a one-game lead in the Rex trophy series, and tied the six-year series between the two teams at three games each. The two teams were comprised of area Masons who starred for local sandlot teams. Among the players selected were Carl Schlee, Art Heiden, Rube Marquardt, Arlie Tarbert, Ed Hovlik, and Lee Meadows, who once pitched for the Pittsburgh Pirates. Tickets were priced at 50¢, 75¢ and $1, with all proceeds going to the Shrine Crippled Children's and Grotto Charity funds.

Al Koran-6	Al Sirat-1
Reeves cf	Arndt rf
Cochran ss	Smith 2b
Roberts lf	Tarbert cf
Hughes rf	Abel ss
Kimmick 2b	Heiden lf
Boone 3b	Schlee lb
Krause lb	Vaughn c
Kress c	Fleck 3b
Doak p	Hovlik p

Substitutes/
Al Koran- Stewart p

Al Sirat- Krejci lf
           Johns
           Keenan p
           Marquardt p

Time of Game: 3:10

Grand Summer Opera Week

(Right) To promote Opera Week at the Stadium, a special Summer Opera Festival front was built on the Cleveland Press Want Ad Headquarters at 227 Euclid Ave., one of several places where tickets could be purchased. A special 20' by 30' white flag with a broad red diagonal stripe was flown at exactly 4 P.M. each evening from the top of Terminal Tower to let opera goers know that the evening performance would take place as scheduled. In the event of rain, the flag would not be raised, indicating that the opera was called off.

(Right) Children from one of the city playgrounds promote the upcoming Summer Opera Festival. The camel, on loan from the Hagenbach-Wallace circus, was used in the scene of the triumph of Rhadames in the second act of "Aida." The Cleveland Press was very active in recruiting youngsters from local playgrounds to sell opera tickets through an "Around The World Flight" contest. Area youngsters were given books made up of ten 25¢ tickets to sell. Each ticket sold represented another step around large global maps found at each playground. Selling a complete book won the child a 25¢ opera ticket and a "pilot's insignia," indicating a successful trip around the world.

Only twelve days after the second staging of the Shrine spectacle "A Night in the Orient" on July 16th, the city's inaugural Summer Opera Festival opened at the Stadium. The six-night musical affair was organized by Cleveland's Civic Summer Grand Opera Co., "to make great grand opera on a truly magnificent scale available to every purse in a depression season." Tickets prices were the lowest on record for grand opera, ranging from 25¢ to $2 for individual seats, and from $3 to $5 for individual seat packages. Proceeds went to the Cleveland Press Milk Fund, a program used to supply milk to needy children through city schools and playgrounds. Verdi's "Aida," was chosen as the opening night presentation on Tuesday, July 28th, with Anna Roselle in the starring role. "Aida" was presented again on Friday, July 31st and Sunday, August 2nd, with new casts each evening. A triple bill of "Cavalleria Rusticana," act three of "La Gioconda," and the final scene of "Die Meistersinger," was offered on Wednesday and Saturday, also with new casts each night. Act two of "Carmen," act three of "The Bartering Bride," and the final scene of "Die Meistersinger," was presented on Thursday, July 30th.

(Above right) Metropolitan Opera prima donna soprano Elda Vettori visited the city's East Madison playground on Friday, July 10th, where 14-year-old Helen Kundrot (right), was leading The Cleveland Press "Around the World" ticket sales contest. On Wednesday, July 29th, Vettori sang the lead role of Santuzza in "Cavalleria Rusticana," the lead role in "La Gioconda," and played Eva in "Die Meistersinger." Vettori was called the greatest Santuzza in the world. On August 2nd, Vettori sang the title role in "Aida." **(Above)** Rita De Leporte, premiere danseuse of the Metropolitan Opera Co., receives a gift from her dance troupe. De Leporte and chorus director Maestro Giacomo Spadoni were the first professionals signed by director Guy Golterman to lead the Cleveland Civic Summer Grand Opera Co. **(Below)** De Leporte, in the lower right corner, oversees a rehearsal conducted at Public Hall in preparation for the outdoor performances. The dancers are practicing a scene from the invocation of the priestesses from the first act of "Aida." De Leporte and her dancers took eleven bows for their colorful presentation of the "Dance of the Hours," which climaxed the third set of "La Gioconda," on Wednesday night.

(Above) The Cleveland Summer Opera Company's massive 250' x 125' all-wood main stage under construction was billed as "the largest opera stage in history." The two-level stage was built under the direction of celebrated Vienna-born stage director Dr. Ernst Lert, who joined the Cleveland Opera Company after serving as stage director for La Scala in Milan, Italy and New York's Metropolitan Opera.

(Below) A pre-performance rehearsal at the Stadium. Nearly an acre and a half of usable performance area was provided by the stage and surrounding Stadium infield. The opera orchestra performed in an area near the pitcher's mound. The area was illuminated by 40' light towers placed on either side of the stage. 20,000 seats were set aside for the opera festival, arranged in thirteen sections around home plate.

(Right) Among the record-breaking opening night audience of 18,063 were Harry F. McNutt (at left), and John L. Severance (right), president of the Cleveland Musical Arts Association, who only six months earlier, celebrated the opening of Severance Hall, home of the Cleveland Orchestra. When the final performance of "Aida" on Sunday night attracted over 14,000 patrons, the Summer Opera Festival's six-night attendance total reached 88,708, setting a new American record for open air opera fes-

tivals. The single night record was set on Friday, July 31st, when 19,147 watched the second performance of "Aida," with European soprano Alida Vane performing the title role in her American debut, and celebrated tenor Pasquale Ferrara performing the role of Rhadames, in his local debut.

(Far right) Thursday, July 30th was "Governor's Night" at the opera, as Ohio governor George White (center), and his daughter Mary (right), joined U. S. Senator Robert J. Bulkley, president of the Northern Ohio Opera Association (left). 18,364 saw the performance that night, setting an American open air opera record. On opening night, Bulkley stated, "The Stadium Opera far exceeds anything I thought was possible."

(Right) The patrons at right were among the 8,201 attending the second night of opera on the 29th, as the threat of inclement weather severely curtailed attendance. Though rain delayed the opening, and caused some scenes to be conducted without a sound system, the entire performance went on as planned.

(Below) On August 2nd, the final night, cast members gathered behind behind the elaborate set built for "Aida."

The First Major League Baseball Game

The first major league baseball game at Municipal Stadium was set to be played on Sunday, July 26, 1931, between the Cleveland Indians and the Philadelphia Athletics. But on Tuesday, July 14th, lease negotiations between Cleveland Baseball Co. and city officials broke down, forcing Indians general manager Billy Evans to continue playing home games at aging League Park. It also forced Evans to return $30,000 generated from 14,000 tickets sold for the July 26th contest. Negotiations continued until Saturday, July 23, 1932, when Evans announced he would sign a short term lease to have his team play its remaining home games at the Stadium- a 14-game home stand beginning on July 31st, and an 18-game home stand starting on September 8th. On Saturday, July 30th, as the Olympic Games got underway in Los Angeles, third-place Cleveland lost to the second-place Philadelphia Athletics, 7-2, before 5,000 at League Park. The following day, the Indians left the park at E. 66th and Lexington Ave. for the first time in 41 years, moving to Municipal Stadium where they faced the Athletics in a Sunday contest before a major league record crowd of 80,124. That morning, 38,000 tickets went on sale at the Stadium- 17,000 unreserved grandstand seats at $1.10; 11,000 unreserved pavilion seats (covered) at 85¢; and 10,000 bleacher seats at 55¢. The festivities began at 12:30 P.M., with Jimmy Johnston's 60-piece orchestra leading an informal parade to the Stadium. Formal ceremonies began at 1:30 P.M., with the introduction of veteran Cleveland baseball stars who paraded before their fans and helped local Marines raise the American flag. Gov. George White threw the first pitch to Mayor Ray T. Miller, as baseball commissioner Judge Kenesaw Mountain Landis played umpire. The Athletics won, 1-0, as the A's Robert Moses (Lefty) Grove pitched a four-hitter, outdueling young Tribe starter Mel Harder, who threw a six-hitter. Both men pitched shutout ball until the eighth inning, when Philadelphia scored the only run. The next day, the Indians lost again to the Athletics, 1-0, as starter Wes Ferrell took the loss. The Cleveland club continued playing at the Stadium until October 13, 1933, when Tribe president Alva Bradley, citing poor attendance and high costs, informed the city he was cancelling the lease and moving back to League Park. The next Indians contest played at the Stadium took place during the Great Lakes Exposition on Sunday, August 2, 1936, when 65,342 watched Cleveland play the New York Yankees to a thrilling 4-4, 16-inning tie. Denny Galehouse shut out the Yank's "Murderer's Row" from the 9th to 16th innings, until darkness halted the classic match. Games continued at both ballparks until 1947, when new Tribe president Bill Veeck moved his club to the Stadium permanently.

(Right) Mrs. E. S. Barnard, widow of former Cleveland Indians president and president of the American League, Ernest S. Barnard, heads to her seat before the game begins. With Mrs. Barnard, who sat next to baseball commissioner Judge Kenesaw Mountain Landis, is National League President John Heydler (left), Cleveland Indians president Alva Bradley (with hat), and Philadelphia Athletics president Tom Shibe (right). A Cleveland Plain Dealer headline on Monday, August 1, 1932 offered, Mrs. Barnard Sees 'Barney's' Dream Come True." Before his death, (Barney) Barnard played an instrumental role in developing the Stadium as a house for baseball.

(Right) Before the game, twenty-five former Cleveland baseball players were introduced to the massive crowd. Among those honored were Bill (Wamby) Wambsganss (left), who pulled off an unassisted triple play during the 1920 World Series; Tris Speaker, who served as player-manager of the 1920 team; Charlie Jamieson, who joined the Indians in 1919 and played for the 1932 squad; Larry (Nap) Lajoie, who from 1902 to 1914 played for the Cleveland Bronchos, the Cleveland Blues and later served as player-manager of the Cleveland Naps; and Charles Louis (Chief) Zimmer (right), a member of the 1895 World Champion Cleveland Spiders, who played for Cleveland teams from 1887 to 1899. Others introduced included Cy Young, Lee Fohl, Joe and Jim Delahanty, Ed Zmich, Jack Graney, Dode Paskert, Les Nunamaker and Elmer Smith, who hit the first World Series grand slam in 1920.

THE STARTING LINEUPS

Cleveland Indians-0	Philadelphia Athletics-1
Dick Porter, rf	Max Bishop, 2b
Johnny Burnett, ss	Mule Haas, cf
Earl Averill, cf	Mickey Cochrane, c
Joe Vosmik, lf	Al Simmons, lf
Eddie Morgan, 1b	Jimmie Foxx, 1b
Luke Sewell, c	Eric McNair, ss
Bill Cissell, 2b	Bing Miller, rf
Willie Kamm, 3b	Jimmy Dykes, 3b
Mel Harder, p	Lefty Grove, p
Roger Peckinpaugh, Manager	Connie Mack, Manager
Winning Pitcher: Lefty Grove	Losing Pitcher: Mel Harder

Time of Game: 1:50

Attendance: 80,184: Paid 76,979 / Passes 3,005 / Employees 200

(Right) Before the game, Tris Speaker (left), and Nap Lajoie posed with former Cleveland pitching great Denton True (Cy) Young (far right). Young won a total of 270 games for two major league Cleveland teams, the National League Spiders (241 from 1890 to 1898) and the American League Naps (29 from 1909 to 1911.) The three Cleveland greats were honored in 1937 by being the second set of players elected to baseball's Hall of Fame.

(Opposite page) Photographers wait for Tribe starter Mel Harder to throw the first pitch as Athletics lead-off hitter Max Bishop heads to home plate. With the home run distance set at 470' to deep center field, 435' to left and right fields and 320' down both lines, six games were played before the first major league home run was hit. After a two-game series with the Athletics, and a four-game series with the Boston Red Sox, Tribe shortstop Johnny Burnett hit the first Stadium home run before 21,818 on Sunday, August 7th, in the first game of a 7-4, 6-2, doubleheader win over the Washington Nationals. Burnett's blast traveled into the lower right field stands. Indians center fielder Earl Averill, who was robbed of hitting the first homer in the first game, hit the second Stadium homer in the second game, his 26th of the year, into the lower right deck.

The Golden Autumn Festival

Part three-ring circus, part sports carnival, the city's first Golden Autumn Festival was held at the Stadium on Thursday, October 12, 1933. The festival was organized by the Cleveland Advertising Club's Come to Cleveland committee under the direction of former Public Hall manager Lincoln G. Dickey, who brought in CBS radio announcer Ted Husing from New York to serve as master of ceremonies. Choral numbers, fencing exhibitions featuring 200 fencers, acrobatics by the German Turnverein, military drills, relay races, a roller skating race, horse races, a horse show, tap dancing, a football game, boxing matches from the Cleveland News stage and even a hog calling contest, despite only one contestant showing up, were among the sixty distinct acts and events that took place simultaneously on three separate stages and around the Stadium grounds. The Dorothy Frank dancers, the Corley dancers and Alice Brueggemann, the city's first

acrobatic fan dancer, were among the local acts featured that night. At 7 P.M., the Louis Rich orchestra kicked off the festival's diverse musical program, which moved from the swinging sounds of Sammy Kaye and his band, to the Cleveland Orchestra performing "America," conducted by Artur Rodzinski, the Orchestra's new musical director, who was making his first local appearance. At 9:29 P.M., daredevil Capt. Ed MacDonald, with his gasoline-soaked uniform set afire, jumped 85 feet into a shallow flame-filled water tank. Forty-five minutes later, "The Great Wilno," a human cannonball making his 3,356th attempt, was shot from a canon into a net over 150 feet away. Adding to the excitement were the death-defying aerial acrobatics of "The Five Peerless Potters" and "The Fearless Falcons." Fireworks concluded the ambitious program, with marching bands playing "The Star Spangled Banner," as the sky above erupted in color.

(Above) Over 50,000 paid either 35¢ for general admission tickets or 75¢ for reserved seats, to attend the city's first Golden Autumn Festival. The entertainment began at 6:30 P.M. with a horse-pulling contest in left field, where a new world record was set. At 7 P.M., as the Louis Rich orchestra played "The Stars and Stripes Forever," to open the festival's musical program, the Cleveland News Skippies' football team was scrimmaging in the Stadium outfield and local runners were competing in a series of track events on the outdoor arena's cinder track. At 7:30 P.M., as the first parade groups entered the Stadium through the northeast gate, boxing matches were taking place on the Cleveland News stage near first base. At 10:23 P.M., the special event portion of the show ended with "capture the machine gun nest," a military drill conducted by the 145th Infantry.

When the marching groups, floats, bands, drill teams and costumed characters of the Golden Autumn Festival Bell Ringers' parade entered the Stadium at 7:30 P.M., bedlam broke out, as bands began playing, fireworks were exploded and bells of all sizes were rung. It took nearly two hours for the parade to circle the Stadium. The parade began at E. 22nd and Euclid Avenue, with the city's mounted police force in the lead, followed by the mayor's car and the Cleveland Grays.

(Above) Ladies of the G. A. R. proceed around the Stadium infield during the Bell Ringers' Parade. Over 8,000 area residents were involved in the parade and Stadium events.

(Below) The Ladies Auxiliary Drill Team of the Knights of St. John marches patriotically before the Stadium spectators. Police estimated that over 60,000 onlookers lined Euclid Avenue to view the Columbus Day procession as it headed to the Stadium.

(Right) Event organizer Lincoln G. Dickey (left), studies the pre-event set-up with Indians business manager Walter A. McNichols from the main stage at home plate.

(Below) The three Golden Autumn Festival stages sponsored by The Cleveland News at first base, The Cleveland Plain Dealer at second base and The Cleveland Press at home plate are visible below. The cannon used by the "Great Wilno" sits near third base. Along the first-base line is the high wire apparatus used by the "Five Fearless Potters."

One of the Golden Autumn Festival's many high points was the awarding of travel prizes at 9 P.M., to the twenty "Emissaries of Good Will 'round the U. S. A.," at right, who won their prizes by selling the most Golden Autumn Festival tickets. The free trips were awarded by the Come to Cleveland committee as a way for the twenty hard workers to help 'sell' Cleveland to the nation as they traveled around the country. Mayor Ray T. Miller awarded the top two ticket sellers their prizes from the special "coronation stage" at second base. Mrs. Bertha H. McKenzie and Miss Eunice M. Brown won the grand prize awards which were thirty-day trips around the country by way of New York City; Havana, Cuba; the Panama Canal; San Francisco; Los Angeles; the Grand Canyon and Chicago. Prizes won by the eighteen other emissaries included trips to Bermuda, Florida and the World's Fair at Chicago.

(Right) **Mayor Ray T. Miller and the Contest Winners**

Mayor Ray T. Miller is joined by Mrs. Bertha H. McKenzie (left), and Miss Eunice M. Brown (right), winners of the "Emissaries of Good Will" contest.

At left are three of the "Mae West" girls who participated in the Golden Autumn Festival Bell Ringers' parade on October 12th. That evening, women dressed in Mae West attired were spared the admission price of 40 cents (plus tax), for the special midnight premiere of Paramount's "I'm No Angel," starring Mae West and Cary Grant at Loew's State Theater on Playhouse Square. "Come downtown for the gigantic Autumn Festival parade... then be a member of the FIRST audience in Cleveland to see torso-tossin', curvacious Mae in the most sensational screen entertainment ever to come out of Hollywood," coaxed a newspaper advertisement promoting the local premiere. Before the movie began, several hundred West look-a-likes competed for $25, $10 and $5 prizes in a theater-sponsored "Mae West Figure Contest," won by Miss Helen Hunter over Rosalie Naderson and Anna Fall. The next day, Cleveland Press reporter George Davis wrote, "Mae West's newest movie was shown last night at the State to the largest midnight movie audience we remember having seen in Cleveland." Among the spectators filling the theater's lobby as the figure contest began were, according to another newspaper account, "quite a few young men who were ready, it seemed, to go 'West.'"

The Seventh National Eucharistic Congress

Before departing by train from Cleveland's Union Terminal on Thursday, September 26, 1935, His Eminence Patrick Cardinal Hayes remarked, "After these days of glorious triumph, I feel that I have been living in a spiritual wonderland. I seem to know no time when I was so lifted up to the heaven of heavens as in these magnificent days." Cardinal Hayes made his remarks after having just presided as personal representative of Pope Pius XI over the Seventh National Eucharistic Congress, a three-day spiritual rally that attracted over 200,000 faithful Catholics to Cleveland. On Tuesday, September 24th, over 43,000 attended an evening session at Municipal Stadium, when the event was moved from the city's 10,000-seat Public Hall because of the immense crowd. The principal speaker that evening was former New York Governor Alfred E. Smith, who assailed communism as a foe to the church. On the morning of September 25th, over 40,000 attended a Mass for Children at the Stadium. That evening, a holy hour and midnight mass for men (and women) attracted over 150,000 worshippers to the Stadium, arguably the

(Top) His Eminence Patrick Cardinal Hayes (center), the first American prelate to be so named, leaves Union Terminal on Monday, September 23rd, after arriving to act as Pope Pius XI's personal representative during the Eucharistic Congress. Second from right is Bishop Joseph Schrembs, who served as Congress president.

(Above) On July 25th, over 150,000 worshippers were bathed in candlelight at the Stadium during an 11 P.M. holy hour and pontifical low mass at midnight.

(Above right) Part of the three-hour procession heading from St. John Cathedral to the Stadium crosses the walk bridge for closing ceremonies on the 26th.

(Right) Rev. Msr. Fulton J. Sheen, head of Catholic University in Washington, D. C., was among the presenters at the Stadium on Tuesday night, September 24th.

largest single crowd ever entertained at the outdoor arena. When the Congress concluded on the morning of the 26th, over 90,000 witnessed the religious pageantry from the Stadium grandstands, with thousands more turned away when Stadium management was forced to close the gates. The closing ceremonies began with over 22,000 men, women and children marching in a colorful procession from St. John Cathedral to the Stadium, where they formed a human monstrance that filled the playing field. Pope Pius XI later delivered his paternal apostolic benediction to the massed group in Latin by way of radio from Castel Gandolfo, the papal summer residence in Italy, as the crowd knelt in silence. The Pope's message was then translated into English for the Stadium congregation.

(Above) His Excellency Most Rev. Amelto Giovanni Cicognani, archbishop and apostolic delegate to the United States, chanted solemn high mass on the 25th from the altar above.

(Left) Members of the Knights of St. John, who later lined the monstrance below, march through the Stadium during the beginning of closing ceremonies on the 26th.

(Below, left) Formed around the altar in center field, the living monstrance nears completion below, as thousands of devoted Catholics look on. Area school children helped fill the stem.

The Great Lakes Exposition Balloon Race

Sunday, August 2, 1936, was "Akron Day" at the Great Lakes Exposition, the city's summer-long exhibition stretching along the lakefront from Municipal Stadium eastward to E. 18th street. One of the many events held on August 2nd was a special hot air balloon "grudge race" between the Goodyear-X of Akron and the Great Lakes Exposition balloon representing the city of Cleveland. The event was designed to see which balloon could travel the furthest in a fifteen-hour period. The balloons were scheduled to leave Municipal Stadium at 8 P.M., as the second half of a "doubleheader," following a game between the second-place Cleveland Indians and the league-leading New York Yankees, the first Indians game played at the Stadium since 1933. But when the game went into extra innings, the balloon launches were pushed back to the early morning hours. After 16 innings of play, the teams were deadlocked at 4-4, forcing the contest to be called because of darkness at 7:15 P.M. To the delight of several thousand weary spectators, most waiting in the bleachers for the balloons to clear the 112-foot Stadium walls, the Goodyear-X balloon, the first balloon launched, finally lifted off at 1:45 A.M. The Goodyear-X was declared the victor after the Great Lakes balloon was forced down by a thunderstorm 75 miles short of Le Raysville, Pennsylvania, where the Akron entry touched down. The Exposition visitor coming closet to guessing the winning balloon's distance was awarded a season pass to the Great Lakes Exposition and a new set of tires.

(**Above**) An aerial view of the 1936 Great Lakes Exposition grounds showing Municipal Stadium at far right.

(**Left**) Great Lakes Exposition balloon pilot Milford Vanik (in basket), shakes the hand of co-pilot Anthony Fairbanks after arriving in Cleveland for the Akron Day race. The two pilots had just returned from the 24th Annual National Balloon Race at Denver, Colorado, where the Goodyear-X balloon nosed out the Great Lakes Expo entry to win the event. Because of its proximately to Lake Erie and the Canadian wilderness, Cleveland was reported to be one of the more dangerous cities to launch from. On board with the Expo crew was a camping outfit, a shotgun, fishing tackle and an inflatable pontoon. Frank Trotter and John Rieker, pilot and co-pilot of the Goodyear-X, carried a short-wave transmitter as an additional precaution. By finishing first and second in the National Balloon Race, the two balloons qualified to compete in the James Gordon Bennett International Balloon Race on August 30, 1936, in Warsaw, Poland.

(Left) Prior to the launch, Frances Ernst (left), daughter of Great Lakes Exposition Vice-President A. C. Ernst, and Mrs. A. W. Denny, daughter of Goodyear Tire and Rubber Co. president P. W. Litchfield, flipped a coin to see which balloon would be first to leave. Denny, representing the Goodyear-X, won the toss. At the same time the balloons were being prepared for launch on August 2nd, the Marx Brothers, Harpo, Chico and Groucho, who had entertained fans before the Indians-Yankees game, were performing at Loew's State on Playhouse Square. Next to the State, the Palace Theater was swinging to the sounds of Duke Ellington and his orchestra. One of the songs Ellington performed that night was "The Expo Swing," written for the Great Lakes Exposition. On August 3rd, articles about the balloon race shared newspaper space with the exploits of former East Tech High track star Jesse Owens, who had just captured his first of four gold medals by winning the 100-meter dash at the Summer Olympic Games in Berlin, Germany.

(Below) The Goodyear-X is set for launching while the Great Lakes Exposition balloon is being filled with highly flammable hydrogen gas under the illumination of Stadium floodlights. Because hydrogen was being used, military men were positioned around the Stadium playing field to prevent anyone from smoking near the balloons. The Goodyear-X balloon lifted off at 1:45 A.M., followed by the Great Lakes Expo balloon at 2:07 A.M. The two balloons headed northeast by east toward Buffalo at a speed of 12 miles per hour. With Vanik and Fairbanks in the basket of the Great Lakes balloon were eight carrier pigeons. A bird was set to be released at daybreak with information on the balloon's position.

The Stadium Gas Explosion

On Monday, October 12, 1936, the city's impressive Great Lakes Exposition ended its 108-day run along the lakefront after attracting nearly four million visitors. The next day, Expo workers began moving items to the Stadium for storage. At 5:50 P.M. that afternoon, wardrobe man James A. Cosgriff entered a storage room below Section 12 at the Stadium. Cosgriff told investigators that after pulling the cord to an overheard light in the middle of the room, "There was a flash and the room was immediately filled with flame." An electrical short in the light fixture reportedly sparked a buildup of natural gas in the room. The flash fire, which enveloped part of the building near Gate B, triggered a terrific explosion that rocked the five-year-old structure. Initial estimates placed the damage at $100,000. In the spring of 1936, leaking gas claimed the life of a circus employee at the Stadium who was sleeping in one of the upstairs rooms. When the circus they were performing in failed after attempting a number of shows in the Stadium, a number of performers were allowed to sleep in the building. All were overcome by the fumes that took the life of their fellow performer.

(Left) The blast was so violent that it twisted huge cantilever beams supporting the upper deck, hurled huge concrete blocks forty feet in the air and blew seats onto the playing field. Hundreds of windows and scores of doors were blown out by the blast. Almost every window on the south side of the structure was shattered.

(Left, Below left) Much of the lower deck seating in Section 12 was blown away by the blast. Brick walls around the section were also destroyed. The explosion could be heard throughout much of the downtown area.

(Below) Debris covers the storage room were the blast occurred. Cosgriff was severely injured with severe burns to the head, shoulders and chest, but survived the blast after being hurled through the storage room door before the debris. He was taken to Charity Hospital. Three other workers in a guard room across from the storage room were slightly injured.

(Above, Right) Firemen inspect the blast damage while searching the debris for injured persons. "I was telephoning at the time and the cradle phone was wrenched right out of my hand," Miss Mabelle Radigan told reporters. Radigan recounted, "A change box fell to the floor and we thought the whole stadium was coming down. Then we started running and saw other people running from all parts of the building." Some 200 workers, most Great Lakes Exposition employees, were in the Stadium when the blast occurred. All were badly shaken. Stadium officials said that since the floodlighting system was not damaged, a football game between John Carroll University and Adrian (Mich.) College set for Friday, October 16th, would go on as planned. The Blue Streaks of John Carroll beat Adrian, 7-0. The game was played in a steady drizzle before 800 spectators.

Baseball at the Stadium

June 11, 1933
Walter "Big Train" Johnson's First Day as Manager

On Saturday, June 10, 1933, the Cleveland Baseball Co. welcomed future Hall of Fame pitcher Walter "Big Train" Johnson to town as the team's new manager. On Sunday, June 11th, the Indians played their first game under the watchful eye of Johnson before 8,000 at the Stadium. Cleveland beat the St. Louis Browns, 1-0, in ten innings when reliever Oral Hildebrand, who got the win, singled to score left fielder Joe Vosmik for the winning run. Hildebrand relieved Mel Harder who battled Browns starter Irving "Bump" Hadley for nine innings, before leaving with the bases loaded in the tenth.

(Left) Johnson, who succeeded Roger Peckinpaugh, addresses his team before his first game. The new skipper began his debut by throwing out the first pitch. Johnson compiled a 179-168 record with Cleveland before being replaced by Steve O'Neill in 1935.

Played before an "embarrassingly large crowd," of 31,606 at the Stadium on Tuesday, April 19, 1938, rookie manager Oscar Vitt's Cleveland Indians faced manager Gabby Street's St. Louis Browns in the season opener. Pitching for Cleveland was talented right-hander Johnny Allen. At third base was rookie Ken Keltner, who started 149 games that season. The Indians banged twelve hits off Browns starter Bobo "Buck" Newsom, including a 6th-inning homer by Hal Trosky, but lost, 6-2. Keltner went 2 for 4. The next day Tribe ace Bob Feller pitched a one-hitter, beating the Browns, 9-0, before 3,500 at League Park.

(Left) The 1938 baseball season begins at the Stadium.

May 30, 1938
Cleveland vs. Chicago

The first-place Cleveland Indians battled the seventh-place Chicago White Sox in a holiday doubleheader on Monday, May 30, 1938, before 38,618 at the Stadium. Pitching the first game for Cleveland was 19-year-old right-hander Bob Feller who made his major league debut as a 17-year-old on July 17, 1936. Feller pitched a five-hitter for a 5-2 win. Veteran Johnny Allen won the second game, 8-1, on a four-hitter. It was the sixth win for both men. Allen finished the 1938 season with a 14-8 record. Second baseman Odell Hale went 5 for 7 in the two games.

(Right) Indians manager Oscar Vitt congratulates Feller (14), after winning the first game. Feller won 17 games in 1938 and led the major leagues in strikeouts with 240. In 1939, Feller led the American League in wins with 24 and the majors with 246 strikeouts.

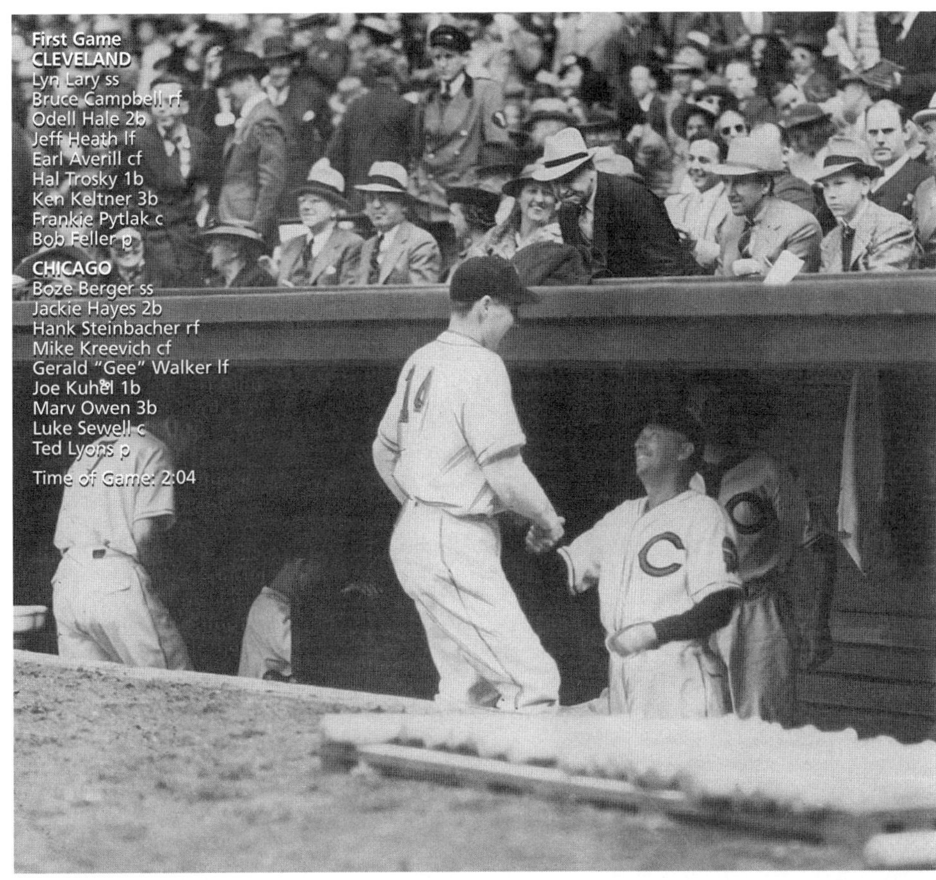

July 10, 1938
Johnny Allen Day

It was "Johnny Allen Day" at the Stadium on Sunday, July 10, 1938, as the first-place Indians (43-25), faced the last-place St. Louis Browns before 27,700 at the Stadium. Cleveland won the game, 8-7, when Jeff Heath singled in the bottom of the ninth to drive in Skeeter Webb. Though Allen started, reliever Danny Galehouse got the win. Allen, who struck out four, was in search of his 13th straight win against only one loss. Allen had won 28 out of his last 30 games, giving him a career winning percentage of .758 (97-31).

(Right) Before the game, Tribe hurler Johnny Allen was honored as the Sporting News' outstanding pitcher for 1937 after posting a 15-1 record. Local sportscaster Jack Graney (left), presents a scroll to Allen recognizing his achievement, as manager Oscar Vitt looks on.

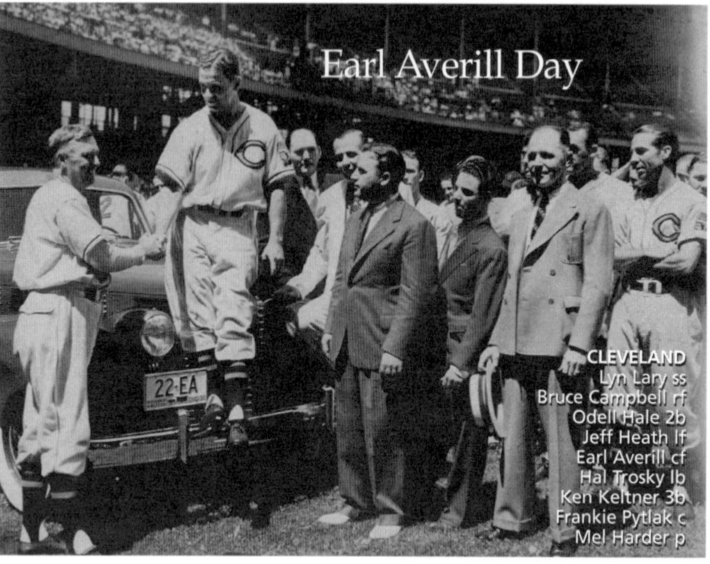

Fighting to remain in second place, the Cleveland Indians, two games behind the league-leading New York Yankees in the American League standings, hosted the third-place Boston Red Sox in a Sunday doubleheader on August 7, 1938. Prior to the game, veteran Tribe All-Star center fielder Earl Averill was honored before 35,000 at the Stadium for his ten seasons with the club. Though Averill helped by hitting a triple, Cleveland lost the first game, 4-3, as Boston starter Jack Wilson got the win. Tribe starter Mel Harder took the loss. In the second contest, starter Earl Whitehill, Johnny Humphries and Bob Feller combined to beat Boston, 8-6. All eight Tribe runs were scored in the first six innings, before the Red Sox tallied for the first time. Averill went 1 for 3 in the second game with a single.

(Left) Averill shakes hands with Tribe manager Oscar Vitt in front of the $2,500 Cadillac Averill received during a pre-game ceremony.

(Above right) Earl Averill (right), is joined by Boston slugger Jimmie Foxx. Averill was batting .354, second to Foxx in the American League batting race. Foxx was hitting .359. The Indians' Hal Trosky was fifth in the A.L. standings, with a .337 average. Foxx went on to win the A.L. batting title with a .349 average, but it wasn't Averill or Trosky, who finished second to Foxx. It was Cleveland left fielder Jeff Heath, who ended the year with a .343 average and led the league with 18 triples. Heath was batting .314 on August 7th.

June 27, 1939 / Major League

Baseball Under Lights Comes to Cleveland

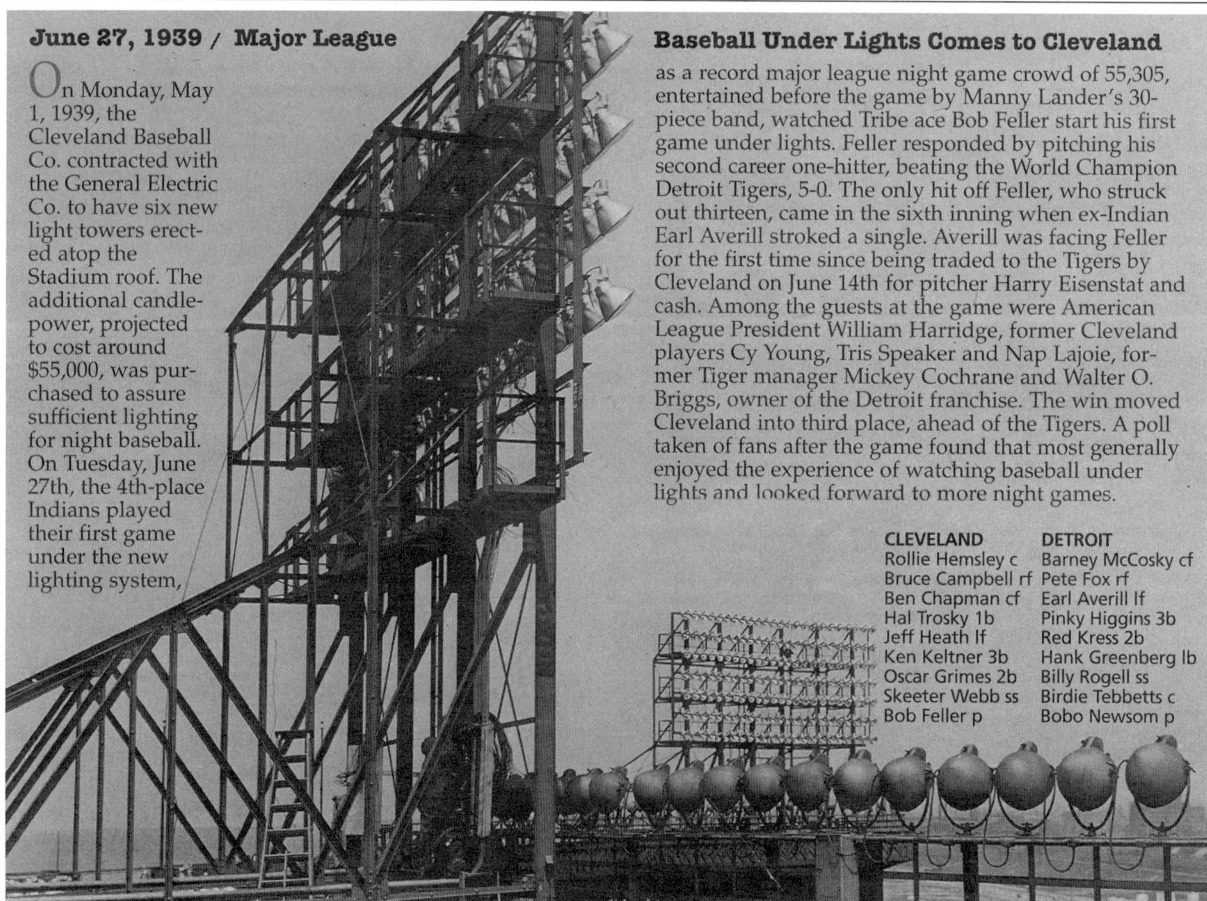

On Monday, May 1, 1939, the Cleveland Baseball Co. contracted with the General Electric Co. to have six new light towers erected atop the Stadium roof. The additional candlepower, projected to cost around $55,000, was purchased to assure sufficient lighting for night baseball. On Tuesday, June 27th, the 4th-place Indians played their first game under the new lighting system, as a record major league night game crowd of 55,305, entertained before the game by Manny Lander's 30-piece band, watched Tribe ace Bob Feller start his first game under lights. Feller responded by pitching his second career one-hitter, beating the World Champion Detroit Tigers, 5-0. The only hit off Feller, who struck out thirteen, came in the sixth inning when ex-Indian Earl Averill stroked a single. Averill was facing Feller for the first time since being traded to the Tigers by Cleveland on June 14th for pitcher Harry Eisenstat and cash. Among the guests at the game were American League President William Harridge, former Cleveland players Cy Young, Tris Speaker and Nap Lajoie, former Tiger manager Mickey Cochrane and Walter O. Briggs, owner of the Detroit franchise. The win moved Cleveland into third place, ahead of the Tigers. A poll taken of fans after the game found that most generally enjoyed the experience of watching baseball under lights and looked forward to more night games.

CLEVELAND	DETROIT
Rollie Hemsley c	Barney McCosky cf
Bruce Campbell rf	Pete Fox rf
Ben Chapman cf	Earl Averill lf
Hal Trosky 1b	Pinky Higgins 3b
Jeff Heath lf	Red Kress 2b
Ken Keltner 3b	Hank Greenberg lb
Oscar Grimes 2b	Billy Rogell ss
Skeeter Webb ss	Birdie Tebbetts c
Bob Feller p	Bobo Newsom p

Ray Mack & Lou Boudreau
August 7, 1939

Before the 1939 regular season began, second baseman Ray (Mlckovsky) Mack (left, at right), and infielder Lou Boudreau (right), two of the Indians' top prospects, were sent down to the Tribe's minor league club in Buffalo for several months of training under the watchful eye of Bisons manager Steve O'Neill. On Monday, August 7, 1939, Mack and Boudreau made their big league debut as a double-play tandem in a night game between the fourth-place Indians and the last-place St. Louis Browns before 16,467 at the Stadium. Both 22-year-olds played a role in the Tribe's 6-5 win over St. Louis. In the fourth inning, Boudreau, after hitting a triple to right field, scored the Tribe's first run on a wild pitch. With the score tied in the eighth inning, hits by pinch-hitter Roy Weatherly and catcher Rollie Hemsley scored Mack for the winning run, after Mack had driven in the tying run with a fielder's choice. Right-hander Willis Hudlin started, but reliever Johnny Broaca captured the victory, the Tribe's fourth win in five nighttime contests. Boudreau told reporters after the game, "I don't want to appear cocky, but I think I can make the grade. I'm not worried about my fielding, but I'll admit that I have been a little scared about not being able to hit big league pitching."

(Left) Before the game began on August 7th, Cleveland native Ray Mack (second from right), a former local sandlot star and All-Ohio fullback at Case Tech, was honored at home plate by hometown friends with a floral wreath as teammate Lou Boudreau (second from left), looked on. Both men fielded a number of infield smashes to display their defensive skills, but missed the chance to combine on a double play. After the game, Mack and Boudreau were the guests of honor at a banquet held at Otto Poschke's Poschke Barbeque, 8905-23 Lake Avenue. Mack played for Poschke Barbeque in the Cleveland Baseball Federation's Class A Division.

THE LINEUPS

CLEVELAND	ST. LOUIS
Lou Boudreau ss	Don Heffner ss
Bruce Campbell rf	Joe Grace cf
Ben Chapman cf	George McQuinn 1b
Hal Trosky 1b	Moose Solters lf
Jeff Heath lf	Harlond "Darkie" Clift 3b
Ken Keltner 3b	Billy Sullivan rf
Ray Mack 2b	Joe Glenn c
Rollie Hemsley c	Johnny Berardino 2b
Willis Hudlin p	Howard Mills p

Time of Game: 2:16

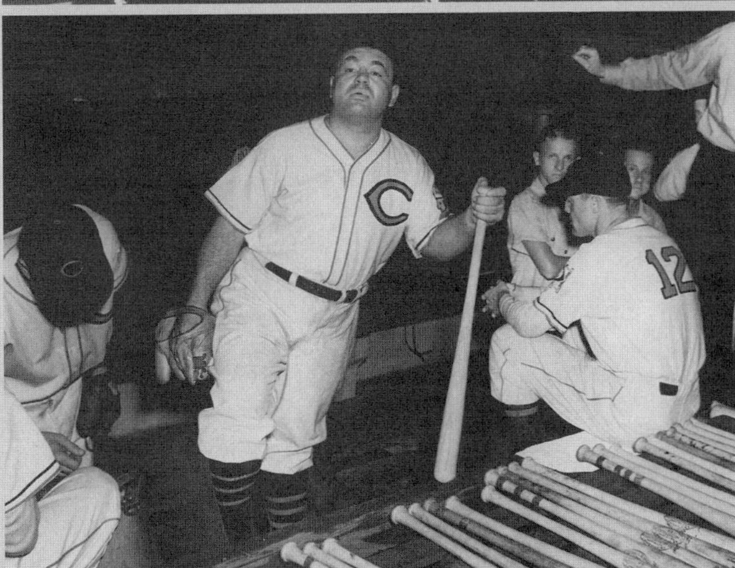

(Left) Heavyweight boxer "Two-Ton" Tony Galento (with bat), was brought in by local Italians to entertain Stadium fans on August 7th. Columnist Ben Williamson wrote in The Cleveland Press the following day, "Signor T. T. T. Galento hit a dozen pitches, pushed Umpire Cal Hubbard around a few times and, perspiring nobly, came back to the dugout and allowed, "this ain't no business for me." That made it unanimous. It was reported that Galento's fee was one grand. They should have had him at the Poultry Congress (at Public Hall,) instead of the ball game, for Tony laid one grand egg." Miss Cleveland of 1939 was also introduced before the game.

The 1940's
Festivals of Freedom

Tuesday, July 4, 1940

The Come to Cleveland Committee and the American Legion joined forces to sponsor the city's first Festival of Freedom at the Stadium on Tuesday, July 4, 1939. Though rain washed out the final half of the show, and moved the fireworks display to the following Sunday, the foundation was laid for another Independence Day festival. Over 75,000 attended the second Festival of Freedom at the Stadium on Thursday, July 4, 1940. When all the Stadium seating was taken, loudspeakers were employed outside the Stadium to direct an additional 50,000 spectators to a section behind City Hall where they could watch the fireworks. Inside, William Ganson Rose presided over the array of speeches by local dignitaries, musical presentation by groups such as the Wings Over Jordan Chorus, and sets of community singing led by the Festival of Freedom orchestra. For a half hour period, Americans from coast to coast followed the event via a live radio broadcast. During the broadcast, 150 Boy Scouts unfurled the world's largest American flag as the Stadium audience rose to join Ohio Supreme Court Chief Justice Carl V. Weygandt in pledging allegiance to the flag. Deputy Traffic Commissioner John R. Sammon later said the second Festival of Freedom brought more people downtown than any event in his memory. Over 200 businesses contributed to making the city's celebration of freedom a success.

(Above) The 1940 Freedom Festival ended with one of the largest and most colorful fireworks displays ever held in the city.

Saturday, July 4, 1942

Over 81,000 spectators, the largest turnout in the event's four-year history, attended the city's first war-time Festival of Freedom on Saturday, July 4, 1942. Uncle Sam was there. As was 100-year-old Josiah Williams Hill, who served as a scout for Gen. Sherman in the Civil War. A patriotic music program was offered, with the crowd led in community singing sessions while Dr. Rudolph Ringwall conducted the Festival of Freedom orchestra. Before the annual fireworks display began, a mass induction of 500 men into the Army, Navy, and Coast Guard was held. The Cleveland Grays band played "Yankee Doodle" as the newly-inducted men marched off to war. "God Bless America" followed, draining the emotions of those singing along.

(Right) A military parade opened the free event with area infantry marching along downtown streets to the Stadium. The convoy of military vehicles at right included vehicles built locally by the White Motor Co.

Tuesday, July 4, 1944

On the European front, General Omar Bradley was leading Allied forces in a new offensive, only days after the invasion of Normandy, when Cleveland held its sixth annual Festival of Freedom at the Stadium on Tuesday, July 4, 1944. Before the show concluded with the annual fireworks display, band leader Benny Goodman performed with his trio, "producing several potent samples of his rhythmic elixir." Adding to the musical program were the 68-piece Silver Band of the Canadian Air Force from Ottawa, the Festival of Freedom orchestra led by Dr. Rudolph Ringwall and Donald Dickson of the Metropolitan Opera, who delivered stirring renditions of "Old Man River" and "One Alone." Hollywood stars Susan Hayward and Alan Marshall, on tour with the fifth War Loan Drive, also made brief bond-buying appeals to the crowd of over 70,000. Preferred seating was offered to attendees who received tickets in exchange for purchasing War Bonds at $18.75.

(Upper left) Hollywood stars Susan Hayward, Alan Marshall and baritone Donald Dickson, a former Clevelander (right), join band leader Benny Goodman (far left), at the Stadium during the Festival of Freedom.

(Left) The Cleveland Kilty Band (at left), the Civil Air Patrol Cadets, the Cleveland Grays band and the Boy Scouts were among the groups participating in a ninety-minute all-military parade that opened the Festival of Freedom. Over 2,000 area fighting men marched in the display of local patriotism.

Thursday, July 4, 1946

The city's first post-war Festival of Freedom was held at the Stadium on Thursday, July 4, 1946, in celebration of the nation's 170th Independence Day and the city's sesquicentennial. Over 80,000 attended the gala event that began at 7:45 P.M. with six B-26 bombers and six P-47 Thunderbolts from the famous All-Negro 99th Fighter Squadron flying over the Stadium. Music was provided by the Festival of Freedom orchestra, joined by a 1,500-member chorus. The massive fireworks display (at right), which began at 9:55 P.M., was highlighted by a simulated atomic bombing of the fleet at Bikini with, "the biggest boom heard here in years." Among the many celebrities introduced that evening were Miss Mary Dublin, the city's sesquicentennial queen and Miss Marguerite Bacon, great-great-great-great-granddaughter of Moses Cleaveland.

The Army War Show

When the U. S. Army's 2,000-member Army War Show opened its five-night stand at Municipal Stadium on Friday, September 18, 1942, the newspaper advertisement called it, "the greatest spectacle ever staged in America, with roaring guns, rumbling tanks, zooming planes, charging cavalry, medical corps, combat engineers, flame throwers, signal corps, Army chaplains, mobile artillery, a jeep jamboree and realistic battle action." Under the direction of Col. Wilson T. Bals, "Here's Your Army," played to 43,789 spectators on opening night, with all proceeds from each show going to Army Emergency Relief. Music was provided throughout the 23-scene show by the sixty-piece Army War Show Task force band. Each night, a short fireworks display and the singing of the national anthem ended one of the smokiest, noisiest and most patriotic events ever held at the Stadium. On Sunday, September 20th, 81,009 attended the military extravaganza, making it at the time, the largest paid attendance to see a Stadium event, surpassing the previous record set in 1932 during the first professional baseball game at the Stadium, by 825 visitors. When 76,113 attended the final performance on Tuesday, September 22nd, the Army War Show had drawn over 340,000 spectators to its five-day military tribute.

(Above) At 9:59 P.M., huge searchlights cut through the evening sky as a 90-mm. gun commanded by Lieut. J. Cannon (at left), and a 40-mm. Bofors gun commanded by Lieut. Walter Segda, blazed away at planes outlined by brilliant searchlights. Weighing eight and a half tons, the 90-mm. gun fired 25 times a second and had a range of up to six miles. The Bofors gun fired several pounds of explosives at 120 shots a minute. Other demonstrations included a motorized artillery display with four 105-mm. guns at 9:05 P.M., a cavalry display at 9:14 P.M. and an automatic weapons display at 9:15 P.M. At 9:48 P.M., army tanks entered the Stadium and proceeded to crush several cars placed in their way. The tanks were then engaged in a battle with tank destroyers carrying 75-mm. canons.

(Below) A "Battle Depot" was set up directly east of the Stadium to house War Show personnel and equipment during the

five-day show. A special section featuring military exhibits and equipment demonstrations was open to the public from 2 to 10 P.M. each day with tickets priced at 35¢ for adults and 10¢ for children. Visitors, especially mothers of men and boys in the service, were welcomed into the bivouac area from 2 to 4 P.M. each afternoon. "Mothers particularly, are interested in seeing the conditions under which their boys live in the army," declared Colonel Bals.

(Left, below left) Each War Show performance ended with a mock battle, as U. S. forces attacked a tree-studded Japanese stronghold situated in the north section of the Stadium. The action began with two motorcycle scouts entering the infield from the south. Gun fire from the enemy-held village would "kill" one of the scouts, but the other scout would escape to alert the infantry, who advanced in waves on the enemy position under rifle and machine gun cover. The ground troops were then joined by tanks and field artillery, who shot screaming shells into their objective while anti-aircraft guns fired on enemy planes highlighted by ground lights with pinpoint accuracy. The action continued until the "Japanese" soldiers were taken prisoner and the American flag was raised. Ticket prices for the Stadium spectacle were 55¢ for general admission, $1.10 for reserved seats and $2.20 for box seats. At the conclusion of the War Show's five-day run, the Stadium grounds crew was responsible for getting the field in shape for a football game between Cathedral Latin and St. Ignatius high schools on Sunday, September 27th. The heavy tanks, cavalry and artillery pieces dug up the Stadium turf so extensively, that one grounds crew member remarked, "We've been trying to get rid of crabgrass for years and it looks like it took the Army to do it." Cathedral Latin beat St. Ignatius, 22-0, before 9,942 at the Stadium.

(Right) Spewing flames up to 75 feet in the air, flame throwers operated by soldiers of the chemical warfare outfit were brought out for a one-minute demonstration each evening from 9:33 to 9:34 P.M. under the command of Lieut. Marshall Linz. "It was real flame, too, and the heat of that super-charged bit of hell could be felt in the stands," wrote Roelif Loveland in the Cleveland Plain Dealer on Saturday, September 19, 1942. A salute to industry and labor followed at 9:36 P.M. Technicians from the army's signal corps demonstrated at 9:44 P.M. how it took only three minutes to string the communication lines seen in the top photograph.

1940-1945
Baseball at the Stadium

The Cleveland Indians played their home opener of the 1940 season on Friday, April 19th against manager Del Baker's Detroit Tigers before only 26,259 paying fans, in large part because of the 39° game-time temperature. Cleveland beat the Tigers, 4-0, on starter Johnny Allen's three-hitter. Helping the Tribe's cause was a home run by left fielder Jeff Heath.

(Right) Before the game, Tribe manager Oscar Vitt (with jacket, left), was joined by Miss Mary Porter of Memphis, Tennessee, the official "Maid of Cotton," and Chief Oneida, one of the Indians performing with the rodeo at Cleveland Arena. Vitt, who was holding a cotton ball, received the headdress he's wearing from the rodeo Indians. The baseball Indians were guests of the rodeo riders at the Arena that evening.

OPENING DAY LINEUPS

CLEVELAND	DETROIT
Lou Boudreau ss	Barney McCosky cf
Roy Weatherly cf	Bruce Campbell rf
Ben Chapman rf	Charlie Gehringer 2b
Hal Trosky 1b	Hank Greenberg lf
Jeff Heath lf	Rudy York 1b
Ken Keltner 3b	Pinky Higgins 3b
Rollie Hemsley c	Dick Bartell ss
Ray Mack 2b	Birdie Tebbetts c
Johnny Allen p	Cotton Pippen p

Ceremonial first pitch:
Mayor Harold R. Burton

June 23, 1940
Ted Williams' Injury

The first-place Cleveland Indians faced the Boston Red Sox in a Sunday doubleheader before 56,850 at the Stadium on June 23, 1940. Indians starter Al Smith beat Boston's Lefty Grove to the win the first game, 4-1. Smith, who got help from homers by Mack and third baseman Ken Keltner, threw a six-hitter, holding Joe Cronin, Jimmie Foxx and Dom DiMaggio hitless. Two homers by first baseman Jim Tabor off Tribe starter Joe Dobson, gave Boston a 2-0 win in the second game.

(Left) In the eighth inning of the first game, Red Sox left fielder Ted Williams (on the ground), was knocked out when he collided with center fielder Doc Cramer while chasing a drive by Tribe second baseman Ray Mack. Williams, in his second season with the Red Sox, walked off the field, but remained in Lakeside Hospital the next day with a mild concussion.

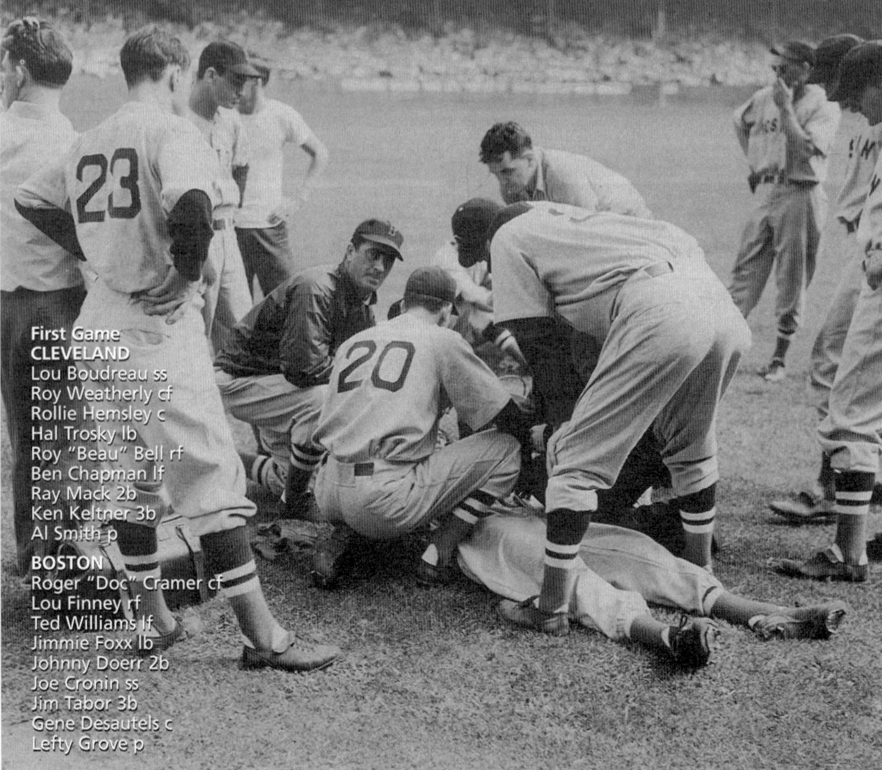

First Game
CLEVELAND
Lou Boudreau ss
Roy Weatherly cf
Rollie Hemsley c
Hal Trosky 1b
Roy "Beau" Bell rf
Ben Chapman lf
Ray Mack 2b
Ken Keltner 3b
Al Smith p

BOSTON
Roger "Doc" Cramer cf
Lou Finney rf
Ted Williams lf
Jimmie Foxx 1b
Johnny Doerr 2b
Joe Cronin ss
Jim Tabor 3b
Gene Desautels c
Lefty Grove p

1940- Lemons, Tomatoes, Oranges & Eggs

Sept. 11, 1940 / Cleveland vs. New York

The Cleveland Indians, fighting to stay in first place, faced the New York Yankees in a crucial doubleheader on Wednesday, September 11, 1940, before 33,471 at the Stadium. In the fourth inning of the first game, a lemon was tossed at Yankee slugger Joe DiMaggio as he came up to bat. This was followed by a barrage of lemons, oranges, tomatoes and eggs hurled at Yankee players, with many aimed at unpopular third base coach Art Fletcher. Though most of the throwing was harmless, in the second game, a beer bottle was tossed toward the Yankees from the upper deck on the third base side. The Indians lost the first game, 3-1, but came back to win the darkness-curtailed second contest, 5-3, with Tribe starter Al Smith getting the win.

(Right) Yankee manager Joe McCarthy (center), reacts to the fruit tosses, as members of the ground crew pick up the debris. McCarthy threatened to take his team off the field if the fruit throwing continued.

September 27, 1940
The Ladies' Day Fruit Barrage

It was Ladies' Day at the Stadium on Friday, September 27, 1940, as the second-place Cleveland Indians faced the Detroit Tigers, who were on the verge of clinching their sixth American League pennant. The game was played before 45,533, with many fans aware that the week before Cleveland players had been hit by fruit thrown by Tigers fans during a crucial series in Detroit. As Tiger left fielder Hank Greenberg took the field during pre-game batting practice, he was showered by apples, oranges, tomatoes and the remains of lunches from women spectators in the upper and lower left field stands. The left fielder became the subject of more fruit tosses as he took the field in the first inning. When Greenberg tried to field a pop fly, he was peppered by even more fruit. Head umpire Bill Summers responded by informing the crowd that any time a Detroit player was interfered with, the Tribe batter would be called out. The next inning, a basket filled with fruit and empty bottles fell from the upper deck into the Detroit bullpen, striking Tiger catcher George (Birdie) Tebbetts in the back of the neck. Tebbetts was knocked unconscious, but recovered enough to leave the field after several minutes of attention. The fans remained calm until the last inning, when eggs were thrown at Tigers players protesting a call at home plate. Facing Cleveland ace Bob Feller on the mound was 25-year-old rookie hurler Floyd Giebell. Feller, who was seeking his 27th win, pitched his best game of the season against the Tigers, a complete-game, three-hitter, but Detroit won, 2-0, to clinch the pennant. The two Tiger runs came in the fourth inning on a pop-fly homer by Rudy York that barely cleared the left field stands. Giebell, who also pitched a complete game, held Cleveland to six hits, while issuing only two walks and striking out six. After getting pinch-hitter Jeff Heath to ground out for the final out, Giebell was carried off the field on his teammate's shoulders. In his column the next day, Plain Dealer sports reporter Gordon Cobbledick wrote that the fruit throwing frenzy, "Only went to prove that the female hoodlum is more vicious than the male."

(Above right) The Stadium grounds crew and Tiger players cleaning up the fruit debris.
(Right) Detroit catcher George (Birdie) Tebbetts (right), eating a piece of fruit with teammate Hal Newhouser during the game. Tebbetts later played 97 games for the Cleveland Indians in 1951 and 1952. Tebbetts also managed the Indians from 1963 to mid-1966.

Al Horwitz's swing band entertained fans before the game, as manager Roger Peckinpaugh's second place Cleveland Indians faced manager Joe McCarthy's league-leading New York Yankees before 67,468, "the greatest crowd in the history of night baseball," at the Stadium on Thursday, July 17, 1941. On the line was Yankee slugger Joe DiMaggio's record-setting 56-game hitting streak. In his first at bat, DiMaggio hit a hard smash off left-hander Al Smith to third baseman Ken Keltner. Keltner made a spectacular back-handed play to stop the ball and then threw to first for the out. In his second at bat, DiMaggio walked. His third time up, DiMaggio hit another hard smash to Keltner, who again threw to first for the out. In his final trip to the plate, DiMaggio (above during his last at bat with Tribe catcher Rollie Hemsley,) stepped up to the plate with the bases loaded and only one out. This time 'Joltin' Joe' faced reliever Jim Bagby, Jr. With the count at one ball and one strike, Joe bounced a grounder to shortstop Lou Boudreau, who combined with Ray Mack and first baseman Oscar Grimes on an inning-ending double play. "That Al Smith pitched a good game, but he didn't break my hitting streak. The guy that turned the trick was that Ken Keltner. He was a little rough on me," explained DiMaggio. Smith and Bagby combined on a seven-hitter, holding DiMaggio, Rosar and Rizzuto hitless, but lost 4-3. Smith held New York hitless until the seventh inning, when Joe Gordon homered. In the eighth inning, Tribe outfielder Roy Weatherly misjudged a low fly to center. The ball rolled to the cinder track, allowing Charlie Keller to reach third. Lefty Gomez singled to drive in Keller. A pop single by Sturm and a double by Rolfe gave the Yankees a 4-1 lead. In the ninth inning, Oscar Grimes and Gee Walker, who hit a fourth-inning inside-the-park homer, scored on Larry Rosenthal's triple, but reliever Johnny Murphy got Weatherly to ground out for the victory. Gomez got the win. Smith took the loss. DiMaggio faced Tribe hurlers 26 times in 223 at bats during his streak, with ten of his 91 hits coming off Cleveland pitchers. Three of his hits came at League Park on July 16th, when DiMaggio scored three runs to help beat the Tribe.

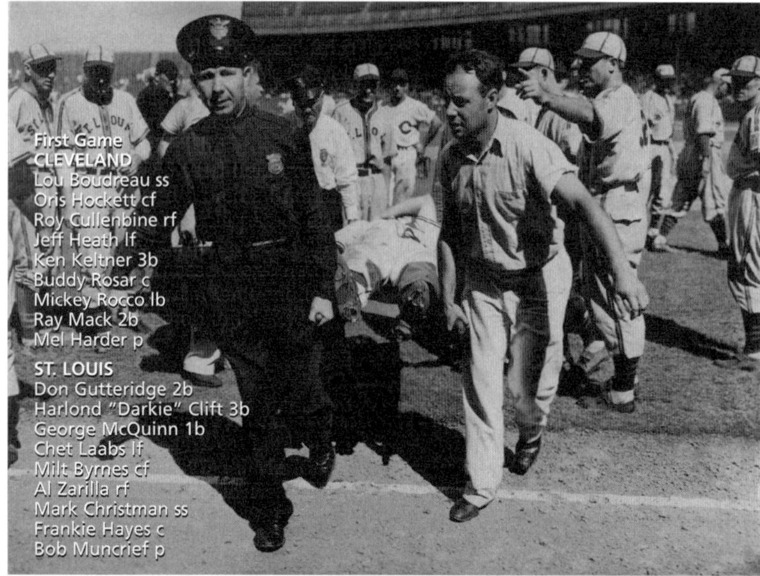

August 8, 1943
Ken Keltner is Injured

The 5th-place Cleveland Indians handed the St. Louis Browns a double defeat on August 8, 1943, taking both games of a Sunday doubleheader, 6-5, and 3-2, before 16,727 at the Stadium. Tribe reliever Cubby Dean got the win in the 14-inning first game. In the second contest, Jim Bagby pitched a complete game to beat starter Bobo Newsom for his 12th victory. The Indians captured the two contests, but lost the services of starter Ken Keltner, when the third baseman was spiked by St. Louis right fielder Mike Chartak in the 12th inning of the first game. Chartak cut Keltner's right ankle to the bone in a gash four inches long.

(Left) Being carried off the field at left, Keltner was transported to Lakeside Hospital in a police ambulance. That night, club physician M. R. Castle said he thought the infielder might be lost for at least a month, and possibly for the season.

May 25, 1944
Mel Harder Night

Thursday, May 25, 1944 was "Mel Harder Night" at the Stadium, as the Cleveland Indians took on the Washington Senators before 18,798 at the Stadium. Harder, who pitched a complete game, was seeking his 202nd career win, but his teammates spoiled the night by losing to the Senators, 4-2, on four unearned runs. Three came in the ninth inning. The loss dropped Cleveland into the American League cellar.

(Right) Tribe ace Mel Harder, the dean of Indians pitchers, (center), is joined during pre-game ceremonies by Cleveland Mayor Frank Lausche (left), and former pitching great Cy Young. Harder, who compiled a 223-186 record in 582 games with the Indians from 1928 to 1947, was being honored for entering the prestigious 200-career win club.

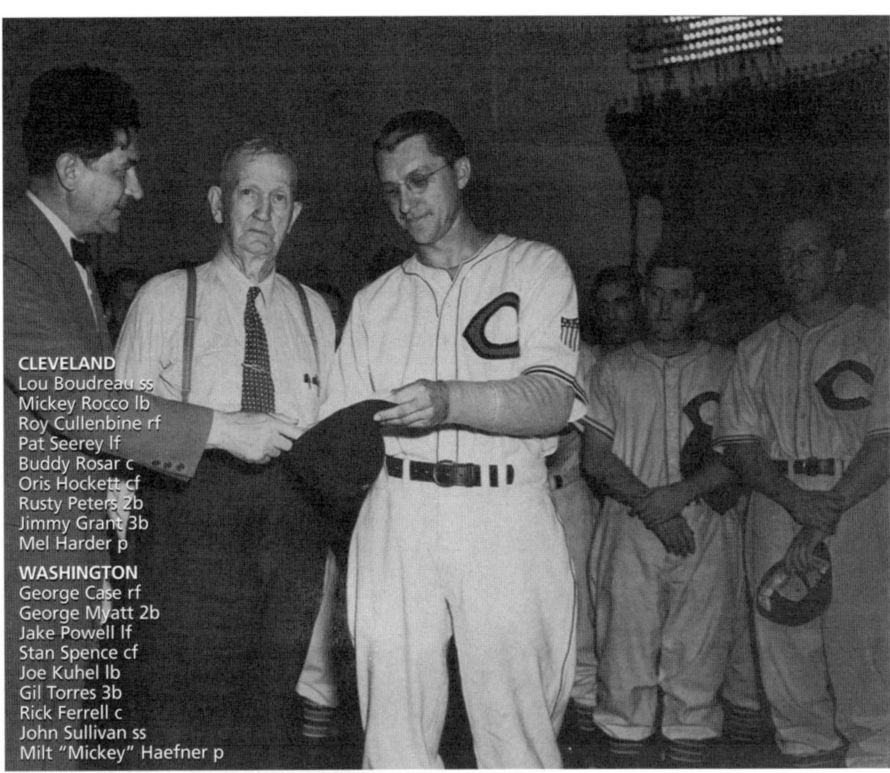

August 24, 1945
Bob Feller Returns to Action

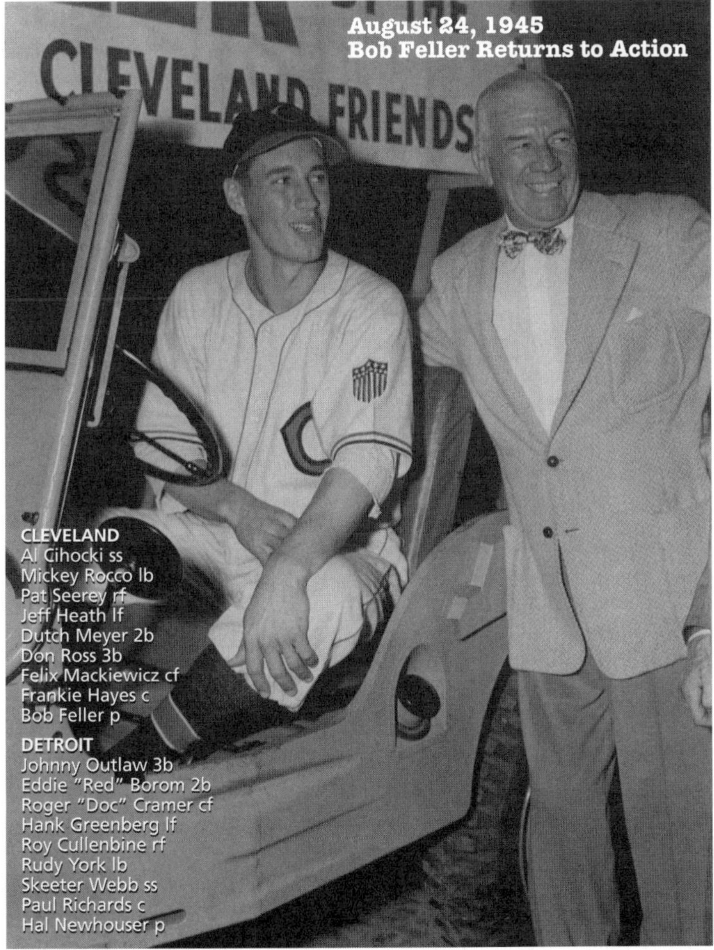

In the early morning hours of August 23, 1945, 26-year-old Chief Specialist Robert W. Feller, N. R., arrived at Cleveland Airport wearing civvies for the first time since enlisting in the Navy on December 10, 1941. Feller returned on an United Airlines Mainliner with his wife from Chicago, where he had been assigned to the Great Lakes Naval Training Station. His return to private life was celebrated with a luncheon that afternoon at Hotel Carter. On Friday, the 24th, Feller made his return "debut" at the Stadium against the first-place Detroit Tigers with Hal Newhouser (who won baseball's pitching triple crown in 1945,) on the mound. Feller delighted the partisan nighttime crowd of 46,477 by beating the Tigers, 4-2, on a four-hitter. Feller captured his 108th career win by striking out twelve, including Hank Greenberg, Rudy York and Johnny Outlaw twice each and fanned every Tiger starter except catcher Paul Richards, at least once. "Bob had very good stuff," reported Tribe catcher Frankie Hayes. "His fast ball was too much for them and he showed me as good a curve as I've seen. He's a helluva good pitcher, allright." Right fielder Pat Seerey helped by hitting a first-inning homer. When Feller returned to the Indians in 1945, only six players remained from the 1941 squad- shortstop Lou Boudreau, who had replaced Roger Peckinpaugh as manager; pitchers Mel Harder, Al Smith and Jim Bagby; outfielder Jeff Heath and Gene Desautels.

(Left) Feller received a number of gifts from Cleveland friends as part of the pre-game activities on August 24th, including the new Jeep at left. Joining Feller is former Cleveland player-manager and Hall of Famer Tris Speaker. Feller also received a pen and pencil set from club manager Lou Boudreau and his teammates.

The 1940's
Cleveland Baseball Federation Amateur Days

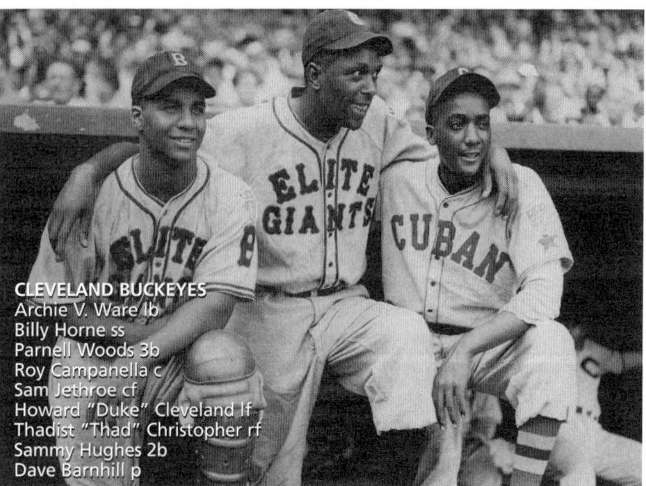

CLEVELAND BUCKEYES
Archie V. Ware 1b
Billy Horne ss
Parnell Woods 3b
Roy Campanella c
Sam Jethroe cf
Howard "Duke" Cleveland lf
Thadist "Thad" Christopher rf
Sammy Hughes 2b
Dave Barnhill p

A crowd of over 20,000 was expected for the Cleveland Baseball Federation's 20th anniversary Amateur Day program at the Stadium on Sunday, August 9, 1942, but only 13,000 showed up because of foul weather. Only two games got underway before rain wiped out further action. The first contest was a Class F game won by Edith Ayres Post 402 over Dudley Blossom Boystown, 9-7. The second game pitted the Negro National League-leading Cleveland Buckeyes against a local Class A All-Nations squad made up of players representing 26 different nationalities. With the addition of Baltimore Elite Giants catcher Roy Campanella, Giants second baseman Sammy Hughes and New York Cubans right-hander Dave Barnhill to their roster, the Buckeyes were much too powerful for the Class A squad. The Negro stars scored five runs in the first inning off All-Nations starter Roy Pinyoun and were leading, 9-0, after five innings, when the game was called. Cleveland Buckeyes star Sammy Jethroe went 1 for 3 with a double. The Class A game for the first half championship between the Rosenblums and Bartunek Clothes teams was rescheduled for the next night. The following week, The Cleveland Plain Dealer reported that Campanella had been fined $250 and suspended from Negro League play for the rest of the year because he failed to get his team's permission to play for the Buckeyes. The paper also suggested that it might cost Campanella a tryout with the Pittsburgh Pirates. Hughes and Barnhill, who were also slated for tryouts with the Pirates, had permission to play from their teams.

(Above left) The Cleveland Buckeyes and All-Nation teams during pre-game ceremonies. **(Left)** Catcher Roy Campanella (left), second baseman Sammy Hughes and pitcher Dave Barnhill. Barnhill gave up four hits, struck out nine and didn't issue a walk in the win.

Amateur Day / July 25, 1943

The annual Cleveland Baseball Federation Amateur Day festival in 1943 was held on Sunday, July 25th, before a record turnout of 20,432 at the Stadium. Before the amateur games began, an impressive patriotic pre-game ceremony was arranged by CBF president Bill Duggan to honor ex-sandlotters in the armed forces. As part of the military tribute, a parade was organized which included a number of local military groups and organizations such as the Weatherhead Co. Band and the Wings Over Jordan Choir. In the Class A game, Norm Schoen's Bartunek Clothes, behind an eight-hitter by John Hvisdos, beat Factory Furnitures, with Frank Pecjak pitching, 3-1. Over $8,500 was raised for the CBF's medical injury fund. Amateur Day chairman Max Rosenblum was also honored on his 25th anniversary of sponsoring local athletic teams.

(Right) Cleveland Baseball Federation president Bill Duggan addresses the Stadium crowd during pre-game ceremonies. Behind Duggan are members of the Wings Over Jordan Choir.

Ty Cobb, Babe Ruth & Tris Speaker

July 27, 1941

The Cleveland Baseball Federation's annual Amateur Day program at the Stadium on Sunday, July 27, 1941, was called both an artistic and financial success, after more than 15,000 came out to watch the amateur games and see three of baseball's living legends, Ty Cobb (left), George Herman (Babe) Ruth, and former Cleveland player-manager Tris Speaker (right). The three men signed autographs and even took a few swings at the plate. Ruth and Cobb also served as honorary managers of a youth game between the Dudley S. Blossom Boystown and Edith Ayres Post No. 402 teams, with Speaker umpiring the contest.

Following the opening flag raising ceremony, the three men were escorted to home plate where broadcaster Tom Manning presented Cobb, Ruth and Speaker to the crowd after remarks by Amateur Day chairman Max Rosenblum and Mayor Edward Blythin. While Cobb was addressing the crowd, the Stadium P. A. system went out, forcing Ruth and Speaker to simply wave to their fans. In the Class A doubleheader, the Bartunek Clothes squad, led by iron man Max Aynik, who pitched both games, beat the Akron Goodyears, 3-2, and Rosenblums, 4-1, to win the first half Class A title.

A record crowd of 64,877 paying 85¢ for reserved seats, and $1.25 for box seats, attended the 26th annual Cleveland Baseball Federation (CBF) Amateur Day program at the Stadium on Wednesday, July 14, 1948. Most came to see the Cleveland Indians battle manager Leo Durocher's Brooklyn Dodgers in the second game of a home-and-home exhibition series. The first contest was won a month before by the Dodgers at Ebbets Field. The game marked the first appearance of a Brooklyn team in Cleveland since the Indians faced the Brooklyn Robins in the 1920 World Series at League Park, and the first time the game's four black players, Jackie Robinson, Roy Campanella, Satchel Paige and Larry Doby, played in the same major league contest. The Cleveland Press reported the next day, "It was only an exhibition game between the Indians and the Brooklyn Dodgers, but it was enough of an attraction to prove once more (as if additional proof is necessary,) that Cleveland is the most astonishing baseball city in the country." The Indians beat Brooklyn, 4-3, in 11 innings, with Tribe hurlers Ed Klieman, Don Black, Gene Bearden and Paige, who struck out the side in the seventh inning, holding Brooklyn to five hits, two by Campanella. Each pitch Paige threw was greeted with a huge roar from the crowd. In the 11th, Tribe catcher Jim Hegan singled to score second baseman Joe Gordon from second base for the win. In the Class A game before the big league contest, Bartunek Clothes beat Wenham Truckers, 3-1. Wally Kloots got the win over Wenham starter Edgar (Special Delivery) Jones.

(Left) Prior to the Indians-Dodgers game, Amateur Day chairman Max Rosenblum (left), presented a plaque to Tribe president Bill Veeck in recognition of his support of the CBF. Tribe Vice President Hank Greenberg (right), accepted the award for Veeck, who was in Chicago visiting his ailing mother.

The NFL Championship

After beating the Chicago Bears and Green Bay Packers twice, and the Detroit Lions, 28-21, in freezing weather on Thanksgiving Day to clinch the Western Division title, the Cleveland Rams (9-1), headed to the NFL championship game for the first time in the club's eight-year history. Their opponent on Sunday, December 16, 1945, was the Washington Redskins led by veteran QB Sammy Baugh, who were seeking their third NFL title. Heavy coats, gloves, ear muffs, and woolen blankets were a must, as the Stadium crowd of 32,178 (paying from $2.40 to $6.00 for reserved seats,) watched the championship contest under frigid winter conditions. The title game was reported to be the coldest on record since 1933, with the temperature never reaching above six degrees. At quarterback for Cleveland was rookie Bob Waterfield, who completed 14 passes for 192 yards, including TD passes to LE Jim Benton and RH Jim Gillette.

THE RAMS' CHAMPIONSHIP LINEUP

POSITION	PLAYER	WEIGHT
L. End	Jim Benton	(206)
L. Tackle	Elbie Schultz	(260)
L. Guard	Riley Matheson	(210)
Center	Mike Scarry	(220)
R. Guard	Milan Lazetich	(215)
R. Tackle	Gil Bouley	(233)
R. End	Steve Pritko	(210)
Quarterback	Bob Waterfield	(191)
L. Half	Fred Gehrke	(190)
R. Half	Jim Gillette	(185)
Fullback	Don Greenwood	(191)

GAME STATISTICS:	Cleve	Wash
First downs rushing:	9	3
First downs passing:	4	4
First downs penalty:	1	1
Total first downs:	14	8
Yds. gained rushing:	180	32
Yds. gained passing:	182	179
Total yds. gained:	372	211
Passes attempted:	27	20
Passes completed:	14	9
Passes intercepted:	1	1

Gillette led all rushers with 101 yards, while the Rams defense held Washington to only 32 yards rushing. The Rams received two fortunate breaks during the hard fought contest. In the first quarter, an end zone pass by Baugh hit the goal post, bouncing back through the end zone for an automatic safety. In the second quarter, after the Rams scored their first TD, Waterfield's partially blocked extra point kick hit the crossbar, but bounced over for the score. The two breaks proved to be the victory margin for Cleveland, who beat the Redskins, 15-14. By capturing the city's first NFL title since 1924, the Rams became the youngest team to win the NFL title. After the game, 33-year-old Rams owner Dan Reeves announced that Waterfield had just signed a new three-year contract worth a reported $20,000 a year, making him football's highest paid player. Waterfield, who after the game headed back to California to be with wife Jane Russell, was reportedly paid $8,000 to play for the Rams in 1945.

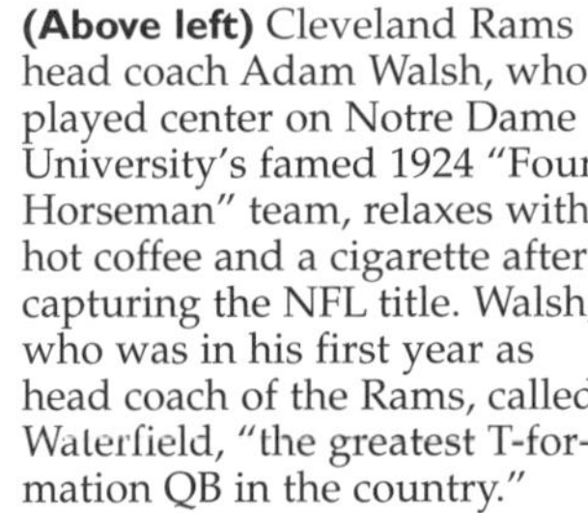

(Above left) Cleveland Rams head coach Adam Walsh, who played center on Notre Dame University's famed 1924 "Four Horseman" team, relaxes with hot coffee and a cigarette after capturing the NFL title. Walsh, who was in his first year as head coach of the Rams, called Waterfield, "the greatest T-formation QB in the country."

(Left) Cleveland Rams Jim Gillette (left), Bob Waterfield, and Jim Benton, who caught nine passes for 125 yards, join head coach Adam Walsh (right), after beating the Redskins. Benton and Gillette both caught TD passes from Waterfield. Each player received $1,469 for winning the title match, $20 more than the winners received in 1944. When the Rams beat the Detroit Lions on Thanksgiving Day, Benton caught ten passes for a 303 yards, an NFL record.

December 22, 1946

The AAFC Championship

When he signed a five-year deal on Thursday, February 8, 1945 to serve as coach and general manager of owner Mickey McBride's Cleveland franchise in the new All-America Football Conference, former Massillon High School and Ohio State University head football coach Paul Brown declared, "You know me- I'm going to try to build a football dynasty in Cleveland." Under Brown's leadership, the Browns compiled an astonishing 47-4-3 record, dominating the AAFC by winning four straight championships. After beating the Buffalo Bisons, 42-17, to clinch their first Western Division title before 37,054 at the Stadium on Sunday, November 24, 1946, Cleveland faced the New York Yankees in the inaugural AAFC title game on Sunday, December 22nd, before 40,469 at the Stadium. Led by the play of Lou "The Toe" Groza, Edgar (Special Delivery) Jones, Marion Motley, Mac Speedie, Dante "Glue Fingers" Lavelli, and QB Otto Graham, who completed 16 passes for 213 yards, Cleveland beat the Yankees, 14-9, to clinch the AAFC crown. New York's score came on a two-yard, third period run by HB Orban "Spec" Sanders. Each Browns player received $931.00 as their share of the winners' pool.

THE CHAMPIONSHIP LINEUP

Position	No.	Player	Weight
L. End	-58-	Mac Speedie	(192)
L. Tackle	-48-	Ernie Blandin	(249)
L. Guard	-36-	Ed Ulinski	(200)
Center	-20-	Moe Scarry	(208)
R. Guard	-32-	Lin Houston	(205)
R. Tackle	-44-	Lou Rymkus	(229)
R. End	-56-	Dante Lavelli	(194)
Quarterback	-60-	Otto Graham	(190)
L. Half	-90-	Dub Jones	(192)
R. Half	-85-	Don Greenwood	(190)
Fullback	-76-	Marion Motley	(218)
PK/Tackle	-46-	Lou Groza	(226)

(Top) Browns FB Marion Motley (left), with guard Bill Willis (right), after beating the Yankees. Motley, who rushed 13 times for 98 yards, scored Cleveland's first TD on a one-yard run. Another time, Motley rambled 51 yards before being tackled by former local grid star Eddie Prokop.

(Above) Head coach Paul Brown savors the win in the locker room with QB Otto Graham (left), Dante Lavelli and Mac Speedie (right). Speedie and Lavelli were Graham's favorite targets. Lavelli caught a game-winning 16-yard TD pass from Graham with less than five minutes to play. A shoestring catch by Speedie set up the TD pass. Brown later stated, "I wouldn't trade these three boys for any six football players."

(Left) While some jubilant fans rushed the field to tear down the goal posts, others mobbed the victors as they headed to the locker room after winning the AAFC championship.

September 21, 1947
Cleveland-28, Baltimore-0

After opening the season with a 30-14 win over the Buffalo Bills at home, and a 55-7 victory over the Brooklyn Dodgers in Brooklyn, the Cleveland Browns (2-0), returned home to play the Baltimore Colts at the Stadium on Sunday, September 21, 1947. Playing before 41,206, coach Paul Brown's talented champions kept their undefeated streak alive, defeating the Colts, 28-0. With the win, Cleveland took over sole procession of first place. The Browns scored three times in the first period, on TDs by FB Marion Motley, HB Bill Boedeker and DB Tom Colella, who scored after intercepting a pass from Colts QB Bud Schwenk. In 1946, Colella led the AAFC with 10 pass interceptions. Cleveland's final score came in the second period on a half-yard plunge by HB Bob Cowan. Brown pulled his starting lineup after the fourth score.

(Left) Cleveland Browns owner Mickey McBride (far left), is joined on the bench during the Baltimore Colts game by left halfbacks Edgar Jones, out with a broken elbow, and Bill Lund (second from right), who was sidelined with a broken thumb.

October 5, 1947 / Cleveland-26, New York-17

After beating the Chicago Rockets, 41-21, the week before in Chicago, the Western Division-leading Cleveland Browns returned home on Sunday, October 5, 1947, to square off against the Eastern Division-leading New York Yankees before a record crowd of 80,067 at the Stadium. Cleveland scored on a first quarter TD pass from QB Otto Graham to HB Bob Cowan, a 29-yard TD run by HB Tommy Colella, a third period TD pass from Graham to E Mac Speedie and two Lou Groza field goals to win 26-7. The Browns played New York again on Sunday, December 14, 1947 in the AAFC championship match before 60,103 at Yankee Stadium. Cleveland won the contest, 14-3, on TDs by Graham and HB Dub Jones, to clinch their second straight AAFC crown.

(Right) Browns place-kicker Lou "The Toe" Groza (46), boots the second of Cleveland's two field goals, a 43-yarder, in the fourth quarter, as Otto Graham (60), spots the ball. Defending against the kick is New York LB Lou Sossaman (25), who had already blocked a Groza extra point attempt and a Groza field goal try.

BROWNS	Att.	Yds.
Colella	5	63
Motley	12	59
Cowan	4	19
Graham	3	31
Greenwood	2	17
Adamle	1	22
Boedeker	1	4
Allen	1	1
Lewis	1	1
YANKEES		
Sanders	11	36
Young	7	41
Sweiger	2	9
Prokop	2	4
Kennedy	1	1

Winning a Third Championship

After winning the All-America Football Conference Western Division title for a third straight year, the Cleveland Browns battled the Buffalo Bills in the AAFC championship game at the Stadium on Sunday, December 19, 1948. Cleveland beat the Bills, 49-7, to capture the AAFC crown for a third straight year. The Cleveland squad carried an 18-game unbeaten streak over two seasons into the Stadium contest, including three regular season wins over the Bills. Cleveland led, 28-0, before the Bills scored their only TD on a 10-yard pass from QB Jim Still to end Alton Baldwin. With the win, the Cleveland Browns became the first franchise in pro football history to finish the season undefeated, and the first to win three straight championship titles. Head coach Paul Brown declared after the win, "This is the best team I've ever coached. Motley, I think, is the greatest fullback in history, greater even than Bronko Nagurski."

(Right) Cleveland scored first at the end of the first quarter, when Edgar (Special Delivery) Jones (with ball), went over from the three-yard line after getting the handoff from QB Otto Graham (60). Helping Jones score are OT Lou Groza (46), C Frank Gatski (22), and OG Ed Ulinski (36). Because only 22,891 fought the winter chill to watch the Browns clinch their third straight AAFC title, each Cleveland player received $594.16 from the players' pool for winning the title. Reserved seats were priced at $6.00, $4.60 and $3.60 with tax. Student tickets were 50¢.

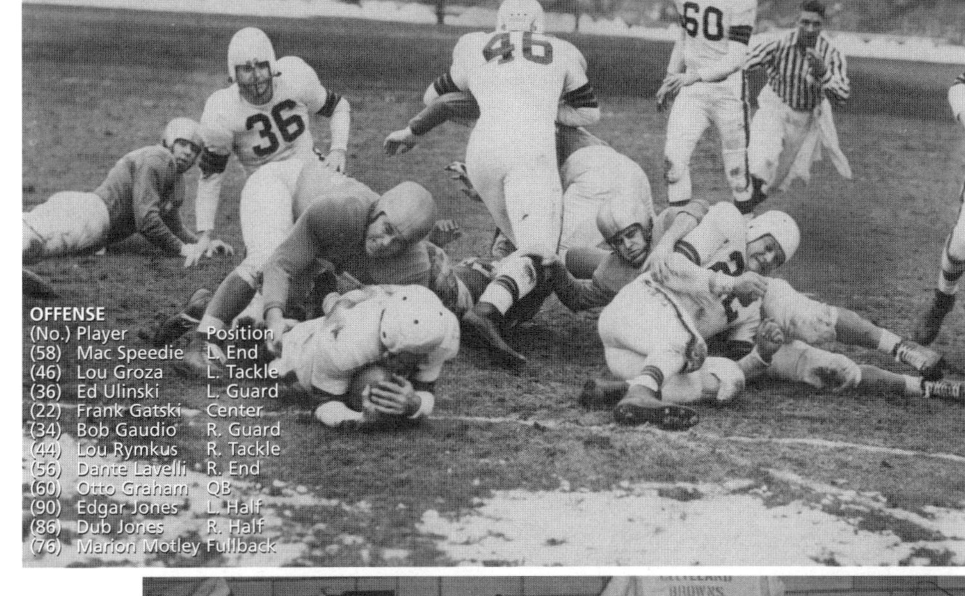

(Below) Cleveland Browns owner Mickey McBride (left), joins head coach Paul Brown in the locker room after watching his team set a new pro football record with its third straight championship.

(Above) Celebrating after the win are HB Edgar Jones (left), who scored twice; QB Otto Graham, who completed 11 passes for 118 yards; FB Marion Motley, who ran for 133 yards, scoring three times on runs of 29, 31 and 5 yards; and team captain Lou Saban (seated), who scored his first career TD on a 39-yard pass interception.

1949- The Final AAFC Season

**September 18, 1949
Cleveland-21
Baltimore-0**

After playing the host Buffalo Bills to a 28-28 tie on Labor Day, the Cleveland Browns opened at home on Sunday, September 18, 1949, against the Baltimore Colts. The game was played before only 19,243 at the Stadium, with the Colts providing little opposition for the Browns who won, 21-0. Cleveland scores came on a 24-yard TD pass from QB Otto Graham to E Dante Lavelli and two TD runs by HB Edgar "Special Delivery" Jones. It was an easy, but costly victory for the Browns, who lost DE George Young with a cracked cheek bone and FB Marion Motley with damaged ribs.

(Right) Browns HB Edgar "Special Delivery" Jones scores one of his two TDs.

INDIVIDUAL RECEIVING		
BROWNS	No.	Yds.
Speedie	6	99
Motley	3	55
Lavelli	3	73
Gillom	1	29
Boedeker	1	15
49ERS		
Cathcart	5	88
Beals	4	56
Schoener	2	24
Eshmont	1	48
Lillywhite	1	1
Salata	1	14

**October 30, 1949
Cleveland-30, San Francisco-28**

After being humiliated earlier in the season by the San Francisco 49ers, 56-28, in San Francisco, the Cleveland Browns (5-1), faced their AAFC rivals a second time on Sunday, October 30, 1949, before 72,189 at the Stadium. The two teams were battling for second place in the All-America Conference behind the league-leading New York Yankees. San Francisco scored first, but the Browns evened the score at 7-7 in the second period, when QB Otto Graham connected with E Dante Lavelli on a nine-yard TD pass. HB Dub Jones scored Cleveland's second TD on a five-yard sweep. In the third period, Graham scored the Browns' third TD on a 20-yard quarterback sneak to give Cleveland a 21-14 lead. Early in the fourth quarter, 49ers QB Frankie Albert hit E Alyn Beals on a 22-yard TD pass to tie the score at 21-21. The Browns immediately broke the tie with a 38-yard field goal by Lou "The Toe" Groza. Cleveland scored a final time when Graham, who completed 14 passes either good for TDs or first downs, connected with E Mac Speedie on an 11-yard TD pass. The 49ers marched 80 yards for a final TD, but it wasn't enough to catch the Browns, who held on to win, 30-28.

(Left) Brown place-kicker Lou "The Toe" Groza (46), kicks a 38-yard field goal to give Cleveland a 24-21 fourth quarter lead as 49ers DB Jim Cason (93), looks on. No. 76 far right is FB Marion Motley. No. 42 is Browns T Darrell Palmer. Tickets for the 2 P.M. contest were priced at $1.80, $2.40, $3.60 (tax included), or 25¢ for student tickets. Game day general admission tickets were priced at $1.25.

November 6, 1949 / Cleveland-35, Chicago-2

Coming off a 30-28 win over the San Francisco 49ers the previous week, on Sunday, November 6, 1949, the Cleveland Browns (6-1-1), hosted coach Ray Flaherty's Chicago Hornets (4-4), before 16,506, the smallest Stadium crowd at the time to watch pro football. During the game, coach Paul Brown used guards Lin Houston and Bob Gaudio to relay messages from the coaching staff to the huddle. After conferring with Brown or assistant coaches Weeb Ewbank, Blanton Collier and Fritz Heisler, Gaudio and Houston alternated bringing in the coach's instructions, while the other man headed to the sidelines for the next play. At left, Gaudio (34), just entering the game, talks with OT Lou Rymkus (44), as teammates QB Otto Graham (with fingers to mouth), E Mac Speedie (58), E Horace Gillom (59), and OT Lou Groza (46), wait for instructions. Also in the huddle were HB Dub Jones, OG Bill Willis, HB Billy Boedeker, C Frank Gatski and OG Ed Ulinski. Cleveland demolished the Hornets, 35-2, with FB Marion Motley and HB Les Horvath each scoring two TDs. One of Motley's scores came on a 49-yard run. Horvath connected on a 59-yard pass from QB Cliff Lewis for one of his scores. HB Dub Jones scored Cleveland's other TD. Two of the Browns' extra points were kicked by Lou Saban, not regular kicker Lou Groza, who got ejected from the game for fighting with the Hornets' Nate Johnson. Chicago's points came after blocking a punt by the Browns' Horace Gillom that rolled out of the end zone for a safety.

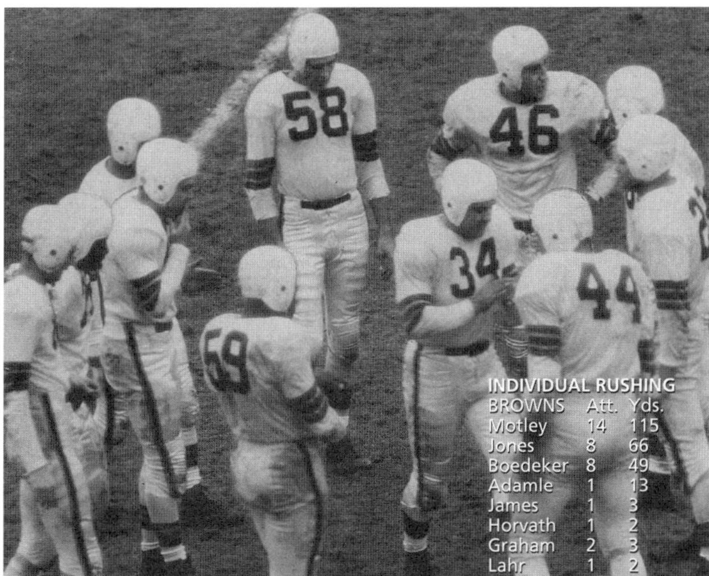

December 11, 1949 / The Last AAFC Championship Game

After beating the Buffalo Bills, 31-21, at the Stadium on December 4th, the Cleveland Browns returned to the Stadium on Sunday, December 11, 1949, to play for the All-America Football Conference championship a record-setting fourth straight year. The game was played against the San Francisco 49ers before only 22,550, partly because of inclement weather and partly because Cleveland was playing the 49ers for the third time that season. Cleveland won the title match, 21-7, on scores by HB Edgar "Special Delivery" Jones, who rushed for 63 yards on 16 carries, FB Marion Motley, who ran 67 yards for the TD, and HB Dub Jones on a four-yard plunge. San Francisco's only score came on a 23-yard pass from 49ers QB Frankie Albert to E Paul Salata. The Browns not only celebrated their AAFC title win that day, but also their move into the new National-American Football League in 1950. Because of the low turnout, each Browns player received $226 for the win.

(Right) Browns head coach Paul Brown sits upon the shoulders of HB Edgar Jones after the game as DE George Young (52), and team captain Lou Saban (20), look on. In the background upper left is Lou "The Toe" Groza. The title match was Saban's last game in a Browns uniform. Before the game, the veteran linebacker announced he was retiring to try coaching in the college ranks.

Baseball And Bill Veeck, Jr.

At 12:50 P.M. on Saturday, June 22, 1946, 32-year-old Milwaukee war veteran Bill Veeck, Jr. stepped out of the law office of local attorney Joseph C. Hostetler and declared, "We're in business as of right now," after completing the purchase of the Cleveland baseball franchise from local businessmen John Sherwin, Jr. and Alva Bradley. Among the men paying around $1.5 million for the American League club, League Park and several minor league teams, was entertainer Bob Hope, who told reporters, "I'm in for one-sixth." Part businessman, part entertainer, Veeck brought a new level of promotion generated enthusiasm to Cleveland baseball with fireworks, giveaways and musical presentations among his innovative special events. Under Veeck's guidance, the Indians rose from a sixth-place finish in 1946, to winning the World Series in 1948, setting attendance records along the way. In 1948, the Indians drew a club-record 2,620,627 spectators. In 1949, the Indians finished in second place, drawing 2,233,771 visitors. On Monday, November 21, 1949, Veeck sold the franchise for a reported $2.2 million to a syndicate headed by 45-year-old insurance salesman Ellis W. Ryan.

July 23, 1946 / "Veeck's Varieties of '46"

The fifth-place Cleveland Indians faced the Philadelphia Athletics before an announced crowd of 25,399 on Tuesday, July 23, 1946. Many fans were attracted by the first special promotion of the season planned by new Tribe president Bill Veeck, Jr., (with saxophone). Veeck's inaugural event featured a pre-game fireworks display combined with live music provided by band leader Tony Granata (at far left), and his 15-piece swing band, the Melo Masters. The Melo Masters played before the game and briefly between innings from a specially designed tepee set on the warning track in deep center field. Special ground rules were put in place that night, in event the ball rolled past a protective wire fence and into the tepee. Cleveland beat the A's, 2-0, on a three-hitter by starter Allie Reynolds. It was Reynolds' fourth straight win of the season, and sixth victory of the year. Veeck said he hadn't asked, and wasn't worried, when Cleveland Press reporter Frank Gibbons asked if he had received the American League's permission to place the tent in center field.

August 1, 1946 / Ladies' Day

One of new Tribe president Bill Veeck's first moves was to restore special matinee games for Cleveland's feminine fans. Veeck held the Indians' first Ladies' Day promotion at League Park on Thursday, July 25, 1946. A week later, Veeck held the club's second "Ladies' Day Special," at the Stadium on Thursday, August 1, 1946. Women were admitted free and given the chance to win one of 503 pairs of nylon hose provided by the Indians. Veeck chose the 503 number to better the 500 pairs of nylons given away by another team. The event proved to be a huge success, as 21,371 women joined 14,162 paying customers. Tribe hurler Mel Harder recorded his 215th career win in leading the Indians to a 2-1 win over the first-place Boston Red Sox. The day before, Cleveland ace Bob Feller won his 20th of the year, beating the Red Sox, 4-1, at the Stadium on a one-hitter.

(Left) Veeck (far right), hands out nylons to the contest winners on August 1st.

September 15, 1946

Lou Boudreau Day

Sunday, September 15, 1946 was "Lou Boudreau Day" at the Stadium. Lou's mother and brother Albert were in attendance, as the veteran infielder and team manager was honored between games of a doubleheader between the sixth-place Cleveland Indians (64-78), and the last place Philadelphia Athletics (48-94). Lou was showered with gifts, including a new gray Lincoln and a home refrigeration unit. New team president Bill Veeck presented Boudreau with a gleaming $750 "thing" inscribed with, "to the best shortstop ever left off an All-Star team." Governor Frank Lausche and Mayor Thomas A. Burke were also among the presenters who praised the Tribe leader. Serving as master of ceremonies was Bob Evans on behalf of the Touchdown Club. Cleveland won the first game, 8-1, behind starter Bob Lemon, who pitched the Tribe to victory, but lost the second contest, 2-0, with Indians ace Bob Feller taking the loss. Feller, who lost to rookie hurler Bill McCahan, struck out seven A's in defeat, raising his strikeout total for the season

Second Game
CLEVELAND
George Case lf
Ted Sepkowski 3b
Pat Seerey rf
Les Fleming 1b
Dale Mitchell cf
Lou Boudreau ss
Ray Mack 2b
Jim Hegan c
Bob Feller p

PHILADELPHIA
Elmer Valo rf
Oscar Grimes 2b
Barney McCosky lf
Pete Suder ss
Ben Chapman cf
Don Richmond 3b
Bruce Konopka 1b
Gene Desautels c
Bill McCahan p

to 315, two better than the season strikeout record of 313 set by Walter Johnson in 1910. The doubleheader marked the major league debut of Dale Mitchell and Ted Sepkowski, who were brought up from Oklahoma City. Mitchell, who played center field, got three hits in the opening contest, but went hitless in the second game. Sepkowski, who filled in at third base, got two hits in each contest. With 29,935 in attendance that evening, the Indians set a new club attendance record, going over the million mark for the season with 1,005,111 visitors. Though Veeck announced that Boudreau would be back to manage the team in 1947, the All-Star shortstop failed to receive what he wanted the most on his special night, a two-year contract extension.

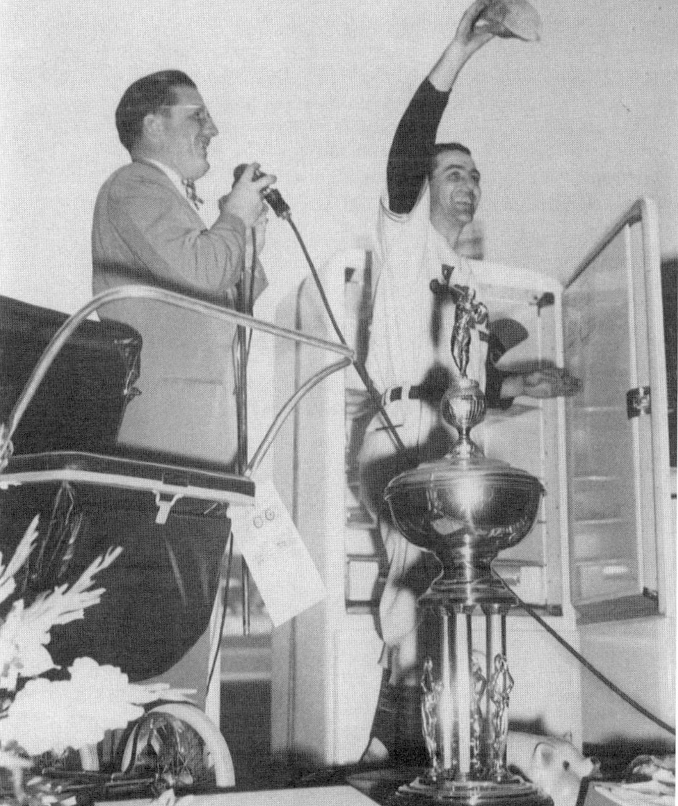

(Above) Boudreau stands in front of some of his gifts as 83-year-old Philadelphia A's manager Connie Mack addresses the crowd. Mack, who was baseball's oldest manager, called Lou, "the best shortstop in baseball." In 1942, Boudreau, at age 24, became the youngest manager in major league history.

(Left) Boudreau holds up a steak found inside the refrigerator he received. At left is master of ceremonies Bob Evans.

November 17, 1946 / Bill Veeck Returns to Action

After entering the Cleveland Clinic on November 1, 1946 to have his right leg amputated below the knee, new Cleveland Indians president Bill Veeck (at left), received a four-hour "pass" from the Clinic on Sunday, November 17, 1946, to attend the All-America Football Conference game between the Cleveland Browns and the Chicago Rockets at the Stadium. Veeck "crutched" up to a box in the upper grandstand where he spent the afternoon with lovely actress Ann Blyth (right), star of the film "Mildred Pierce." Blyth was in town, according to Cleveland Press columnist Stan Anderson, to appear the next night at the Page One Ball in Cleveland Arena. Among the entertainers appearing with Blyth were Edmund O'Brien, Mae West and comedian Bert Wheeler. Veeck and Blyth were among the 60,457 who saw Cleveland beat the Rockets, 51-14. Leading the Browns to victory were Lou "The Toe" Groza, who kicked a 51-yard field goal, the third longest in pro football history; QB Otto Graham, who threw four TD passes, two each to Dante Lavelli and Mac Speedie; HB Edgar (Special Delivery) Jones, who ran for 100 yards on five carries, QB Bud Schwenk, who threw a TD pass to HB Bill Lund, and center Frank Gatski, who scored his first career TD on a pass interception. Groza, who was given a 21-jewel wrist watch by fans from his hometown of Martins Ferry before the game, tied the NFL record of 10 field goals in one season set in 1934. Veeck was scheduled later that week to appear at the Page One Ball, host a party for new local stockholders of the Indians and attend the annual Charity Game at the Stadium where Holy Name and Cathedral Latin high schools played for the scholastic football crown. Veeck awarded prizes to winners of pre-game skills contests at the game.

April 24, 1947
The New Stadium Fence

On Thursday, April 24, 1947, while the Cleveland Indians were playing the Chicago White Sox in Chicago, team president Bill Veeck had the Ferbert Fence Co. install the first temporary fencing at the Stadium. The new 5' high fence reduced the distance from 470' to 410' in deep center and from 435' to 365' in right and left fields. Only the foul poles remained at their original distance of 320'. The first game played with the new fence in place was set for Sunday, April 27th, but was postponed because of rain to the 28th, when 2nd-place Cleveland hosted the Detroit Tigers. The first home run hit over the new fence was by Tiger pitcher Paul "Dizzy" Trout, who drove a third-inning blast off starter Red Embree into the left field stands. Tribe third baseman Ken Keltner hit a blast to deep left field with two on and two out in the ninth inning, but the drive, which would have tied the score, was caught at the fence by Tiger outfielder Dick Wakefield. Cleveland lost to the Tigers, 3-0, before 6,054 "frostbitten fans." **(Above right)** The last pieces of the new Stadium fence are put in place on the 24th.

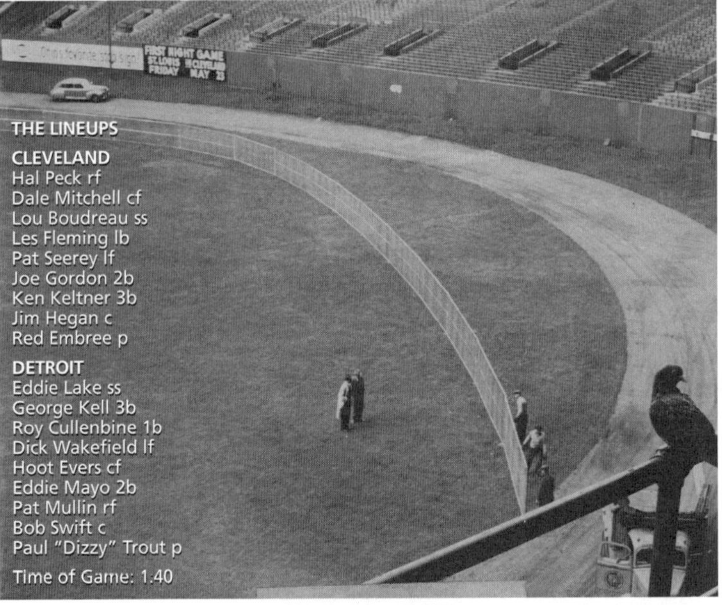

THE LINEUPS

CLEVELAND
Hal Peck rf
Dale Mitchell cf
Lou Boudreau ss
Les Fleming 1b
Pat Seerey lf
Joe Gordon 2b
Ken Keltner 3b
Jim Hegan c
Red Embree p

DETROIT
Eddie Lake ss
George Kell 3b
Roy Cullenbine 1b
Dick Wakefield lf
Hoot Evers cf
Eddie Mayo 2b
Pat Mullin rf
Bob Swift c
Paul "Dizzy" Trout p

Time of Game: 1.40

(Right) June 6, 1947 / Remodeling the Fence

On Friday, June 5, 1947, after watching weak-hitting Washington Nationals catcher Al Evans homer over the new temporary fencing, Tribe owner Bill Veeck remarked, "We'll have to move it back." The next day, sections of the new fencing were removed, pushing the fence back to 362 feet in left and right center. That night, the Indians beat the Philadelphia A's, 7-4, before 19,264 at the Stadium, taking over third place. Homers by Jim Hegan and Dale Mitchell sparked three-run rallies to give starter Mel Harder the win. The homers were the first by both men in the major leagues.

1947- The Season Opener April 15, 1947

After ending the 1946 season in sixth place, with a 68-86 record, the Cleveland Indians opened the 1947 season on Tuesday, April 15th, against the Chicago White Sox before a major league record Opening Day turnout of 55,016 at the Stadium. The season opener began the team's first full year under the leadership of Tribe president Bill Veeck. Gone by way of trades were veteran pitcher Allie Reynolds and outfielder George Case. New to the Tribe roster were outfielders Hal Peck and George (Catfish) Metkovich and second baseman Joe Gordon. New to the coaching staff was former Cincinnati Reds manager Bill McKechnie. Cleveland finished in fourth place (80-74), 17 games behind the New York Yankees. Gordon finished second in the American League to Boston's Ted Williams in home runs with 29, and tied for second with the Yankees' Joe DiMaggio in total bases with 279. Pitching ace Bob Feller led the A.L. in wins (20), shutouts (5), innings pitched (299), and strikeouts (198).

(Far right) Former Cleveland Indians center fielder Tris Speaker (right), spends time before the season opener with Tribe left fielder Pat Seerey, who went 2 for 4 with a double. Speaker was signed by Bill Veeck to serve as a goodwill ambassador and advisory coach for the Cleveland Indians.

(Right) Tribe starter Bob Feller chats with former Cleveland ace Cy Young before the game. During the game, Feller used an electrically-heated jacket to stay warm.

CLEVELAND
Hal Peck rf
Dale Mitchell cf
Lou Boudreau ss
Eddie Robinson lb
Joe Gordon 2b
Pat Seerey lf
Ken Keltner 3b
Jim Hegan c
Bob Feller p

(Above) Rookie southpaws Bob Kuzava (left), Les Willis and Gene Bearden pose before the season opener. Bearden entered only one game in 1947, but went on to win twenty games for the Indians in 1948 and star for Cleveland in the World Series. Kuzava entered just four games for the Indians that season. Willis fared the best, entering 22 games for the Indians in 1947, his only major league season.

(Right) Cleveland ace Bob Feller started against Chicago southpaw Eddie Lopat. Lopat (third from right), is congratulated by a teammate after pitching his team to a six-hit, 2-0, complete-game win over the Indians. Feller, who took the loss, teamed with Tribe reliever Roger Wolff to give up 10 hits, three to Chicago first baseman Don Kolloway.

CHICAGO
Floyd Baker 3b
Luke Appling ss
Dave Philley cf
Bob Kennedy rf
Ralph Hodgin lf
Don Kolloway lb
Casimir "Cass" Michaels 2b
Mike Tresh c
Eddie Lopat P

1947- Midget Auto Racing

In the spring of 1947, Cleveland mayor Thomas A. Burke agreed to let Cleveland Raceways Inc. construct a 40-foot track around the Stadium playing field for a series of midget auto races. The mayor's action ignited a feud between the mayor and Cleveland Indians president Bill Veeck, who was never consulted before the midget race track commitment was made. Veeck told reporters he had received information that when the surface hardened, it would be as hard as concrete which, he claimed, would put his players in constant danger. Veeck asked reporters, "Whose fault would it be if, for instance, Boudreau our manager, runs on it and breaks a leg?" "Mine," he declared. In addition, heavy rains seriously delayed the track's completion, causing concern that the Indians' first night game of the season on Friday, May 23rd, might be cancelled. "We are concentrating now only on getting the place in shape for baseball," a Loesch and Green Construction Co. spokesman said on May 21st, as workers battled to get the track ready for the Friday night contest. On May 22nd, with work on the track progressing slowly, American League Umpire-in-chief Tom Connolly reluctantly ruled that the game could go on after receiving assurances

from mayor Burke that 100 city workers would be loaned to Emil Bossard, the Indians' chief ground keeper, to help complete the project. Bossard's crew, who mixed dry cement and sand with the mud to help solidify the mess, worked overtime to get the track in shape. On Saturday, May 24th, Cleveland Press reporter Frank Gibbons wrote, "The track was not a beauty to behold, but it served no evil part in the overtime defeat of the Indians." A 10-race session had been planned, but the Burke administration exercised a three-race trial option in their contract and permanently suspended midget racing at the Stadium after the third night.

(Top left) Veeck observes work on the race track from the Stadium stands on May 20th. **(Top)** Veeck (left), meets with American League Umpire-in-chief Tom Connolly, Tribe business manager Rudie Schaffer and Earl Hilligan of the A. L. Service Bureau (far right), on May 22nd for a ruling on the field conditions. The responsibility of preparing the field for baseball was shifted to the grounds crew of Emil Bossard. **(Above left)** Al Bonnell of Erie Pa. checks out the quarter-mile race track before the first night of racing on Saturday, June 14, 1947. Many of the 21,157 attending the inaugural race were forced to use blankets, newspapers and even their programs, to shield themselves from flying mud hurled by the race cars.

Wild Bill Boyd lies on the ground after his auto overturned during the second set of midget auto races on Saturday, June 21, 1947. Boyd suffered compound fractures of his right leg, a broken right shoulder, broken ribs and internal injuries.

May 23, 1947   The Midget Race

Baseball's largest crowd of the season, 61,277, turned out for the Cleveland Indians' first night game of the year on Friday, May 23, 1947. The evening began with a fireworks display featuring a mock sea battle, followed by the playing of the national anthem. When the lights came on, the night's master of ceremonies, WGAR Radio baseball announcer Van Patrick, told the crowd that as a special attraction, Tribe president Bill Veeck would present the Stadium's first midget "auto" race. At that moment, the five "lilliputians" above boarded kiddie-cars where the new race track intersected the left field fence and began pedaling toward a finish line at home plate. With the racers at left is Tribe manager Lou Boudreau, who served as the starter. The track was so spongy from the construction work and rain that the five participants were unable to pedal any distance, forcing them to pick up the trikes and run to home plate where they were awarded, according to one newspaper account, "huge cardboard lollipops and real candy peppermint sticks." Veeck had two of the midgets flown in from Chicago to work with Cleveland Browns mascot Tommy Flynn (far right), who organized the race. The stunt was followed by a medley of tunes from a barbershop quartet and a special appearance by Clevelander Bob Hope who joked from home plate, "I've been reading so much about this thing (the midget race track) in the papers, that I didn't know whether to bring a bat or a shovel." Hope finished by posing for photos with Tribe ace Bob Feller after planting a kiss on the starting pitcher's cheek. The last-place St. Louis Browns beat third-place Cleveland, 5-3, in 12 innings, causing Cleveland Press reporter Frank Gibbons to write, "There was no joy in Mudville last night at the Stadium."

(Above) Tribe president Bill Veeck (left), meets with Bob Hope and Del Webb (right), president of the New York Yankees. Hope and Webb arrived at the Stadium just before the game began.

1948- A World Series Season

After finishing the 1947 season in fourth place with an 80-74 record, the team's best finish since 1943, player-manager Lou Boudreau's 1948 Cleveland Indians did something no Cleveland baseball team had been able to accomplish since 1920- win the World Series. Led by pitchers Bob Lemon (20-14), rookie knuckleballer Gene Bearden (20-7), and Bob Feller (19-15), the Indians finished the regular season with a 96-58 record, tied for first place with the Boston Red Sox. On Sunday, October 3rd, the Indians lost the last game of the regular season to the Detroit Tigers, 7-1, at the Stadium, forcing the first playoff game in American League history. Cleveland beat the Red Sox in Boston on Monday, October 4th, 8-3, behind a complete-game, five-hitter by Bearden to clinch the American League pennant. The Indians went on to win the World Series, defeating the National League champion Boston Braves in six games. Cleveland clinched the title in Boston on October 11th, after losing Game 5 to the Braves, 11-5, on Sunday, October 10th, before a record Stadium crowd of 86,233.

THE OPENING DAY LINEUPS

CLEVELAND
Thurman Tucker cf
Larry Doby rf
Lou Boudreau ss
Joe Gordon 2b
Eddie Robinson 1b
Allie Clark lf
Ken Keltner 3b
Jim Hegan c
Bob Feller p

ST. LOUIS
Bob Dillinger 3b
Chuck Stevens 1b
Gerry Priddy 2b
Whitey Platt lf
Al Zarilla rf
Pete Layden cf
Eddie Pellagrini ss
Lester Moss c
Fred Sanford p

April 20, 1948 / The Home Opener

Bill Veeck's Cleveland Indians opened the 1948 season on Tuesday, April 20th against the St. Louis Browns at the Stadium before a major league record Opening Day crowd of 73,163. On the mound for Cleveland was 29-year-old right-hander Bob Feller (at left), who was making his sixth opening day start. Feller pitched a masterful two-hitter in leading the Indians to a 4-0 win over the Browns. Catcher Jim Hegan drove in three of Cleveland's runs with three hits, a 380-foot home run over the right field fence off St. Louis southpaw Sam Zoldak, and two singles. All four runs were scored in the first four innings. The game marked the debut of center fielder Thurman Tucker and rookie left fielder Allie Clark in Cleveland uniforms. It also marked the home opening debut of a rather nervous young Tribe right fielder named Larry Doby, who went 0 for 4.

July 29, 1948 / "Bleacher Bugs"

On Wednesday, July 29, 1948, The Cleveland Press published a front page photostory about the Stadium "bleacherites" who watched the second-place Cleveland Indians battle the Philadelphia Athletics in the hot summer sun. Above the story, the headline read, "Bleacher Bugs' Baseball- Squint, Squirm, Sweat," as the reporter offered, "The shirts come off, even shoes, as the male fans strip for a suntan. The gal fans show up in sun suits, slacks, shorts and halters. Only in the bleachers may a fan occupy three seats for the price of one while watching a game played almost in the next county. The hardy bleacherites are supposedly the real, honest-to-goodness fans because they take their baseball the hard way for 60 cents a head, lowest price charged." The fans at right were among the 23,843 who watched the Indians lose to the Athletics, 4-3, on the 28th. The winning Philadelphia runs were scored in the eighth inning, when Tribe center fielder Larry Doby misjudged a pop fly. The ball fell to the ground after beaning Doby in the head. Cleveland starter Bob Lemon was charged with the loss.

(Right) August 6, 1948 / Possibilities Unlimited

Tribe president Bill Veeck plays first base during a three-inning softball game held before the Cleveland Indians-New York Yankees game at the Stadium on Friday, August 6, 1948. The softball game pitted a Youngstown-based organization of amputees called Possibilities Unlimited, against a group of Cleveland area amputees organized by Veeck, who fouled out in his only trip to the plate. The visiting Youngstown team soundly defeated the local squad, 18-0. After the exhibition game, a packed house of 71,358 watched the first-place Indians battle the Yankees in the opening game of a four-game weekend series. Cleveland won its sixth straight, beating the Yankees, 9-7. Right fielder Allie Clark and second baseman Joe Gordon hit homers in the win, as starter Bob Feller captured his 11th victory of the season. Feller held Joe DiMaggio hitless and struck out George "Snuffy" Stirnweiss for his 100th strikeout of the year. The Tribe win halted New York's win streak at five, and broke Yankee starter Eddie Lopat's personal nine-game win streak.

CLEVELAND	NEW YORK
Dale Mitchell lf	George "Snuffy" Stirnweiss 2b
Allie Clark rf	Tommy Henrich rf
Larry Doby cf	Charlie Keller lf
Ken Keltner 3b	Joe DiMaggio cf
Joe Gordon 2b	Yogi Berra c
Johnny Berardino ss	George McQuinn 1b
Eddie Robinson 1b	Billy Johnson 3b
Jim Hegan c	Phil Rizzuto ss
Bob Feller p	Eddie Lopat p

August 20, 1948
Mayor's Night

CLEVELAND	
Dale Mitchell lf	
Allie Clark rf	
Lou Boudreau ss	
Eddie Robinson 1b	
Ken Keltner 3b	
Larry Doby cf	
Johnny Berardino 2b	
Jim Hegan c	
Satchel Paige p	

CHICAGO	
Ralph Hodgin rf	
Tony Lupien 1b	
Luke Appling 3b	
Pat Seerey lf	
Aaron Robinson c	
Dave Philley cf	
Don Kolloway 2b	
Casimir "Cass" Michaels ss	
Bill Wight p	

(Left) Friday, August 20, 1948 was "Mayor's Night" at the Stadium, as four hundred Ohio mayors and their wives were guests of Gov. Thomas J. Herbert and Bill Veeck at a picnic behind the outfield fence before the first-place Cleveland Indians battled the Chicago White Sox. The Tribe won, 1-0, behind the three-hit pitching of starter Satchel Paige, who ran his scoreless inning streak to 26 1/2 innings. Paige's roommate, center fielder Larry Doby, drove in shortstop Lou Boudreau for the winning run. The game was played before 78,382, a new major league record for night game attendance. It was also the fourth straight no-run game hurled by Cleveland pitchers. The Indians' scoreless inning streak stood at thirty after consecutive shutouts by Paige and fellow starters Bob Lemon, Gene Bearden and Sam Zoldak.

September 13, 1948 / Don Black's Injury

The third-place Cleveland Indians faced the St. Louis Browns before 7,008 on Monday, September 13, 1948, with 31-year-old right-hander Don Black pitching for the Indians. Black, who hurled a no-hitter for Cleveland in 1947, began the game by pitching two strong innings against the Browns. In the bottom half of the second, Black was the fourth batter to face former teammate Bill Kennedy. He took the first pitch for a ball and then took a vicious swing at the next pitch, fouling it into the stands. Suddenly, Black stepped out of the batter's box and began walking around in a small circle to the left of umpire Bill Summers. Black, who had suffered a cerebral hemorrhage, spoke briefly to Summers and then sank to his knees as trainer Lefty Weisman (left, at right), and coach Bill McKechnie (right), rushed to assist Black before he was carried off the field and taken to St. Vincent Charity Hospital. Black recovered, but never pitched in the majors again. Cleveland lost the game, 3-2, with reliever Sam Zoldak taking the loss. The following day, a crucial home series with the New York Yankees awaited the Indians.

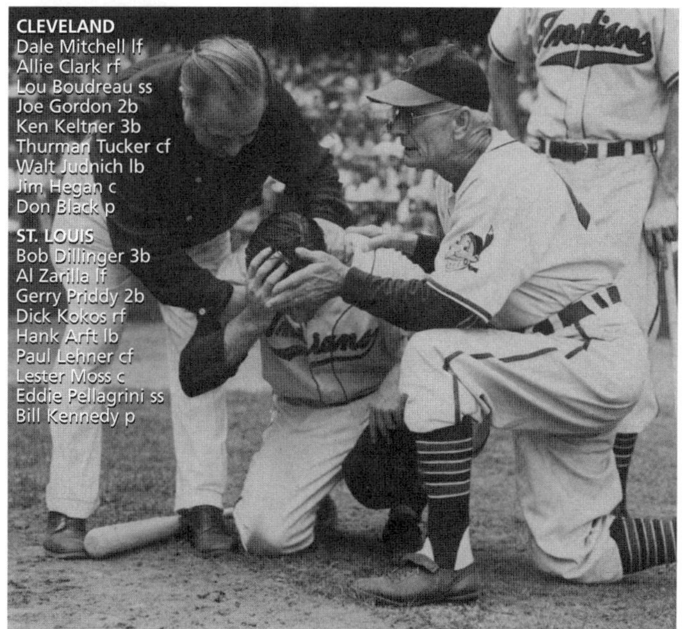

CLEVELAND	
Dale Mitchell lf	
Allie Clark rf	
Lou Boudreau ss	
Joe Gordon 2b	
Ken Keltner 3b	
Thurman Tucker cf	
Walt Judnich 1b	
Jim Hegan c	
Don Black p	

ST. LOUIS	
Bob Dillinger 3b	
Al Zarilla lf	
Gerry Priddy 2b	
Dick Kokos rf	
Hank Arft 1b	
Paul Lehner cf	
Lester Moss c	
Eddie Pellagrini ss	
Bill Kennedy p	

(Above) After returning from an exhausting (2-10) Eastern road trip, the 13-17 Cleveland Indians hoisted their World Championship flag at the Stadium on Friday, May 27, 1949. 33,235 watched Tribe starter Al Benton pitch a complete game to beat Frank Lane's Chicago White Sox, 4-0, on a six-hitter.

With only three games remaining in the regular season, the first-place Cleveland Indians battled the Detroit Tigers in a crucial contest on Friday, October 1, 1948, before 15,988 at the Stadium. The Indians lost to the Tigers, 5-3, as utility player Jimmy Outlaw hit a "dinky, two-run single," in the ninth inning to give Detroit starter Virgil Trucks the win. On October 2nd, the Indians clinched a tie for the American League title, with an 8-0 win over Detroit before 56,238 at the Stadium. Tribe starter Gene Bearden won his 19th of the season.

(Above) During the game, after getting Pat Mullin of the Tigers at second base, Tribe short-stop Lou Boudreau (in the air), whipped the ball to first baseman Eddie Robinson to get Tiger first baseman Dick Wakefield for the double play.

(Right) Boudreau argues with Umpire Bill McKinley after McKinley called Wakefield safe at first. Joining Boudreau in the argument is Tribe catcher Jim Hegan, at right, and second baseman Joe Gordon, behind Boudreau. Right fielder Vic Wertz scored from third on the play.

(Left) Fans congregate outside the Stadium before one of the World Series games. After beating the host Boston Red Sox in a one-game playoff in Boston on Monday, October 4, 1948 to clinch the American League pennant, the Cleveland Indians began World Series play against the Boston Braves on Wednesday, October 6th. After splitting the first two games with the National League champions in Boston on the 6th and 7th, the third, fourth and fifth games of the 1948 World Series were played at the Stadium on October 8th, 9th and 10th. The three games drew record-setting crowds of 70,306, 81,897 and 86,288. Cleveland won Games 3 and 4 by scores of 2-0 and 2-1, but lost Game 5, 11-5, as south-paw Warren Spahn pitched the Braves to victory in relief. The loss moved the series back to Boston where Cleveland won Game 6 on Monday, October 11th. Starter Bob Lemon, who got win, teamed with reliever Gene Bearden to beat the Braves, 4-3, before 40,103 at Braves Field to capture the club's first world championship since 1920.

(Right) Boston Braves hurler Warren Spahn, whose brilliant relief pitching led the Braves to a 11-5 win in Game 5, is greeted by catcher Bill Salkeld after the victory.

(Far right) Indians left fielder Dale Mitchell chases a drive by Boston shortstop Alvin Dark into the left field corner during Game 3 on Friday, October 8th. Mitchell held Dark to a double. 70,036 watched Cleveland beat Boston, 2-0, to take a 2-1 lead in the playoffs. Left-hander Gene Bearden, who threw only 53 pitches through the first six innings, pitched a complete game five-hitter for the win.

GAME FIVE

CLEVELAND-5	BOSTON-11
Dale Mitchell lf	Tommy Holmes rf
Larry Doby cf	Alvin Dark ss
Lou Boudreau ss	Earl Torgeson 1b
Joe Gordon 2b	Bob Elliott 3b
Ken Keltner 3b	Marv Rickert lf
Walt Judnich rf	Bill Salkeld c
Eddie Robinson 1b	Mike McCormick cf
Jim Hegan c	Eddie Stanky 2b
Bob Feller p	Nelson Potter p

(Left) With a record crowd of 86,288 at the Stadium for Game 5 on Sunday, October 10th, fans sought

GAME THREE

CLEVELAND-2	BOSTON-0
Dale Mitchell lf	Tommy Holmes rf
Larry Doby cf	Alvin Dark ss
Lou Boudreau ss	Mike McCormick lf
Joe Gordon 2b	Bob Elliott 3b
Ken Keltner 3b	Frank McCormick 1b
Walt Judnich rf	Clint Conatser cf
Eddie Robinson 1b	Phil Masi c
Jim Hegan c	Eddie Stanky 2b
Gene Bearden p	Vern Bickford p
Manager: Lou Boudreau	Manager Billy Southworth
	Time of Game: 1:36

to watch the action from any vantage point possible. Tribe pitcher Satchel Paige made his only World Series appearance in a relief role, retiring two batters in the seventh inning. The Boston Braves won, 11-5, as Warren Spahn pitched a one-hitter over five and 2/3 innings in relief of Nelson Potter for the win. Bob Feller, who gave up seven runs in 6 2/3 innings, took the loss.

(Right) The Stadium bleachers were filled to capacity as the game began on the 10th. The Braves broke a 5-5 tie in the seventh inning, with six runs on five singles off four Cleveland pitchers for the win. Each morning 8,000 bleacher seats ($1), 10,000 grandstand standing room only tickets ($4), and standing room tickets for behind the outfield fence ($2), were placed on sale.

July 7, 1948 / Satchel's Tryout

On July 3, 1947, Cleveland Indians president Bill Veeck obtained the rights to 22-year-old outfielder Larry Doby from the Newark Eagles of the Negro National League. On July 5th, Doby became the first black to play in the American League. Just over a year later, on Wednesday, July 7, 1948, Negro League hurler Leroy (Satchel) Paige showed his "stuff" at the Stadium to Veeck and player-manager Lou Boudreau. His performance impressed Veeck enough to sign Paige that day. Paige later reported that he threw 50 pitches and missed the corner only a couple of times. "I troubled Mr. Lou and got signed," he recalled. When Paige made his debut in an Indians uniform, he became the first black to pitch in the American League. Paige appeared in 21 games during the regular season in 1948, winning six out of the seven games he started (.857), including back-to-back shutouts, with one save and a 2.47 ERA, but failed to accomplish one of his life-time goals- starting a World Series contest. He appeared only once during the 1948 World Series in a relief role. When Paige joined the Tribe roster, Cleveland became only the second major league team with two blacks in uniform. (Jackie Robinson and Roy Campanella were teammates on the Brooklyn Dodgers.)

(Left) Satchel Paige with Bill Veeck at the Stadium on Wednesday, July 7, 1948.

Leroy (Satchel) Paige

August 3, 1948 Satchel's First Start

Tribe hurler Satchel Paige made his first major league start for the Indians on Tuesday, August 3, 1948, as the Indians faced the Washington Nationals with Early Wynn on the mound. The game was played before 72,434, the largest night game crowd in Cleveland Indians history at the time. Paige, who struck out six, pitched seven solid innings before being relieved for a pinch hitter. Cleveland won the contest, 5-3, taking over first place with the victory.

(Left) Satchel Paige at bat during his first start. In addition to winning the game, Paige also got his first major league hit, a deep grounder to short in the sixth inning.

'Good Old Joe Earley' Night

(Right) Joe and June Earley join Cleveland Indians president Bill Veeck as he addresses the Stadium crowd from home plate.

(Above) Ted Brooks, an old friend of Earley, made his Jack & Jill Shop at 15015 Detroit Ave. in Lakewood a "Joe Earley Night" headquarters. Money raised was donated to the American Cancer Fund.

A yellow 1949 Ford convertible with red upholstery, a refrigerator, a television set, a radio, a new dishwasher, and a lifetime pass to any American League baseball park were among the many gifts bestowed on Joe Earley and his wife June, during 'Good Old Joe Earley' Night at the Stadium on Tuesday, September 28, 1948. The 24-year-old war veteran received his special evening after winning a "Mr. Average Baseball Fan" letter writing contest sponsored by the Indians and The Cleveland Press. Not forgetting the 60,405 in attendance, Veeck gave away "prizes" including live turkeys, 100-pound cakes of ice, step ladders, white rabbits, guinea pigs and bushels of peaches, apples and tomatoes. Veeck also presented orchids, flown in from Hawaii at a cost of $30,000, to the first 20,000 women entering the stadium. After the last animals were chased from the field, rookie Gene Bearden took the mound for first-place Cleveland, beating the Chicago White Sox, 11-0, on a four-hitter. Outfielders Dale Mitchell and Allie Clark, who went 3 for 5, homered in the win. Earlier in the day, workers for the Indians began opening sacks of mail requests for World Series tickets.

(Above) Joe Earley (right), studies the caricature drawn by Cleveland Press artist Walt Ditzen. **(Right)** Among the gifts Earley received from the Indians were a horse described as "only a medical checkup away from a baseball cover factory," a cow, a calf, seven pigs, a goat and some chickens. Earley lived with his wife in an upstairs apartment in Lakewood.

The Holy Name Society Holy Hour

When the Holy Name Society of the Cleveland Catholic Diocese held its second Holy Hour at the Stadium on Sunday, June 4, 1950, Municipal Stadium was transformed into a giant open-air cathedral, with a 36-foot oil painting of Our Lady of Fatima on a 55-foot altar as the centerpiece. Over 65,000 attended the spiritual rally "held under a blue canopy of the heavens in a star-studded sky." A colorful procession began the celebration with more than 500 clergy filing into the Stadium, followed by uniformed ranks of the Knights of Columbus, Knights of St. John, Catholic War Veterans and thousands of Catholic school girls who later participated in a field ceremony. The keynote address was delivered by Archbishop of Chicago, Samuel Cardinal Stritch, who spoke about how "in the aftermath of the most destructive war in all history, there is no peace." He was introduced by Bishop Edward F. Hoban who presided at the Holy Hour. Music that evening was offered by the choir of St. Mary's Seminary and a massed band of 250 led by Jack Hearns. The first Holy Hour was held at the Stadium on Sunday, May 21, 1949, when widely known radio orator monsignor Fulton J. Sheen, delivered an 18-minute presentation to over 50,000 Catholics in a pouring rain.

(Top) As the presentations came to an end, thousands of area Catholic high school girls with flashlights began forming a living rosary in the Stadium infield.

(Above) After the Stadium lights were dimmed, groups of the high school girls lighted their flashlights in unison to denote the saying of a bead as Auxiliary Bishop Floyd L. Begin led recitation of the rosary. The gigantic altar erected in center field can be seen beyond the living rosary.

(Left) At benediction, Clevelanders prayed for peace with the Stadium aglow in candlelight. Several thousand nuns occupied reserved sections of the Stadium after being given special permission to attend the holy hour by Auxiliary Bishop Begin. The Rev. Fr. Thomas F. Carey, O. P. of New York, assistant national director of the Holy Name Society, led the Holy Name pledge.

June 28, 1953

The Family Rosary Crusade

Six-hundred thousand daily recitations of the holy rosary by area Catholics was the goal of the Holy Name Society, when it sponsored the Family Rosary Crusade at the Stadium on Sunday, June 28, 1953. Over 55,000 attended the public demonstration of faith that climaxed a prayer crusade by the Cleveland Diocese. The keynote address was delivered by Rev. Patrick Peyton, C. S. C., who appealed for 10 minutes of prayer each day from "every father, mother and their children." Peyton spoke from a 60-foot outdoor sanctuary, shaped like a cross, in the Stadium outfield. Archbishop Edward Cardinal Mooney of Detroit, Archbishop Edward F. Hoban, Auxiliary Bishop Floyd L. Begin, who served as the crusade committee's local chairman, and Mayor Thomas A. Burke also spoke at the rally, which was arranged as a spiritual bouquet to Archbishop Hoban's golden jubilee in the priesthood. The next day, 20,000 members of the Holy Name Society began visiting Catholic homes to get signed statements pledging daily recitation of the rosary.

(Top) Archbishop Edward F. Hoban (at the microphone), is dressed in protective rain gear as he led in open recitation of the rosary during the solemn and sacred benediction ceremony. It rained through much of the ceremony.

(Above) The gates opened at 2 P.M. to let the 55,000 devoted Catholics in attendance enter the Stadium. The musical program began at 3 P.M.

(Above left) A colorful procession opened the crusade at 3:40 P.M., as Catholic hierarchy and clergy were joined by members of the Knights of Columbus, the Knights of St. John and the Knights of St. Gregory, who later lined the giant cloth cross at left.

(Left) A two-foot width of cloth laid in the shape of a cross outlined a 60-foot square outdoor sanctuary built for the Crusade. Music was provided during the rally by the Parmadale band, trumpeters from the John Carroll University Band and the combined bands of St. Ignatius, St. Edward, Holy Name, Cathedral Latin and Benedictine high schools.

Baseball at the Stadium

June 22, 1950
Bob Feller's 199th Win

The second-place Cleveland Indians faced the first-place New York Yankees before 18,407 at the Stadium on Thursday, June 22, 1950. On the mound for the Indians was ace Bob Feller. Cleveland beat the Yankees, 6-2, giving Feller his seventh victory of the year and 199th career win. Feller got help from two homers by first baseman Luke Easter, one by shortstop Ray Boone and two by catcher Jim Hegan. The two Yankee runs came on homers by Johnny Mize and Joe DiMaggio. The next day Easter, in his second season with the Indians, hit a towering 477-foot home run that sailed above the scoreboard on the right-center field stands. It is thought to be the longest home run ever hit at the Stadium. Easter's 28 home runs in 1950 were second on the Cleveland roster to third baseman Al Rosen, who led the American League with 37 homers.

(Left) Bob Feller (lower right), is joined by home run hitters Luke Easter (far left), Ray Boone (center), and catcher Jim Hegan (upper right), after the game.

June 20, 1952
Cleveland-9, Boston-2

The fourth-place Cleveland Indians, only game behind manager Lou Boudreau's second-place Boston Red Sox, opened a crucial four-game series with Boston on Friday, June 20, 1952. Played at the Stadium before 28,949, the Indians won the night game, 9-2, as rookie Jim Fridley (left, at right), pitcher Bob Lemon and center fielder Larry Doby (far right), all homered for the Indians. Lemon (6-7), held the Red Sox to five hits, striking out four and walking only one.

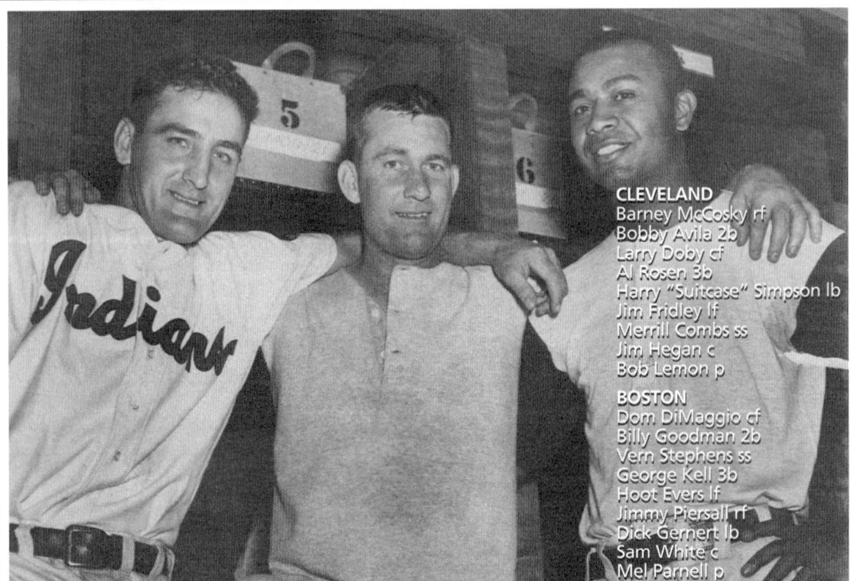

(Left) When the Cleveland Indians opened their series with the Red Sox on June 20th, Boston's starting lineup featured sluggers Dom DiMaggio, George Kell and Billy Goodman, who were first, second and fourth in American League hitting. In third was Tribe third baseman Al Rosen, who was batting .326. Tribe outfielders Dale Mitchell and Larry Doby followed in fifth and seventh place. Also starting in the Boston lineup was colorful rookie right fielder Jimmy Piersall (at bat left), who was making his Stadium debut. Piersall later played in 359 games for the Indians from 1959 to 1961. In 1961, Piersall finished the year with a .322 average and six homers.

Bob Feller is Honored

August 13, 1951

It was "Bob Feller Night" at the Stadium on Monday, August 13, 1951, as the first-place Cleveland Indians played the Detroit Tigers before 46,290 at the Stadium. Feller, who was being honored for his fifteen seasons with the Indians, received a number of gifts before the game, including the souvenir newspaper front page at right, a key to the city from Cleveland Mayor Thomas A. Burke and congratulations from former pitching great Cy Young. Feller started for the first-place Indians, pitching a complete game, seven-hitter to beat the Tigers, 2-1. The 32-year-old right-hander raised his record to 19-4 with his 227th career victory. Feller held the Tigers to one hit in the first four innings and scoreless until the eighth. He received help from Tribe third baseman Al Rosen, who hit a fourth-inning homer and Indians left fielder Dale Mitchell, who extended his hitting streak to 21 games with a single. The win was the Indians' 11th straight. Feller, who led the American League with 22 wins in 1951, had broken the Indians' all-time win record of 223 held by Mel Harder earlier in the season.

(Right) Tribe third baseman Al Rosen (left), who hit his 20th homer of the season, holds the souvenir front page presented to Feller before the game. The front page, created for Feller by the Cleveland Chapter of the Baseball Writer's Association of America, listed many of the famous pitcher's achievements on the baseball diamond. Copies of the page were also shared with fans at the Stadium that evening, and made available through the offices of the Cleveland Press.

September 9, 1956

The Cleveland Indians honored the 20-year career of veteran hurler Bob Feller at the Stadium on Sunday, September 9, 1956, during a doubleheader with the Chicago White Sox. Joining the 28,457 in attendance were former Indians great Tris Speaker, who served as master of ceremonies; Steve O'Neill, who served as Feller's catcher and first major league manager; C. C. Slapnicka, the scout who signed Feller and former hurler Harry Eisenstat, who beat Feller the day Feller struck out 18 Detroit Tigers in 1938. Among the gifts Feller received were a 1957 Cadillac from team owners and telegrams from President Dwight Eisenhower and team stockholder Bob Hope. Tribe starter Herb Score won his 16th of the year, beating the White Sox, 4-1, in the first game. Chicago won the second game, 6-2, with Tribe starter Hank Aguirre taking the loss.

(Left) Feller (left) with his family on September 9th.

1952- Three Twenty-Game Winners

In 1952, right-handers Early Wynn, Bob Lemon and Mike Garcia each won more than twenty games for manager Al Lopez's 93-61 Cleveland Indians, who finished in second place, two games behind the New York Yankees. Wynn (2.90 ERA) ended the year with 23 victories, second in the American League to Philadelphia Athletics hurler Bobby Shantz's 24 wins. Garcia (2.37) and Lemon (2.50) each won 22 games. The three men combined for a total of 106 starts, 852 innings pitched, 66 complete games, 427 strikeouts and 11 saves over the 130 games they appeared in. The 1952 season was the fourth time since Cleveland joined the American League as a charter member in 1901 that three starters each won 20 or more games in one season. The three seasons were: 1906 (Rhoads-22/Joss-21/Hess-20); 1920 (Bagby-31/Coveleskie-24/Caldwell-20); and 1951 (Feller-22/Wynn-20/Garcia-20).

September 11, 1952
Cleveland's 20-Game Winners

Indians center fielder Larry Doby and first baseman Luke Easter were leading the American League in home runs with 30 and 29, when the second-place Cleveland Indians faced the Philadelphia Athletics in the final game of a three-game series on Thursday, September 11, 1952. Played at the Stadium before 7,903, Cleveland moved to within a half game of the league-leading New York Yankees after beating the Athletics, 1-0, to sweep the series. The Tribe's lone run came on a 4th-inning homer by second baseman Bobby Avila.

(Left) Starter Mike Garcia (left), celebrates with teammate Early Wynn after hurling a two-hit shutout for his his 20th win of the year. With the win, Garcia became the league's third 20-game winner. Wynn won his 20th on September 9th. It was the third straight shutout and sixth of the year for Garcia, who lowered his earned-run-average to a league-low 2.26.

September 21, 1952 / Bob Lemon's 21st Win

Trailing the league-leading Yankees by one and a half games with six games remaining in the season, the second-place Cleveland Indians faced the Detroit Tigers on Sunday, September 21, 1952, before 22,436 at the Stadium. On the mound was right-hander Bob Lemon, who was seeking his 21st win of the season. Lemon pitched a complete game, leading the Tribe to a 7-1 win. The win gave Cleveland its fifth straight victory and 14th win in the last 16 games. In the remote chance that Cleveland would win the American League pennant, team management announced during the game that it was beginning to accept World Series ticket orders. Ticket prices were set at $24 per three-game set for box seats and $18.75 per set for reserved seats. After the game, several thousand fans remained to hear play-by-play of the Yankees-Athletics game offered over the Stadium public address system. New York won the game, 1-0, keeping the Tribe a game and a half behind the American League champions.

(Left) Tribe third baseman Al Rosen (left), points to Tribe starter Bob Lemon's jersey number after Lemon recorded his 21st win of the year. Rosen hit his 27th homer of the season, a three-run blast, off loser Art Houtteman. Rosen finished the game with 101 runs-batted-in, giving him his third straight year of 100 or more RBI. Lemon ended the 1952 season with a 22-11 record, leading the American League in complete games (28), and innings pitched (310). Lemon also allowed the fewest hits per nine innings (6.86).

April 14, 1953 / The Season Opener

Coming off a second place finish, two games behind the World Champion New York Yankees in 1952, Manager Al Lopez's Cleveland Indians opened the 1953 season on Tuesday, April 14th against the Chicago White Sox before 53,698 at the Stadium. Veteran right-hander Saul Rogovin started for the White Sox. On the mound for Cleveland was 32-year-old right-hander Bob Lemon, who pitched a complete-game one-hitter to beat Chicago, 6-0. Former Indian Minnie Minoso got the only hit off Lemon, a first-inning single. The Indians tagged White Sox pitchers, Rogovin, Mike Fornieles and Gene Bearden, for eleven hits, including homers by Lemon, the Tribe's first of the year, and second baseman Bobby Avila. Shortstop Ray Boone added a triple and a single. The only Tribesman who failed to hit safely was catcher Jim Hegan.

(Right) Only two other Chicago batters reached base, both on errors by Indian infielders. One error came late in the game, when Tribe third baseman Al Rosen failed to field a hard smash. The other error occurred when shortstop Ray Boone fielded an easy grounder by Rogovin, but threw wildly to first, well over the head of first baseman Luke Easter, jumping to catch the throw at right. Easter went 2 for 3, hitting two hard singles.

(Left) Tribe second baseman Bobby Avila (left), congratulates starter Bob Lemon after the win. Both men homered in the victory. The shutout extended Lemon's innings of no-run ball against the White Sox to 24 and gave the veteran hurler his second win in three opening day assignments. Only three of the putouts recorded by the Tribe were made by Indian outfielders.

July 3, 1953
Cleveland-8, Detroit-1

Tribe third baseman Al Rosen (right, at left), was leading the American League in home runs (19), and runs-batted-in (58), when the second-place Cleveland Indians hosted the last-place Detroit Tigers on Friday, July 3, 1953, before 17,219 at the Stadium. On the mound for Cleveland was Early Wynn (center), who pitched a six-hitter to beat the Tigers, 8-1. Wynn got help from home runs by shortstop George Strickland (left), and Rosen, who hit his 20th homer. It was Rosen's fifth homer in five games, one game short of the league record for home runs in successive games. Of the six hits Wynn surrendered, three came off the bat of rookie shortstop Harvey Kuenn. Rosen, who hit 43 home runs and knocked in 145 RBI in 1953, was voted the league's Most Valuable Player, but missed claiming baseball's triple crown by a single point. Rosen, who hit .336, finished second to Mickey Vernon, who batted .337.

1953- Beethoven and Baseball at the Stadium

"Considering it was a pioneering venture, it was absolutely amazing," reported Thomas J. Sidlo, president of the Cleveland Musical Art Association, after the Cleveland Summer Orchestra opened its 15th season with a concert at the Stadium on Tuesday, June 2, 1953. The musical affair was held before the Cleveland Indians - Boston Red Sox game, with Louis Lane conducting the 70-piece ensemble from a canopied stage located behind the home run fence in center field. Over 9,000 came early to hear the Cleveland News-sponsored concert, which was the first of a 12-set series of 7 P.M. pops concerts scheduled before Indians games. A new "three-dimensional" sound system was installed to enhance the sound. The "Indipops" concept was so unique, that Life magazine sent a crew to photograph the opening performance.

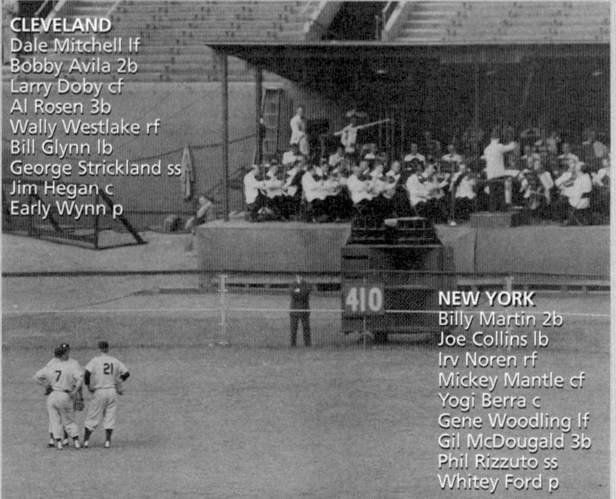

(Above) New York Yankee players Mickey Mantle (7), and Bob Kuzava (21), talk with an unidentified player while being serenaded during the fourth Cleveland Summer Orchestra concert on Friday, June 12, 1953. The second-place Cleveland Indians lost to the first-place Yankees, 4-2, before 43,157, the largest night game crowd of the season. Yankee starter Whitey Ford (7-0), got the win over Early Wynn (3-4), who took the loss. Part of the specially-installed speaker system can be seen immediately behind the 410' sign.

(Left) The Cleveland Summer Orchestra practices on Saturday, May 29th before their first performance on Tuesday, June 2nd. The 7 P.M. concert offered a wide variety of music from Cole Porter to the "Blue Danube Waltz," and Sousa's "Semper Fidelis." 17,386 watched Cleveland lose the baseball half of the doubleheader to manager Lou Boudreau's Boston Red Sox, 7-3.

September 5, 1955
Cleveland vs. Kansas City

The Kansas City Athletics were in town on Monday, September 5, 1955, to play a Labor Day doubleheader with the league-leading Cleveland Indians before 20,947 at the Stadium. The Indians dropped the first game, 5-4, with Tribe reliever Don Mossi taking the loss, but rallied to win the second game, 9-2, as rookie southpaw Herb Score raised his record to 15-10 on a four-hitter. Score struck out 11, raising his AL-leading total to 220. Score was aided by back-to-back homers from Doby and third baseman Al Rosen, who hit his 20th of the year. The doubleheader split gave the Indians a 17-5 edge for the year over the A's, who were under the guidance of first-year manager Lou Boudreau. 1955 was also the first season for the Athletics franchise away from Philadelphia, the city it called home since becoming a charter franchise of the American League in 1901. After finishing 60 games behind the American League champion Cleveland Indians in 1954, the Mack family sold the club to Chicagoan Arnold Johnson, who moved the franchise to Kansas City.

(Right) In the sixth inning of the first game, Tribe center fielder Larry Doby hit his 22nd homer of the year into the right field stands. First base umpire Lou Paparella ruled the homer, which barely cleared the foul pole, a fair ball. Kansas City manager Lou Boudreau (left), rushed out of the dugout to protest the call with Paparella (center), as Kansas City first baseman Vic Power (at right), looked on. Doby's homer drove in Gene Woodling and Bobby Avila to tie the score at 3-3. After going 1 for 4 in the first game, Doby went 2 for 4 in the second game, adding a triple to his two home runs.

1956-
Cleveland's 20-20 Men

September 25, 1956

A new low in night game attendance at the Stadium was set on Tuesday, September 25, 1956, when only 3,604 watched Cleveland Indians right-hander Early Wynn (left, at right), capture his 20th win of the year, a 4-1 victory over manager Lou Boudreau's Kansas City Athletics. The win gave Wynn, who pitched a four-hitter, his fourth season of twenty or more wins and his 221st career victory. Shaking Wynn's hand at right is rookie Tribe right fielder Rocky Colavito, who hit his 21st homer of the year, a three-run blast, in the 10th inning to give Cleveland the win. The game was sent into extra innings when Preston Ward hit a two-out, ninth inning pinch-hit homer off rookie starter Wally Burnette over the 380-foot sign on the right field fence. Tribe left fielder Joe Caffie went 3 for 5 in the win.

September 26th / Score Wins His 20th

Left-hander Herb Score won his 20th game of the year on Wednesday, September 26, 1956, beating the Kansas City Athletics, 8-4, before 3,630 at the Stadium. The 23-year-old pitched a 7-hitter, fanning twelve to run his league-leading strikeout total to 263. Score became the fifth American League hurler to win twenty or more games for the year. Two of the four in the elite club were teammates Bob Lemon (20-9), and Early Wynn (20-14). (Chicago's Billy Pierce and Detroit's Frank Lary were the others.) Indians first baseman Vic Wertz went 5 for 5 in the win, hitting a single and four straight doubles. Wertz singled in the first inning, and then hit doubles in the third, fourth, fifth and seventh innings, tying a major league record. The Indians' last four runs were driven in by Wertz.

(Left) Bob Lemon (left), and Early Wynn (right), join Score (center), after the game. Score finished the year with a 20-9 record- five wins were shutouts- and a 2.53 ERA. Score allowed the American League's fewest hits per nine innings, (5.85).

June 16, 1957 / Father's Day at the Stadium

Between games of a Father's Day doubleheader with the Baltimore Orioles on Sunday, June 16, 1957, the sons of Cleveland Indians players and former players took the field for a two-inning game against their big-league fathers who batted from the opposite side of the plate. To make the game "competitive," a rubber ball that had been frozen until it lost its bounce was used by the tiny Tribesman who beat their fathers, 3-0. When the youngsters batted, a regular softball was used. Their big league fathers of the fourth-place Indians beat the Orioles in the first game, 4-3, as rookie Tribe right fielder Roger Maris hit a two-run, 8th-inning single to give Tribe reliever Ray Narleski the win. In the second game, starter Early Wynn pitched a six-hit complete game on two days rest, to beat Baltimore, 5-1. Wynn got help from homers by third baseman Al Smith and center fielder Dick Williams. Attending the doubleheader was profitable for several of the 19,000 fans who won Father's Day gifts including a lawn mower, contour lawn chairs, barbecue grills and clothing. The grand prize was a $175 power lawn mower complete with a driver's seat.

(Left) Bob Feller's son, 9-year-old Marty Feller, pitches against the fathers. His teammates included Larry Dolin, Joe Early Wynn, Glenn and Steve Greenberg, Jeff Lemon, Mike and Pat Hegan, Steve Feller, Bobby Busby and Ben Farrell. Umpire Bill Summers, a father of eight, called the game.

First Game
CLEVELAND
Al Smith 3b
Bobby Avila 2b
Vic Wertz 1b
Gene Woodling lf
Rocky Colavito rf
Roger Maris cf
Chico Carrasquel ss
Hal Naragon c
Don Mossi p

BALTIMORE
Billy Gardner 2b
Bob Boyd 1b
Joe Durham lf
Gus Triandos c
Jim Busby cf
Jim Pyburn rf
Billy Goodman 3b
Willie Miranda ss
Connie Johnson p

May 7, 1957 / Cleveland-2, New York-1

Manager Kerby Ferrell's third-place Cleveland Indians faced manager Casey Stengel's World Champion New York Yankees in the opening game of a three-game series before 18,386 at the Stadium on Tuesday, May 7, 1957. On the mound for Cleveland was 23-year-old southpaw sensation Herb Score, the American League Rookie-of-the-Year in 1955. Pitching against Score was right-hander Tom Sturdivant. Score, who finished the 1956 season with a 20-9 record, a 2.53 earned-run-average and 263 strikeouts, was looking for his third straight shutout against the Yankees. The Yankee roster included triple crown winner Mickey Mantle and 20-year-old rookie Tony Kubek, who was a pre-season favorite to

challenge Tribe outfielder Roger Maris for rookie-of-the-year honors. After retiring lead-off hitter Hank Bauer for the first out, Score faced Yankee shortstop Gil McDougald. Only three minutes into the game, McDougald hit Score's 12th pitch sharply back to the mound, striking Score squarely in the nose and right eye socket. Score fell to the ground as the ball ricocheted toward third base. Third baseman Al Smith picked up the ball and threw to first for the out. Score later reported that he didn't see the ball until the last couple of feet. Indians hurler Bob Lemon stepped in to complete the game, holding the Yanks to six hits for a 2-1 Tribe win. Just prior to the accident, the Indians had turned down a million dollar offer from the Boston Red Sox for Score, who had fanned 39 batters in the last 36 innings.

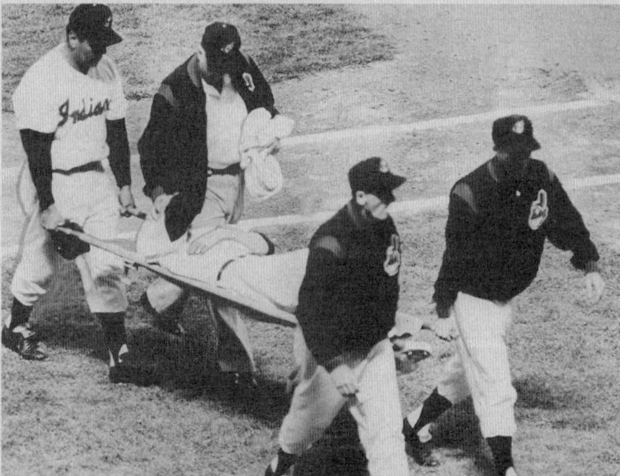

NEW YORK	CLEVELAND
Hank Bauer rf	George Strickland 2b
Gil McDougald ss	Gene Woodling lf
Mickey Mantle cf	Al Smith 3b
Yogi Berra c	Vic Wertz 1b
Bill "Moose" Skowron lb	Roger Maris cf
Billy Martin 2b	Rocky Colavito rf
Elston Howard lf	Chico Carrasquel ss
Andy Carey 3b	Jim Hegan c
Tom Sturdivant p	Herb Score p

(Above) Bobby Avila, far right, and Mike Garcia, third from right, are among the Indians gathered around Score as trainer Wally Bock prepares to transfer the injured pitcher to the stretcher in front. Score's close friend Rocky Colavito stands in the rear, sixth from right.

(Left) Score was carried to the locker where he was initially examined by team physician Dr. Don Kelly. Score was then transported to Lakeside Hospital, where he was examined by eye specialist Dr. Charles Thomas.

April 23, 1958 / Cleveland-2, Chicago-0

Returning in solid form from his injury on May 7, 1957, Tribe southpaw Herb Score raised his record to 2-1 on Wednesday, April 23, 1958, beating the Chicago White Sox, 2-0, before 2,391 at the Stadium. Score pitched a three-hit complete game, striking out thirteen Chicago batters. Score recorded least one strikeout in each inning except the fifth, and fanned the side in the sixth inning. It was Score's first shutout for the Cleveland Indians in exactly a year. Tribe second baseman Bobby Avila's first homer of the year, a third-inning blast off White Sox starter Billy Pierce, gave Cleveland its final run. Colavito went 3 for 3 with a double.

(Left) Starter Herb Score brushes back White Sox shortstop Luis Aparicio. Score gave up three hits, all singles, in the first to second baseman Nellie Fox, Aparicio in the third and third baseman Sammy Esposito in the seventh inning.

CHICAGO			CLEVELAND
Luis Aparicio	ss	rf	Roger Maris
Nellie Fox	2b	3b	Bobby Avila
Al Smith	lf	lf	Minnie Minoso
Sherm Lollar	c	lb	Rocky Colavito
Ron Jackson	1b	ss	Chico Carrasquel
Bubba Phillips	rf	cf	Carroll Hardy
Jim Landis	cf	c	Dick Brown
Sammy Esposito	3b	2b	Billy Moran
Billy Pierce	p	p	Herb Score

August 10, 1958 / Cleveland vs. Kansas City

The Cleveland Indians faced the Kansas City Athletics in a Sunday doubleheader before 25,300 at the Stadium on August 10, 1958. Cleveland starter Cal McLish won the first game, 11-2, with help from homers by first baseman Vic Power and center fielder Larry Doby. In the second game, the Indians sent rookie southpaw Hal Woodeshick to the mound. Woodeshick threw hitless ball for six innings, but the A's scored twice in the ninth inning to take a 2-1 lead. Cleveland's first run came in the seventh, when Tribe right fielder Rocky Colavito, celebrating his 25th birthday, drove a pitch from starter Bud Daley into the left field stands for his 24th homer of the year. Cleveland tied the game in the ninth inning, but failed to win in the ninth, when Athletics reliever Dick Tomanek struck out Doby, Colavito and catcher Dick Brown with the bases loaded.

(Right) In the 10th inning, Ex-Indian Roger Maris (right), hit his 19th homer of the year off reliever Jim (Mudcat) Grant, giving the A's a game-winning 4-2 lead. Tomanek then set the Indians down in order for the win. Maris and Tomanek were traded with Preston Ward by Cleveland on June 15, 1958 to Kansas City for Woody Held and Vic Power.

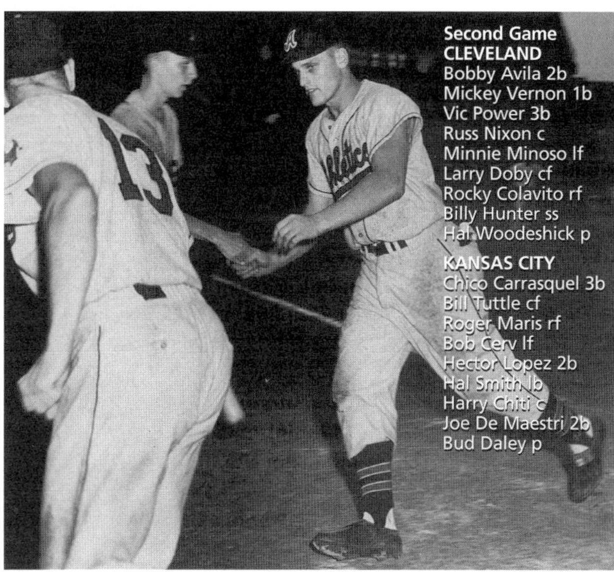

Second Game
CLEVELAND
Bobby Avila 2b
Mickey Vernon 1b
Vic Power 3b
Russ Nixon c
Minnie Minoso lf
Larry Doby cf
Rocky Colavito rf
Billy Hunter ss
Hal Woodeshick p

KANSAS CITY
Chico Carrasquel 3b
Bill Tuttle cf
Roger Maris rf
Bob Cerv lf
Hector Lopez 2b
Hal Smith 1b
Harry Chiti c
Joe De Maestri 2b
Bud Daley p

July 12, 1959 / Family Day

One of the largest gate sales in Cleveland Indians history took place on Sunday, July 12, 1959, when nearly 32,000 tickets were sold before the Family Day doubleheader between the first-place Indians and the Detroit Tigers. Cleveland lost the opener, 6-2, as Tiger hurler Paul Foytack held the Indians to six hits, but rallied to win the second game, 8-4. Rookie reliever Jim Perry raised his record to 4-1, with help from Tribe right fielder Rocky Colavito who hit two homers, his 27th and 28th, and second baseman Minnie Minoso, who hit a solo blast. Tribe starter Bobby Locke took the loss in the first game.

(Left) The line for tickets at Gate A stretched all the way up W. 3rd St. to the bridge over the railroad tracks. The crowd was set at 54,727 (including 13,079 children who got in for free,) making it the third home game of the year to draw over 50,000 fans. The other two home games were against the World Champion New York Yankees.

July 28, 1959
Billy's Inside-The-Park Homer

Manager Joe Gordon's second-place Cleveland Indians faced manager Billy Jurges' last-place Boston Red Sox in a twi-night doubleheader at the Stadium on Tuesday, July 28, 1959. Played before 29,529, the Indians won the first game, 5-2, with starter Gary Bell pitching a six-hitter, but lost the second contest, 8-4, as rookie starter Jim Perry saw his record drop to 6-3. Indians lead-off hitter, third baseman Billy Martin, opened the Tribe's scoring in the second game with a rare first-inning inside-the-park homer. Martin added a double to go 2 for 4. Malzone and Runnels homered for the Red Sox. The split left the Tribe a half game behind the first-place Chicago White Sox.

(Right) Martin (right), is congratulated after his inside-the-park homer by second-baseman Jim Baxes (32), and pitcher Cal McLish (22). In the forefront is utility infielder Granny Hamner.

Second Game
BOSTON   **CLEVELAND**
Pumpsie Green 2b   3b Billy Martin
Pete Runnels 1b   1b Vic Power
Jim Busby cf   lf Minnie Minoso
Dick Gernert lf   cf Tito Francona
Frank Malzone 3b   rf Rocky Colavito
Jackie Jensen rf   ss George Strickland
Pete Daley c   2b Jim Baxes
Jim Mahoney ss   c Ed Fitzgerald
Bill Monbouquette p   p Jim Perry

The Bronx Bombers Invade the Stadium

July 12, 1951 /
Allie Reynolds' No-Hitter

New York Yankee starter Allie Reynolds raised his record to 10-5 on Thursday, July 12, 1951, beating the Cleveland Indians, 1-0, with his first major league no-hitter. Played before 39,185 at the Stadium, the 33-year-old Reynolds was embroiled in a pitching duel with Tribe starter Bob Feller, who had a no-hitter going until the sixth inning, when rookie right fielder Mickey Mantle doubled to left-center. In the seventh inning, former Indian Gene Woodling homered off Feller for the Yankees' only run. Feller's record fell to 12-3. Reynolds walked three, struck out four, and retired the last seventeen men in succession. Reynolds' no-hitter came only 12 days after Feller became the first hurler in modern times to throw three career ho-hitters. Feller beat the Detroit Tigers, 2-1, on July 1st, in the first game of a Sunday doubleheader before 42,891 at the Stadium. Feller duplicated the feat accomplished by Cy Young in 1897, 1904 and 1908.

(Top) Yankee starter Allie Reynolds is greeted by teammates Gene Woodling (left), Joe DiMaggio, trainer Gus Mauch, manager Casey Stengel and catcher Yogi Berra (with arm around Reynolds), after pitching his no-hitter. **(Top right)** Reynolds during his no-hitter. **(Above)** With New York Yankees manager Casey Stengel. The loss placed the fourth-place Indians 4 1/2 games behind league-leading Boston.

(Right) May 4, 1955 / New York-11, Cleveland-5

The first-place Cleveland Indians (13-6), played the fourth-place New York Yankees (10-8), on Wednesday, May 4, 1955, before 27,160 at the Stadium. Tribe starter Bob Lemon (5-1), held Mickey Mantle and Gil McDougald hitless, but lost, 11-5. "I was too cautious," Lemon reported after walking three Yankees in the eighth inning, when New York scored four runs. Yankee homers were hit by catcher Yogi Berra and right fielder Hank Bauer. Center fielder Dave Pope, who went 2 for 3, homered for Cleveland. The next day, former Tribe player-manager Lou Boudreau made his Stadium debut as manager of the "Missouri Miracles" Kansas City Athletics.

(Right) Yankee manager Casey Stengel (left), argues with home plate umpire Larry Napp over a half-swing call at home plate. New York played part of the game without Stengel, who was thrown out by Napp.

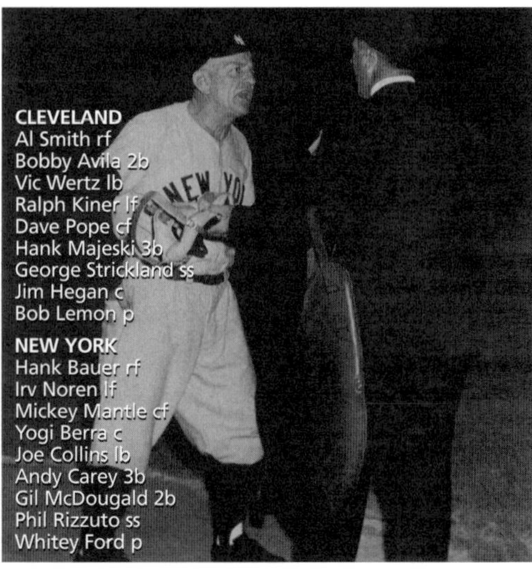

September 16, 1956 / Mantle Hits His 49th

The New York Yankees, on the verge of clinching the American League pennant, faced the Cleveland Indians in a Sunday doubleheader before 39,651 at the Stadium on September 16, 1956. The Yankees won the first game, 10-3, foiling Tribe starter Bob Lemon's bid to become a twenty-game winner. A win in the nightcap would have clinched the title for New York, but the Yanks went down to defeat, 4-3, as Early Wynn, who won his 18th game, pitched a complete-game, three-hitter to postpone New York's victory celebration. On September 18th, as the Yankees clinched the pennant against the Chicago White Sox in Chicago, the Indians won a doubleheader before 4,305 at the Stadium. Tribe pitchers Herb Score and Mike Garcia won their 18th and 10th games of the year. Score pitched a four-hitter, striking out 14, to give him 242 strikeouts for the year.

(Right) Yankee center fielder Mickey Mantle is congratulated by teammate Yogi Berra after hitting his 49th homer of the season in eighth inning of the night-cap. The homer was Mantle's 10th in 22 games against the Indians and his first hit into the Stadium's upper right field stands. Mantle ended the year batting .353, with 52 homers and 130 RBI to win the American League's triple crown and the league's Most Valuable Player award, with Berra finishing second in the MVP balloting. Cleveland ended the year in second place with a 88-66 record, nine games behind the Yankees.

First Game	Second Game
CLEVELAND	**CLEVELAND**
Joe Caffie lf	Joe Caffie lf
Bobby Avila 2b	Bobby Avila 2b
Al Smith cf	Vic Wertz lb
Rocky Colavito rf	Rocky Colavito rf
Al Rosen 3b	Al Rosen 3b
Sam Mele lb	Al Smith cf
Jim Hegan c	Jim Hegan c
George Strickland ss	Chico Carrasquel ss
Bob Lemon p	Early Wynn p
NEW YORK	**NEW YORK**
Hank Bauer rf	Hank Bauer rf
Enos Slaughter lf	Joe Collins lb
Mickey Mantle cf	Mickey Mantle cf
Yogi Berra c	Yogi Berra c
Joe Collins lb	Irv Noren lf
Gil McDougald ss	Gil McDougald ss
Billy Martin 2b	Billy Martin 2b
Andy Carey 3b	Andy Carey 3b
Tom Sturdivant p	Johnny Kucks p

(Left) Cleveland Indians manager Al Lopez (left), enjoys a few laughs with Yankee manager Casey Stengel before the game on September 16, 1956.

June 5, 1959 / New York-11, Cleveland-2

Manager Joe Gordon's Cleveland Indians played the New York Yankees on Friday, June 5, 1959, in the opening game of their first home series of the season against the World Champions. The game was played at the Stadium before 51,935, the American League's largest turnout of the season, with right-hander Gary Bell starting for Cleveland. Bell was soon followed by relievers Bud Podbielan, Al Cicotte and Mike Garcia, who gave up a total of 17 hits to the Bronx Bombers, including at least one to every Yankee except center fielder Micky Mantle, who walked three times and struck out twice. New York won the game, 11-2, with starter Al Ditmar pitching a complete game for the win. The second-place Indians avoided a shutout when second baseman Billy Martin homered in the eighth inning. In the ninth inning, right fielder Rocky Colavito hit his 14th homer of the year to give the Indians their second run. It was the largest crowd to see the Indians play at home since September 4, 1955, when 68,552 watched Cleveland battle New York.

(Right) Yankee catcher Elston Howard is congratulated by teammate Yogi Berra after homering in the seventh inning to give the Yankees a six-run lead.

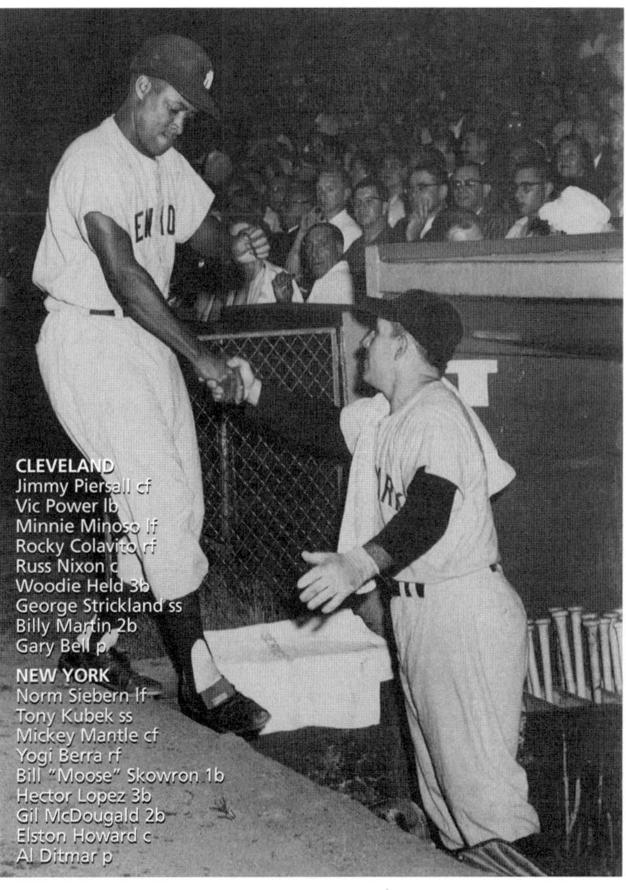

CLEVELAND
Jimmy Piersall cf
Vic Power lb
Minnie Minoso lf
Rocky Colavito rf
Russ Nixon c
Woodie Held 3b
George Strickland ss
Billy Martin 2b
Gary Bell p

NEW YORK
Norm Siebern lf
Tony Kubek ss
Mickey Mantle cf
Yogi Berra rf
Bill "Moose" Skowron 1b
Hector Lopez 3b
Gil McDougald 2b
Elston Howard c
Al Ditmar p

1954- A Record-Setting Season

June 27, 1954 / Cleveland-4, New York-3

After losing the first two games of a three-game series with the New York Yankees by scores of 11-0 and 11-9, the league-leading Cleveland Indians played the final game of the series on Sunday, June 27, 1954, before 47,782 at the Stadium. Pitching for Cleveland against Yankee starter Whitey Ford was Bob Lemon, who was forced to leave in the 3rd inning with a sore back. Thirty-five-year-old reliever Hal Newhouser shut down the Yankees for six innings until Mike Garcia came on to secure a 4-3 win for the Indians. The three hurlers gave up only six hits, holding Collins, Woodling, Carey and Bauer hitless. In the sixth inning, left fielder Wally Westlake, who went 2 for 3, hit a two-run homer to give Cleveland a 3-1 lead. Experimenting to give the lineup more power, Tribe manager Al Lopez had Al Rosen, who normally started at third base, moving to first base. Al Smith started at third in Rosen's place. Smith went 2 for 4 with a double and an RBI. Rosen went 1 for 3. The win gave the Indians a one and a half game lead over the Yanks.

(Left) First baseman Al Rosen (left), prepares to congratulate left fielder Wally Westlake after scoring on Westlake's two-run homer in the sixth inning. Coming up to bat is right fielder Dave Philley, who also homered in the game.

July 4, 1954 / A Three-Way One-Hitter

A holiday crowd of 26,842 at the Stadium watched three Tribe right-handers, Mike Garcia, rookie Ray Narleski and Early Wynn, combine to pitch a one-hitter as the Indians beat manager Paul Richards' Chicago White Sox, 2-1, on Sunday, July 4, 1954. Garcia started the game, but was forced to leave after getting one out in the second inning when a blister formed on the middle finger of his pitching hand (bandaged at right). Narleski, who got the win, retired the next seventeen batters before being replaced by Early Wynn in the 8th inning. Wynn continued to hold Chicago hitless until the 9th inning, when former Tribe infielder Minnie Minoso got the only White Sox hit, a two-out single. Minoso

was then thrown out stealing to end the game. Center fielder Larry Doby drove in both Cleveland runs with a single and his 15th home run, to give the Indians their seventh straight victory and a 4 1/2 game lead over the second-place New York Yankees. First baseman Dave Glynn went 3 for 4 with three singles in the win. The New York Times reported that seven out of ten times, the team in first place on July 4th would finish in first at the end of the season. The Indians won a major league record 111 games (111-43) in 1954 to finish atop the American League.

(Above) Garcia (left), Narleski and Wynn display the number of hits each gave up during the game.

(Left) Wynn (center), is congratulated by catcher Jim Hegan after the win.

The All-Star Game July 13, 1954

On Monday, July 8, 1935, Municipal Stadium played host to the third All-Star game in modern major league history, as 69,812 paid to see Jimmy Foxx's two-run, first inning homer and "Cleveland curve ball specialist" Mel Harder's three innings of scoreless relief pitching lift the American League to a 4-1 win. Nineteen years later, Municipal Stadium hosted its second All-Star contest on Tuesday, July 13, 1954, as 68,751 turned out to watch the 21st annual classic, a slugfest won by the American League, 11-9. With the game tied, 8-8, in the eighth inning, second baseman Nellie Fox of the Chicago White Sox hit a two-out, bases-loaded bloop single to drive in the winning runs. Eight of the American League runs were knocked in by the local heroes. Indians third baseman Al Rosen, the game MVP, tied two records with five runs-batted-in and two home runs. Tribe second baseman Bobby Avila went 3 for 3, driving in two runs with three singles. Center fielder Larry Doby's pinch-hit homer tied the score in the eighth inning at 8-8. A fourth A.L. homer was hit by ex-Indian Ray Boone of the Detroit Tigers. National League homers were clubbed by Cincinnati Reds sluggers Ted Kluszewski and Gus Bell. Seven All-Star marks were set during the nine-inning contest, including most runs (20), most hits by both clubs (31), and most hits by one club- (17- A.L.)

STARTING LINEUPS

American League

Minnie Minoso, Chicago, lf	.313	
Bobby Avila, Cleveland, 2b	.341	
Mickey Mantle, New York, cf	.316	
Yogi Berra, New York, c	.291	
Al Rosen, Cleveland, 1b	.313	
Ray Boone, Detroit, 3b	.303	
Hank Bauer, New York, rf	.306	
Chico Carrasquel, Chicago, ss	.263	
Whitey Ford, New York, p	(7-6)	
Casey Stengel, New York, Manager		

National League

Gran Hamner, Philadelphia, 2b	.323	
Alvin Dark, New York, ss	.293	
Duke Snider, Brooklyn, cf	.367	
Stan Musial, St. Louis, rf	.331	
Ted Kluszewski, Cincinnati, 1b	.313	
Ray Jablonski, St. Louis, 3b	.322	
Jackie Robinson, Brooklyn, lf	.321	
Roy Campanella, Brooklyn, c	.215	
Robin Roberts, Philadelphia, p	(11-8)	
Walter Alston, Brooklyn, Manager		

Winning Pitcher:
Dean Stone, Washington Nationals

Losing Pitcher:
Gene Conley, Milwaukee Braves

Time of Game: 3:10
Receipts $292,678 (Gross) / $259,204 (Net)

(Top) Cleveland Indians third baseman Al Rosen (left), joins Boston Red Sox left fielder Ted Williams, first baseman Mickey Vernon of the Washington Nationals and New York Yankees center fielder Mickey Mantle before the game. Williams and Vernon were held hitless, but Rosen went 3 for 4 with two homers. Mantle added two singles in five at bats. **(Above)** Brooklyn Dodgers left fielder Jackie Robinson, who drove in two runs with a fourth-inning double, chats with New York Giants center fielder Willie Mays before the game. Mays went 1 for 2 with a single.

July 30, 1954
Larry Doby's Sensational Catch

The first-place Cleveland Indians faced the Washington Nationals in a night game on Friday, July 30, 1954, before 17,504 at the Stadium. In the third inning, Senator right fielder Tom Umphlett hit a drive to the fence in left center. Tribe center fielder Larry Doby, "launched himself like a rocket," to snare Umphlett's hit. Doby landed on the bullpen awning

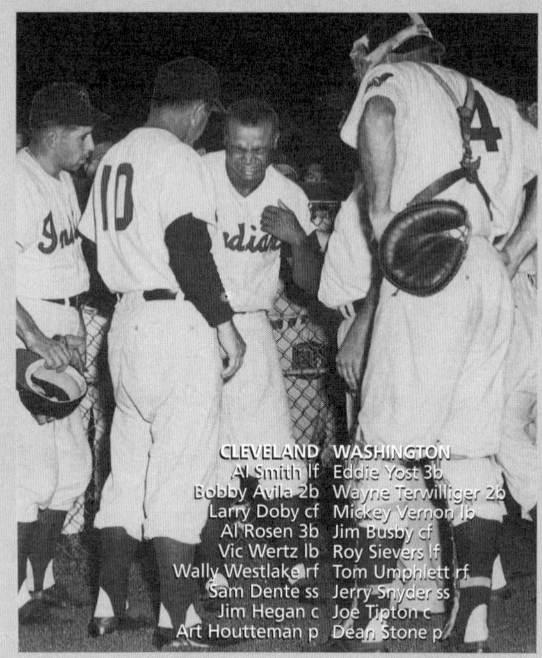

CLEVELAND	WASHINGTON
Al Smith lf	Eddie Yost 3b
Bobby Avila 2b	Wayne Terwilliger 2b
Larry Doby cf	Mickey Vernon 1b
Al Rosen 3b	Jim Busby cf
Vic Wertz 1b	Roy Sievers lf
Wally Westlake rf	Tom Umphlett rf
Sam Dente ss	Jerry Snyder ss
Jim Hegan c	Joe Tipton c
Art Houtteman p	Dean Stone p

and outfield fence before hitting the ground. Umphlett later said, "If this wasn't one of the catches of the century, it must be a match for any other." Baseball great Dizzy Dean, in town for a national TV broadcast the next day, told reporters he'd be a skunk's uncle if it wasn't one of the greatest catches he has ever seen. Dean remarked, "I've seen them all, Moore, DiMaggio and this here fellow named Mays, but I never seen a catch as good as this one and that pitcher ought to pay that Doby a month's salary." Doby's teammate Al Smith said, "He really took off and most of him was over the fence when he back-handed the ball. He bounced off that awning like a rubber ball. I thought he broke his back until he held up his glove with the ball in it." Later in the game, Doby hit his 21st home run of the season, tying him for the American League lead with New York Yankees slugger Mickey Mantle. The Indians won the game, 8-3, with Art Houtteman (10-5) getting the win. Tribe catcher Jim Hegan drove in four runs with a double and home run.

(Above) Tribe center fielder Larry Doby lays on the ground after making his dramatic catch. **(Left)** Third baseman Sam Dente (left), manager Al Lopez (10), and catcher Jim Hegan look on as Doby recovers after the play.

September 10, 1954
Cleveland-4, Boston-2

The first-place Cleveland Indians (101-40), won their 101st game of the 1954 season on Friday, September 10th by beating manager Lou Boudreau's Boston Red Sox, 4-2, before 34,561 at the Stadium. Tribe starter Mike Garcia held Red Sox sluggers Ted Williams and Jackie Jensen hitless, striking out six, including Williams twice, for his 17th win of the year. In the fourth inning, Tribe catcher Jim Hegan, who went 2 for 3, belted a homer off starter Leo Kiely for the final run.

(Right) Tribe manager Al Lopez (far right), congratulates Lou Boudreau before the game, as the former Indians player-manager received a clock from Cleveland Press sports writer Frank Gibbons, president of the Cleveland Chapter of the Baseball Writers of America. The gift was in honor of Lou's induction into the Indians' Hall of Fame. 1954 was Boudreau's last season as manager of the Red Sox.

CLEVELAND	
Al Smith lf	
Bobby Avila 2b	
Larry Doby cf	
Vic Wertz 1b	
Rudy Regalado 3b	
Dave Philley rf	
George Strickland ss	
Jim Hegan c	
Mike Garcia p	
BOSTON	
Billy Goodman 2b	
Ted Williams lf	
Jackie Jensen cf	
Harry Agganis 1b	
Grady Hatton 3b	
Jimmy Piersall rf	
Sam White c	
Bill Consolo ss	
Leo Kiely p	

The 1954 World Series October 1-2, 1954

(Below right) Former Cleveland Indians center fielder and Hall of Famer Tris Speaker (left), shares batting tips with New York Giants center fielder and future Hall of Famer Willie Mays before the first World Series game at the Stadium. Mays made a sensational catch during Game 1 in New York to rob first baseman Vic Wertz of a hit and the Indians of victory.

(Below) Fans root on the Indians from outside the Stadium prior to the playoffs. The four-game series attracted 251,567 spectators, setting a new World Series attendance mark for a four-game series. The old mark of 201,805 was set in 1927, when the Babe Ruth-led New York Yankees swept the Pittsburgh Pirates.

On Friday, October 1, 1954, the Cleveland Indians, down two games in the World Series, faced the New York Giants before 71,555 at the Stadium. Tribe first baseman Vic Wertz (the only Indian to hit safely in all four games,) homered in the 7th inning, but it was too little, too late. The Giants had already scored six runs with Willie Mays and Dusty Rhodes each knocking in two runs. New York won the game, 6-2, as right-hander Ruben Gomez got the win with help from reliever Hoyt Wilhelm. Cleveland starter Mike Garcia took the loss. **(Right)** Outfielder James (Dusty) Rhodes (center), celebrates with Gomez (left), and Hoyt Wilhelm (right), after winning Game 3. **(Below)** New York skipper Leo Durocher (center), was mobbed by reporters after Game 3. The Giants were 8 to 5 favorites to sweep the series, but the cautious Durocher told reporters, "All I'll say is that we're playing here tomorrow at 1 o'clock. It's been a hard, close Series so far and I'm not making any predictions."

On Saturday, October 2nd, 81,102 watched the Giants beat the Indians, 7-4, to sweep the series. Yankee southpaw Don Liddle got the win, with help from relievers Hoyt Wilhelm and Johnny Antonelli, giving Durocher his first World Series title in three tries. Tribe starter Bob Lemon, who struck out five, took the loss. Right fielder Don Mueller went 3 for 4 and shortstop Alvin Dark, 3 for 5, for the victorious Giants.

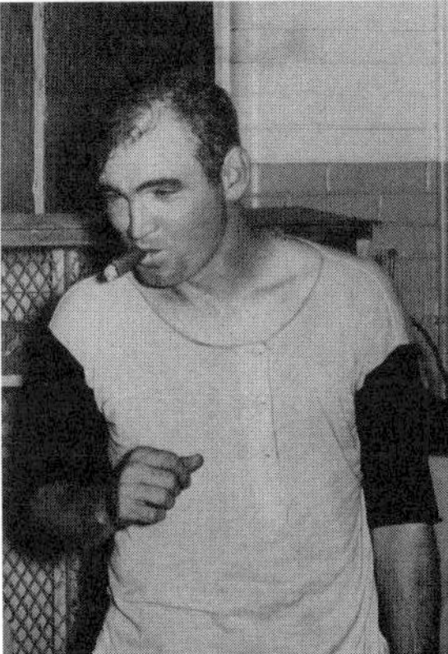

(Above right) Dusty Rhodes celebrates with a cigar after winning the World Series. Rhodes came to the plate only six times, but batted .667 with four hits including homers in Games 1 and 2. Rhodes drove in seven of the team's 20 runs.

The NFL Championship Game

After finishing their first regular season in the National Football League tied for first place with the New York Giants at 10-2, the Cleveland Browns faced the Giants in a playoff for the Eastern Conference title on Sunday, December 17, 1950. Cleveland beat New York, 8-3, before 33,054 half-frozen spectators at the Stadium, setting the stage for a battle with coach Joe Stydahar's Western Division-winning Los Angeles Rams for the NFL championship. Intermittent snow flurries were mixed with chilling winds and a game-time temperature of 15°, as the two teams took the field before 29,751 at the Stadium on Sunday, December 24, 1950. At quarterback for the Rams was Bob Waterfield, who as a rookie, led the Cleveland Rams to the NFL title in 1945. On the first play from scrimmage, Waterfield, who completed 18 of 31 for 312 yards, connected with LH Glenn Davis on a playoff-record 82-yard pass play to give the Rams a 7-0 lead, only 27 seconds into the game. First and third period scores by FB Dick Hoerner and a third quarter fumble by Browns FB Marion Motley that LE Larry Brink turned into six points, accounted for the Rams' other scores. Cleveland scored on TD passes from QB Otto Graham to HB Dub Jones, RE Dante Lavelli (2), and HB Rex Baumgardner. A missed extra point however, put the Browns down, 28-27, late in the game. After forcing the Rams to punt, Cleveland got the ball back on its own 32-yard line with 1:50 remaining.

The drive started with Graham running 14 yards for a first down. He then threw to HB Rex Baumgardner for 13 yards, HB Dub Jones for 16 yards and Baumgardner again for 12 more, putting the ball at the Rams' 11-yard line. With seconds remaining, Lou "The Toe" Groza kicked a 16-yard field goal giving the Browns a thrilling 30-28 victory and their fifth straight pro football championship. Graham completed 22 of 32 passes for 298 yards in leading his team to victory.

Turf Shoes

(Left) To help maneuver on the frozen Stadium turf, Browns players switched between their cleated shoes, and the tennis shoes worn by Browns QB Otto Graham below left.

(Left) Browns receiver Dante Lavelli blocks Rams DE Bob Boyd as Browns QB Otto Graham (60), prepares to be tackled in the fourth quarter. Other Browns in the play are guard Abe Gibron (34), center Frank Gatski (22), and Lou "The Toe" Groza (46), far right. Lavelli, who scored twice, broke an NFL playoff record with 11 pass receptions. Gross receipts totalled $157,078, including about $45,000 from radio and television rights. The total players' pool was $76,272.18 or 70% of the game net of $108,960.25. Each Browns player received $1,113.16 from the winning players' pool of $41,186.98. Game tickets were priced at reserved seats ($4 and $5); general admission ($2); and student section ($1).

1950 CLEVELAND BROWNS

L. End-	Speedie, Young, Gillom
L. Tackle-	Groza, Palmer, Kissell
L. Guard-	Gibron, Humble, Agase
Center-	Gatski, Herring, Thompson
R. Guard-	Houston, Willis
R. Tackle-	Rymkus, Grigg, Sandusky
R. End-	Lavelli, Martin, Ford
QB-	Graham, Gorgal, C. Lewis
L. HB-	Baumgardner, Lahr, Carpenter, Moselle
R. HB-	Jones, James, Phelps
Fullback-	Motley, Adamle, Cole

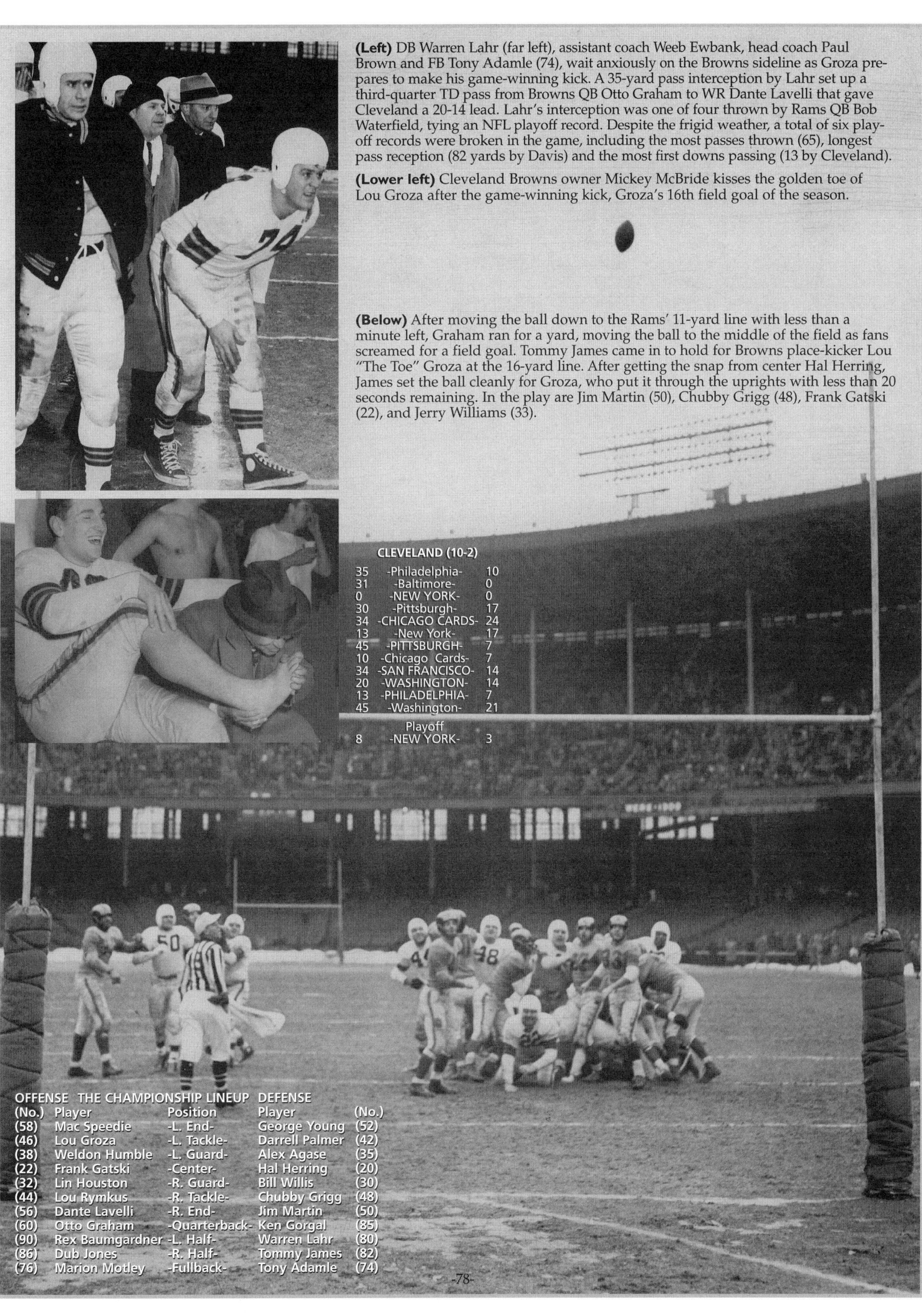

(Left) DB Warren Lahr (far left), assistant coach Weeb Ewbank, head coach Paul Brown and FB Tony Adamle (74), wait anxiously on the Browns sideline as Groza prepares to make his game-winning kick. A 35-yard pass interception by Lahr set up a third-quarter TD pass from Browns QB Otto Graham to WR Dante Lavelli that gave Cleveland a 20-14 lead. Lahr's interception was one of four thrown by Rams QB Bob Waterfield, tying an NFL playoff record. Despite the frigid weather, a total of six playoff records were broken in the game, including the most passes thrown (65), longest pass reception (82 yards by Davis) and the most first downs passing (13 by Cleveland).

(Lower left) Cleveland Browns owner Mickey McBride kisses the golden toe of Lou Groza after the game-winning kick, Groza's 16th field goal of the season.

(Below) After moving the ball down to the Rams' 11-yard line with less than a minute left, Graham ran for a yard, moving the ball to the middle of the field as fans screamed for a field goal. Tommy James came in to hold for Browns place-kicker Lou "The Toe" Groza at the 16-yard line. After getting the snap from center Hal Herring, James set the ball cleanly for Groza, who put it through the uprights with less than 20 seconds remaining. In the play are Jim Martin (50), Chubby Grigg (48), Frank Gatski (22), and Jerry Williams (33).

Football at the Stadium

September 14, 1951
Cleveland-7, Los Angeles-6

The Cleveland Browns battled the Los Angeles Rams in the last pre-season game of 1951 on Friday, September 14th, before 38,851 at the Stadium. It was Cleveland's first appearance at home since beating the Rams in the 1950 NFL title game and marked the local debut of several promising rookies, including HB Chick Jagade and former John Carroll U. stars Carl Taseff and Don Shula. With the Rams leading, 6-0, on two Bob Waterfield field goals, Browns QB Otto Graham led the team on a final drive. Only minutes remained as Graham moved the ball 68 yards to the Rams' 12-yard line. Two plays later, Graham hit WR Horace Gillom for six points. With 39 seconds left, Lou Groza kicked the extra point for a 7-6 victory.

(Left) Rams DB Norb Hecker, who played collegiate football at Baldwin-Wallace College in Berea, Ohio, knocks Browns QB Otto Graham (60), out of bounds during Cleveland's game-winning drive. Graham gained nine yards on the play.

November 25, 1951 / Cleveland-42, Chicago-21

In the first regular season meeting between the two clubs, the American Conference-leading Cleveland Browns (7-1), faced the Chicago Bears (6-2), of coach George "Papa Bear" Halas on Sunday, November 25, 1951, before 40,969 at the Stadium. The Browns beat Chicago, 42-21, as 6' 4" LH Dub Jones tied an NFL record by scoring all six Cleveland TDs. The Browns gained

550 yards in total offense (277 passing,) but were penalized 21 times for 209 yards, eclipsing the NFL record of 17 penalties for 185 yards set by Green Bay in 1945. The Bears, who got nine of their 22 first downs on Cleveland penalties, lost 165 yards on 16 penalties. The 374 penalty yards racked up by the two teams were 216 more than the Bears gained on offense. One penalty, a roughing the passer call, nullified a 94-yard pass interception TD by Browns DB Don Shula. Cleveland QB Otto Graham, who completed 19 of 21 for 277 yards, suffered a broken nose in the battle. In the fourth quarter, Browns players Horace Gillom and Tommy Thompson were ejected with the Bears' George Blanda for throwing punches. Jones' six TDs tied the mark set by the Chicago Cardinals' Ernie Nevers in 1929.

(Left) Browns FB Marion Motley (with ball), runs against the Bears. Motley gained 36 yards on six carries. His teammates in the play are OT Lou Groza (46), C Frank Gatski (22), HB Ken Carpenter (84), OG Lin Houston (32), and OT John Sandusky (49). No. 32 is the Bears' Johnny Lujack.

November 24, 1951 / At the Charity Game

The Collinwood High marching band at right, was one of the 26 high school marching bands performing at the Stadium on Saturday, November 24, 1951, during the 21st annual Plain Dealer Charity Game for the city high school football championship. Before the game, the golden chariot ridden by actor Robert Taylor in the film, "Quo Vadis," was pulled into the Stadium by a team of horses. The chariot, later used to pull Indians pitcher Bob Feller and his wife around the Stadium, was on loan from M.G.M. studios and Loew's Stillman, where the motion picture was playing. Played before 18,759, the 10-0-0 Rhodes High Rams of head coach Andy Moran beat the Collinwood Railroaders of coach Frank Lauterbur, 21-14. On the Rhodes sideline was a live ram, rented by students to serve as the team's mascot.

October 12, 1952 / New York-17, Cleveland-9

With both teams possessing identical 2-0-0 records, first place in the Eastern Conference was at stake on Sunday, October 12, 1952, when the New York Giants battled the Cleveland Browns of coach Paul Brown, who had just received a new five-year contract, before 51,858 at the Stadium. The Browns, playing without starting end Dante Lavelli and halfback Ken Carpenter, picked up only 21 yards rushing in their 17-9 loss to the Giants. The rushing yardage total was the lowest at the time in Browns history. Lou "The Toe" Groza provided all the scoring for Cleveland with three field goals- one a 52-yarder. Cleveland's offense was held to only ten first downs by the tough Giant defense. With the win, the Giants joined the 49ers as the only other NFL team to have beaten the Browns three times. The two New York scores came when QB Charley Conerly connected with E Bob Wilkinson on a 70-yard pass play in the first quarter and DB Tom Landry returned an intercepted pass 70 yards for a TD.

(Far left) Lou "The Toe" Groza kicks his third field goal of the day, a 21-yarder, to give Cleveland a 9-7 lead.

(Left) WR Mac Speedie (83), is pushed out of bounds by Giants DB Emlen Tunnell after making the reception. One of the bright spots for Cleveland was the play of Speedie, who caught eight passes for 161 yards.

**November 9, 1952
Cleveland-28, Chicago-13**

The Chicago Cardinals, featuring rookie sensation Ollie Matson at fullback, faced the Cleveland Browns on Sunday, November 9, 1952, before 34,097 at the Stadium. Cleveland scored its first points in the second period on a four-yard run by HB Ken Carpenter. In the second half, the Browns scored on a 57-yard screen pass from QB Otto Graham to FB Marion Motley, a 57-yard pass play from Graham to end Mac Speedie, and a fourth-quarter run by HB Ken Carpenter to win, 28-13. Graham completed 18 of 24 attempts for 249 yards, throwing 11 times to E Mac Speedie for 157 yards. Matson, a former Olympic sprinter, scored the Cardinals' second TD on a 17-yard run in the second period, shortly after teammate HB Charlie Trippi sprinted in for the team's first score.

(Upper right) Cardinal FB Ollie Matson (33), scores his first points at the Stadium on a 17-yard run. Matson gained 63 yards on 10 carries.

(Right) Browns HB Ken Carpenter (20), is slowed down by a Cardinal defender before being stopped on the one-yard line by Chicago RE Tom Bienemann. Carpenter rushed for 37 yards on 13 carries and caught three passes for 27 yards. Motley gained 94 yards on 13 carries for the Browns.

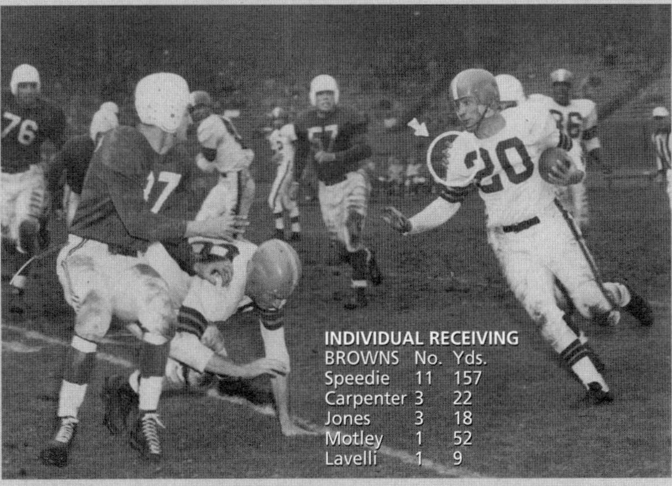

INDIVIDUAL RECEIVING		
BROWNS	No.	Yds.
Speedie	11	157
Carpenter	3	22
Jones	3	18
Motley	1	52
Lavelli	1	9

The NFL Championship

Played before 50,934, the largest turnout to watch a pro football title game at the Stadium, the Cleveland Browns battled the Detroit Lions on Sunday, December 28, 1952, for the NFL championship. It was Cleveland's third straight NFL title game appearance. "The difference between champ and chump is a flimsy margin," remarked Browns head coach Paul Brown after his team went down to defeat, 17-7. The Browns outgained head coach Buddy Parker's Lions on offense, but penalties, missed field goals and turnovers plagued the team throughout the

INDIVIDUAL RUSHING		
BROWNS	Att.	Yds.
Motley	6	74
Carpenter	3	13
Renfro	3	13
Graham	7	23
Jagade	15	104
LIONS	Att.	Yds.
Harder	8	28
Layne	9	47
Walker	10	97
Hoernschemeyer	7	27

(Above) Rookie RH Ray Renfro picks up eight yards before being tackled by Detroit defenders. Renfro finished with 13 yards rushing and 26 yards receiving. No. 78 OT John Sandusky.

game. Detroit's two TDs came on a quarterback sneak by QB Bobby Layne, who completed seven passes for 68 yards, and a 76-yard off-tackle run in the third period by HB Doak Walker, who rushed 10 times for 97 yards. Cleveland's lone score came in the third quarter on a seven-yard sweep by HB Chick Jagade, who rushed 15 times for 104 yards. The Lions received $2,274.77 per player for winning the title. Each Cleveland player received $1,172.49 in the losing effort.

November 8, 1953
Cleveland-34, Pittsburgh-16

The Eastern Division-leading Cleveland Browns (6-0), hosted the Pittsburgh Steelers (3-3), before 35,592 at the Stadium on Sunday, November 8, 1953. Played in a steady rain, the Browns led 24-16 at halftime, on a 20-yard field goal by Lou Groza, a seven-yard run by HB Ken Carpenter and two spectacular second-period TD runs by HB Ray Renfro. Renfro's first score came after Browns DB Warren Lahr intercepted a pass from Steelers QB Jim Finks and returned it to the Steelers' 44-yard line.

Renfro slashed off right tackle on the next play for the score. Renfro scored his second TD when he blocked a Steelers field goal attempt by Nick Bolkovac and returned it 79 yards untouched for the score. Cleveland added 10 points on a field goal and a 17-yard pass from QB Otto Graham to E Dante Lavelli in the fourth quarter to win 34-16. The three Pittsburgh scores came on a field goal by Bolkovac, who also kicked an extra point, a two-yard TD run by HB Ray Matthews and a 77-yard TD pass from Finks to Matthews.

(Right) Browns defenders Tom Catlin (50), and DB Ken Konz (22), chase Steelers HB Lynn Chadnois. Chadnois rushed 11 times for 73 yards and caught seven passes for 38 yards in the Steelers loss.

INDIVIDUAL RUSHING		
BROWNS	Att.	Yds.
Motley	3	39
Carpenter	4	17
Renfro	9	67
Graham	3	4
Jagade	7	53
Reynolds	3	13
Jones	2	9
STEELERS	Att.	Yds.
Chadnois	11	73
Rogel	16	48
Matthews	8	29
Brandt	3	11

Otto Graham's Lip

The Cleveland Browns (7-0), battled the San Francisco 49ers on Sunday, November 15, 1953, before 80,698, at the time, the second largest Stadium turnout to see the Browns play. With Cleveland ahead, 10-7, in the second period, Browns QB Otto Graham ran for 19 yards before being knocked out of bounds by the 49ers' Rex Berry (23). As he laid on the ground, 49ers guard Art Michalik elbowed Graham in the face, splitting open Otto's lip. Backup QB George Ratterman replaced Graham while his gashed lip was repaired. Fifteen stitches held the lip together when Graham returned to the sideline in the third period with a special face mask attached to his helmet. Upon returning to the game, Graham threw a 34-yard TD strike to WR Ray Renfro, giving Cleveland a 20-7 lead. A 31-yard pass from 49ers QB Y. A. Tittle to RB Hugh McElhenny reduced the lead to 20-14. With four minutes to go, place-kicker Lou Groza's 28-yard field goal, one of three by "The Toe," gave Cleveland a 23-14 lead. Groza's kick provided the margin of victory, when Tittle returned to score a last minute TD. The game ended with the Browns ahead 23-21. Graham completed 17 of 24 for 286 yards, despite the injury. His favorite target was WR Dante Lavelli, with six catches for 137 yards.

(Upper right) Browns QB Otto Graham is about to be knocked out of bounds by 49ers DB Rex Berry (23). **(Far right)** Graham walks along the sideline after returning to the game with his lip stitched. **(Right)** The injury.

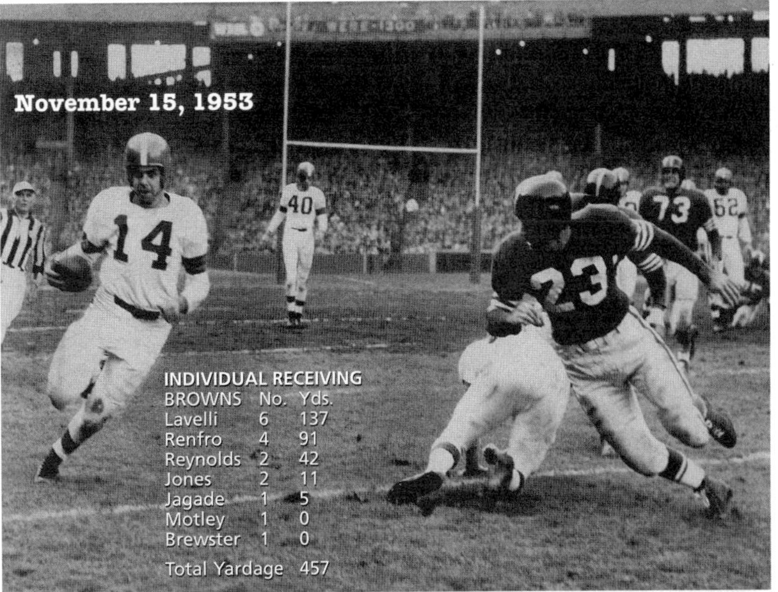

INDIVIDUAL RECEIVING

BROWNS	No.	Yds.
Lavelli	6	137
Renfro	4	91
Reynolds	2	42
Jones	2	11
Jagade	1	5
Motley	1	0
Brewster	1	0
Total Yardage		457

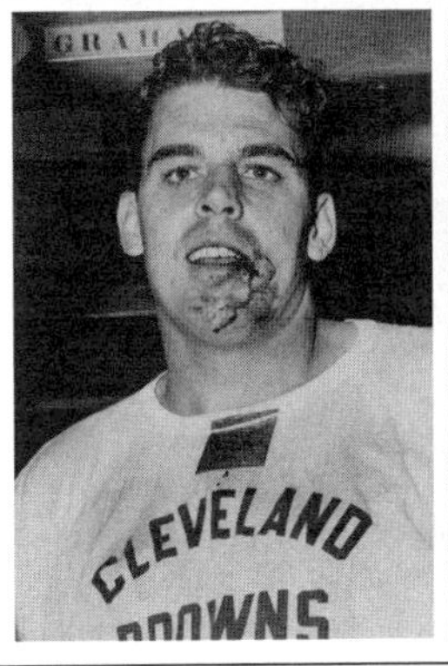

December 6, 1953 / Cleveland-62, New York-14

With the division title under wraps, the Cleveland Browns (10-0), faced the New York Giants on Sunday, December 6, 1953, before 40,235 at the Stadium. After scoring only nine TDs against the Giants in eight previous meetings, the Browns rolled to their most one-sided win since joining the National Football League in 1950, beating the Giants, 62-14. Making his debut as a starter was Browns QB George Ratterman, who completed 15 passes for 235 yards and three TDs. Ratterman played all but a brief period in the third quarter, when QB Otto Graham, who was celebrating his 32nd birthday, went 4 for 4 for 116 yards and two TDs. Cleveland TDs were scored by WR Darrell (Pete) Brewster (3), who caught seven passes for 182 yards; HB Ken Carpenter (2), HB Ray Renfro (2), and LB Walt Michaels. Lou "The Toe" Groza added eight extra points and two field goals, setting a new NFL mark with 21 field goals in a season. The two Giant scores came on QB Charley Conerly passes to HBs Cutter Long and Frank Gifford.

(Left) HB Ken Carpenter (40), scores his second TD on a two-yard plunge. At far left is Browns OG Chuck Noll (65). Behind Noll is QB Otto Graham. Carpenter's first score came on a 22-yard pass from QB George Ratterman.

INDIVIDUAL RECEIVING

BROWNS	No.	Yds.
Brewster	7	182
Gillom	3	52
Renfro	2	71
Lavelli	2	25
Jones	2	18
Motley	2	10
Carpenter	1	22
Reynolds	1	9

GIANTS	No.	Yds.
Long	5	118
Gifford	3	32
Grandelius	3	26
Anderson	2	30
Stribling	2	21
Pelfry	1	2

1954- A Championship Year

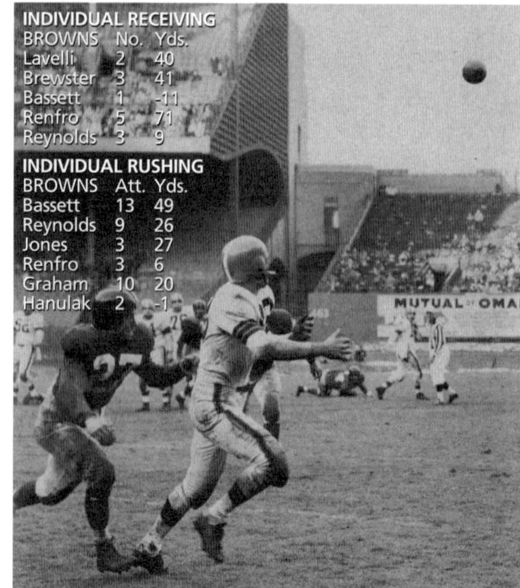

October 31, 1954 / Cleveland-24, New York-14

The Cleveland Browns (3-1), played the New York Giants (3-1), before 30,448 at the Stadium on Sunday, October 31, 1954. The second-place Giants entered the game leading the National Football League in scoring with 161 points after five games, against only 61 points scored by their opponents. The Browns defense met the challenge, holding Giants QB Charley Conerly to 5 completions on 15 attempts for 64 yards, as Cleveland beat the Giants, 24-14. Conerly was also intercepted twice by safety Kenny Konz. Browns QB Otto Graham, who completed 14 of 26 passes for 160 yards, ran the ball 10 times, twice for TDs. Graham also passed 16 yards to WR Dante "Glue Fingers" Lavelli for another score. Browns kicker Lou "The Toe" Groza cemented the win with a fourth-quarter field goal. The two New York scores came on a run by Conerly and an 83-yard pass from HB Frank Gifford to FB Eddie Price, who rushed for 65 yards and caught three passes for 99 yards. Cleveland also dominated the punting game, with Horace Gillom averaging 43 yards per punt to Giant DB Tom Landry's 33-yard per punt average. Browns FB Maurice Bassett led all rushers with 89 yards on 12 carries.

(Left) WR Darrell (Pete) Brewster prepares to catch a fourth-quarter pass from QB Otto Graham with Giant defender Herb Rich (27), in pursuit. The pass was one of three caught by Brewster for 41 yards.

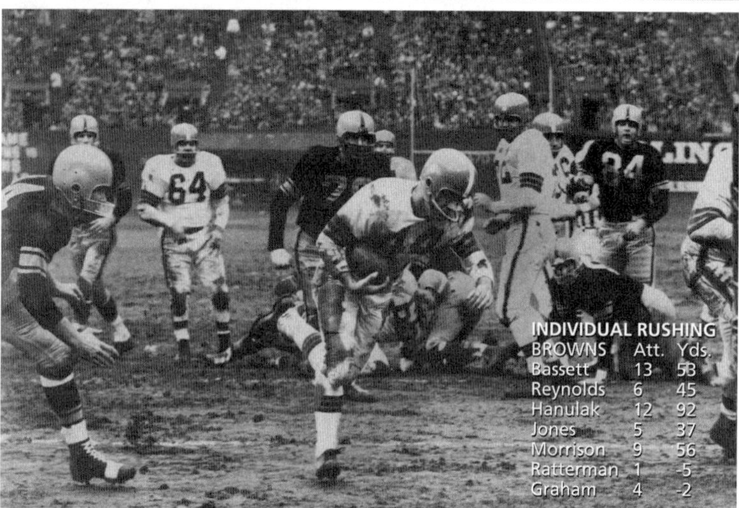

December 12, 1954
Cleveland-42, Pittsburgh-7

The first-place Cleveland Browns avenged an earlier 55-27 loss to the Pittsburgh Steelers, by beating the Steelers, 42-7, on Sunday, December 12, 1954, before 28,064 at the Stadium. Cleveland TDs were scored by rookie HB Chet Hanulak, FB Curley Morrison, HB Billy Reynolds and safety Ken Konz, who intercepted a pass from Steelers QB Jim Finks. The Browns clinched a record-setting fifth straight National Football League division title with the win. It was Cleveland's ninth straight division title dating back to 1946.

(Left) Rookie HB Chet "The Jet" Hanulak scores the first of his three TDs. Hanulak ran for 92 yards on 12 carries in his first starting assignment. No. 64 is Browns OG Abe Gibron.

December 19, 1954
Detroit-14, Cleveland-10

In a tune-up for the NFL title game the following week, on Sunday, December 19, 1954, the Cleveland Browns played the Detroit Lions before 34,168 at the Stadium. Led by QB Bobby Layne, who completed 18 of 36 for 186 yards, the Lions beat the Browns, 14-10, scoring the winning TD on an 11-yard pass from Layne to HB Earl (Jug) Girard with only 50 seconds left in the game. Cleveland's lone TD came on a one-yard run by QB Otto Graham, who completed only one of six passes. Cleveland's other points came on a 43-yard field goal by Lou "The Toe" Groza. That day, Groza became the first NFL Player of the Year picked by The Sporting News.

(Left) Detroit HB Bob Hoernschemeyer is stopped by Browns DB Tom Catlin (50). Also in the play are DT Mike McCormack (74), DT Don Colo (70), and DE Carlton Massey (82).

The NFL Championship Game

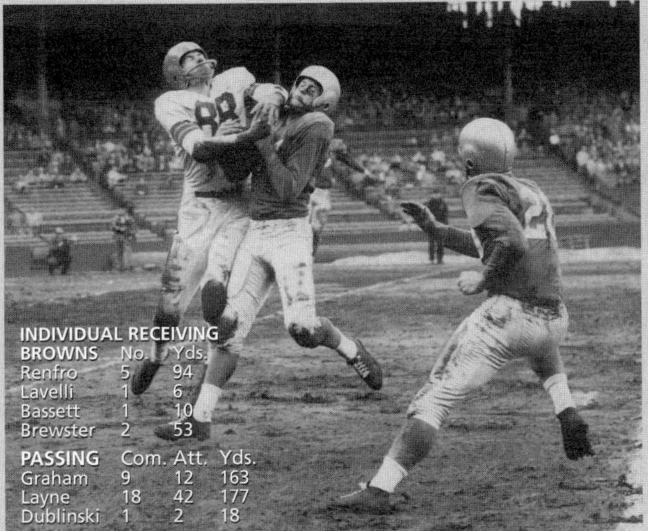

After clinching their fifth straight Western Division crown, the 9-3 Cleveland Browns faced the 9-2-1 Detroit Lions in the 1954 NFL championship game on December 26th. Played at the Stadium before 43,827, (reserved seats were $6, $5 and $4,) Cleveland demolished the Lions, 56-10, avenging a 17-16 loss to Detroit in the NFL title game a year earlier. The Browns set 13 playoff records on their way to winning their second NFL title. Three play-off records set that day belonged to 33-year-old Browns QB Otto Graham, who ran for three scores, and threw for three more to LH Ray Renfro (2), and LE Darrell Brewster. Place-kicker Lou "The Toe" Groza set another playoff record by kicking eight extra points. DE Len Ford also set a playoff record by returning an intercepted pass 45 yards. Each Browns player received a record $2,478.57 from the players' pool for the victory. Detroit players received $1,585.63.

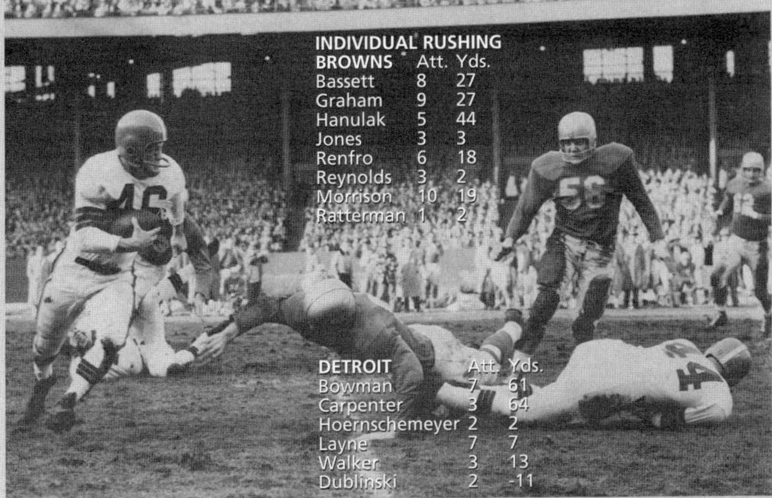

(Above left) Browns LE Darrell (Pete) Brewster fights with Lion defender Carl Karilivacz (21), for a pass from QB Otto Graham. The ball slipped through their grasp, but was grabbed by Browns LH Ray Renfro for the completion. At right is Lion defender Bill Stits (20).

(Left) Browns RH Billy Reynolds (46), returns a punt 42 yards to the 12-yard line with help from a block by LH Chet "The Jet" Hanulak (44). Otto Graham then scored the team's third TD on a one-yard sneak. Graham joined Hanulak, Brewster, FB Fred (Curley) Morrison, Renfro, who scored twice, and Groza, in accounting for Cleveland's 56 points. Renfro led Cleveland with 94 yards on five receptions, despite an ailing knee. No. 56 is LB Joe Schmidt.

(Right) FB Fred (Curley) Morrison breaks through the Lion defense for a 12-yard TD (the team's seventh,) after taking a third-quarter pitchout from QB Otto Graham. Browns OT Lou Groza is No. 76. Morrison carried 10 times for 19 yards. It was not only an emotional day for Graham, who had announced his retirement, but also one of his most memorable. The win gave Graham, who completed 9 of 12 passes for 163 yards, his first victory over the Lions in either regular season or championship play. Detroit QB Bobby Layne completed 18 of 42 attempts for 177 yards, but had six passes picked off by Browns defenders. After the game, the game ball was awarded to veteran DB Warren Lahr. (At the time, Graham had completed 1,375 of 2,417 attempts [56.9%] for 21,874 yards and 162 TDs.)

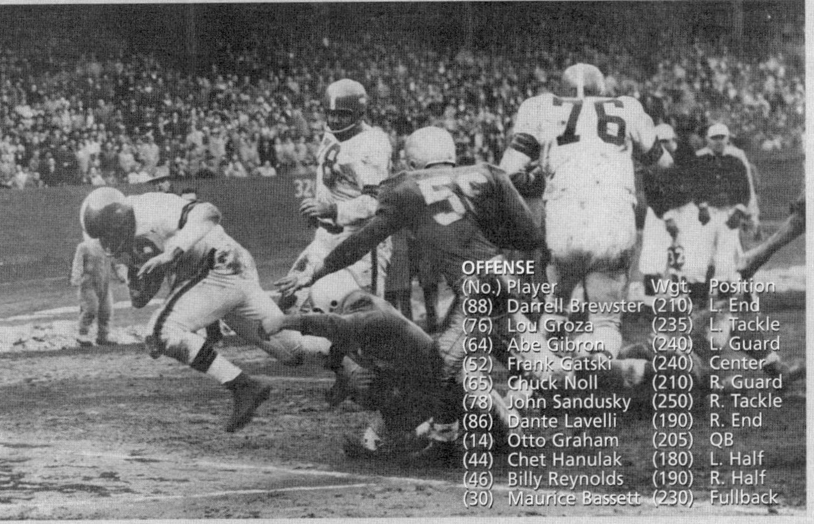

October 23, 1955
Cleveland-41, Green Bay-10

"Never in my whole career have I been rushed like that," said Packer QB Tobin Rote after losing, 41-10, to the Cleveland Browns on Sunday, October 23, 1955, before 51,482 at the Stadium. QBs Otto Graham and George Ratterman, FB Fred (Curley) Morrison, FB Maurice Bassett, RH Dub Jones, RH Pete Brewster and Lou Groza all scored in the win. The two Green Bay scores came on a 100-yard kickoff return by Al Carmichael and a 27-yard field goal by Fred Cone. The Browns won the game, but were left with only two starting linebackers, Walt Michaels and Chuck Noll, when rookie linebacker Sam Palumbo, former Collinwood High and Notre Dame star, left the game with a dislocated left shoulder. Starting center Frank Gatski set a club record by appearing in his 100th straight game.

(Right) Green Bay place-kicker Fred Cone boots a 27-yard field goal. No. 46 is HB Billy Reynolds.

INDIVIDUAL RUSHING		
BROWNS	Att.	Yds.
Graham	3	-7
Morrison	17	87
Smith	7	19
Modzelewski	9	47
Bassett	9	58

INDIVIDUAL RECEIVING		
BROWNS	No.	Yds.
Renfro	3	91
Morrison	1	49
Lavelli	1	17
Jones	1	26
Brewster	4	88

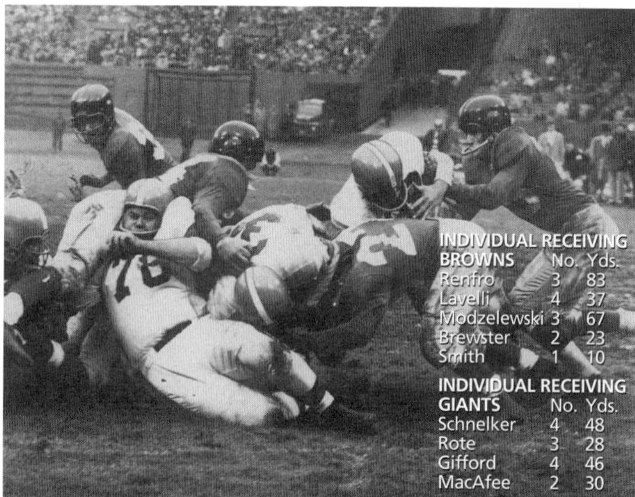

INDIVIDUAL RECEIVING		
BROWNS	No.	Yds.
Renfro	3	83
Lavelli	4	37
Modzelewski	3	67
Brewster	2	23
Smith	1	10

INDIVIDUAL RECEIVING		
GIANTS	No.	Yds.
Schnelker	4	48
Rote	3	28
Gifford	4	46
MacAfee	2	30

November 6, 1955
Cleveland-24, New York-14

After beating the Chicago Cardinals, 26-20, in Chicago the week before, the first-place Cleveland Browns faced coach Jim Lee Howell's last-place New York Giants on Sunday, November 6, 1955, before 46,524 at the Stadium. In the second period, Browns QB Otto Graham was knocked out of the game with a mild concussion. Backup QB George Ratterman rallied the Browns, down 14-3, at half-time, with TD passes to halfbacks Ray Renfro and Pete Brewster for a 24-14 come from behind victory. Ratterman, who completed 10 of 13 for 163 yards, scored the Browns' final TD. The remaining Cleveland points came on a 17-yard field goal and three extra points by Lou "The Toe" Groza. It was the sixth straight regular season win for the 6-1-0 Browns. The Giants scored both TDs in the second period on a six-yard pass from QB Charley Conerly to HB Frank Gifford and a 71-yard pass play from Gifford to HB Kyle Rote. One of the happiest Browns was head coach Paul Brown, who led his team to victory after becoming a grandfather earlier in the day.

(Above left) Browns FB Dick Modzelewski carries the ball to the Giants' four-yard line. No. 78 is Browns RT John Sandusky. On the next play, Ratterman faked to "Big Mo" and then scooted around end to score. Modzelewski ran for 36 yards on 18 carries and caught three passes for 67 yards.

(Left) Browns QB Otto Graham is helped off the field in the second quarter by T Don Colo (70), and John Sandusky (78), after catching an elbow from Giant defender Herb Rich. Graham stretched out behind the bench for a period and then headed to the locker room just before the half. He stayed there until late in the third period, when he returned to the field. Graham, who claimed he didn't know what hit him, later said that it was only the second time he had been knocked out in his football career.

November 20, 1955
Cleveland-41, Pittsburgh-14

The Cleveland Browns (6-2), led the NFL's Eastern Division by a full game over the Washington Redskins after beating coach Walt Kiesling's Pittsburgh Steelers, 41-14, on Sunday, November 20, 1955. Played before 53,509, the largest Stadium crowd of the season, Cleveland scored first when DB Ken Konz intercepted an end zone pass from Steelers QB Jim Finks and returned it 15 yards for six points. Other Cleveland TDs were scored by QB Otto Graham, FB Maurice Bassett, WR Dante Lavelli, who scored twice, once on a 42-yard pass and FB Ed Modzelewski, who scored from the three, after DT Don Colo recovered a fumble by Pittsburgh QB Ted Marchibroda at the Steelers' 14-yard line. The relentless Browns defense allowed Finks and Marchibroda to cross the fifty-yard line only once in the second half.

(Above) Backup Steelers QB Ted Marchibroda is forced to scramble by Browns DB Don Paul in the third quarter. Marchibroda gained 10 yards to put the ball at the Pittsburgh 18-yard line. Browns FB Fred (Curley) Morrison led all ball carriers with 140 yards rushing, picking up 97 yards on two carries. Cleveland beat the Steelers again on December 4th, 30-7, in Pittsburgh, to clinch their 10th straight conference crown. On Sunday, December 26, 1955, the Cleveland Browns beat the Los Angeles Rams, 38-14, before 87,695 in Los Angeles, to capture the National Football League title for a second straight year.

(Left) LB Chuck Noll (far left), LB Walt Michaels (34), and DB Ken Konz (22), chase E Elbie Nickel (81), who took a Finks' pass for a 43-yard gain. Nickel scored both Steelers TDs.

November 24, 1957
Cleveland-45
Los Angeles-31

"He was terrific, simply terrific," declared head coach Paul Brown, after 21-year old rookie FB Jim Brown set an NFL rushing record in Cleveland's 45-31 win over coach Sid Gillman's Los Angeles Rams on Sunday, November 24, 1957. Played before 65,407, the largest Stadium turnout since 1953, Brown rushed for 237 yards on 31 carries and scored four TDs-one on a 69-yard run. After starting QB Tommy O'Connell left with an injury in the second period, rookie QB Milt Plum took over,

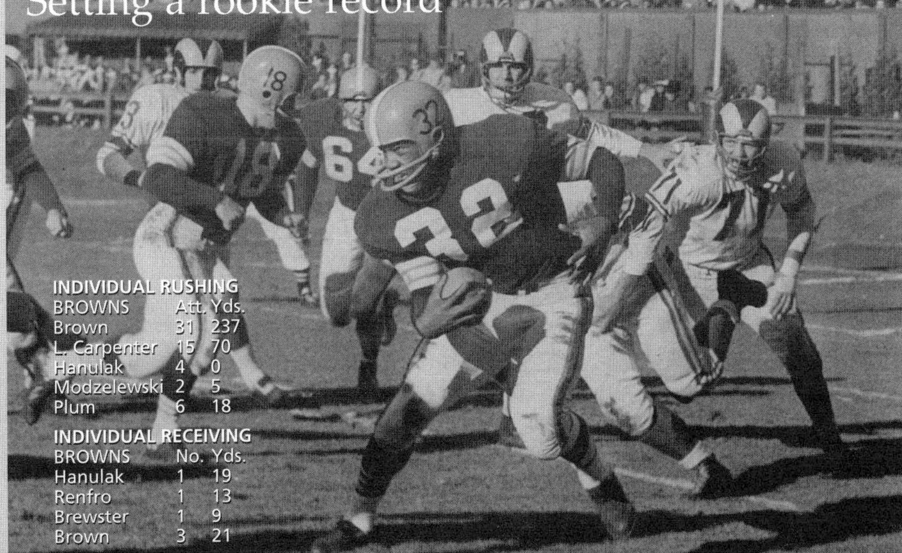

INDIVIDUAL RUSHING		
BROWNS	Att.	Yds.
Brown	31	237
L. Carpenter	15	70
Hanulak	4	0
Modzelewski	2	5
Plum	6	18

INDIVIDUAL RECEIVING		
BROWNS	No.	Yds.
Hanulak	1	19
Renfro	1	13
Brewster	1	9
Brown	3	21

leading the Browns to five TDs and a 48-yard field goal by Lou "The Toe" Groza. The Rams led, 21-17, at halftime, with QB Norm Van Brocklin passing twice to HB Elroy Hirsch for scores. The Browns trailed by 11 points in the third quarter, before scoring 28 points for the win. Cleveland's final score came on HB Lew Carpenter's second TD. After the game, Jim Brown heaped praise on his front line saying, "Give the credit to the blockers. They sure opened holes for me." Brown gained 942 yards on the ground in 1957 to lead the NFL in rushing. Plum completed 6 of 9 for 62 yards in the win.

(Above) Browns FB Jim Brown (32), returns a kickoff in the third quarter with Rams' DT Frank Fuller (71), in pursuit. Also in the play are HB Bobby Freeman (18), and OG Jim Ray Smith (64).

October 12, 1958 / The Home Opener

The Cleveland Browns (2-0), faced new coach Frank (Pop) Ivy's Chicago Cardinals on Sunday, October 12, 1958, before a record home opening crowd of 65,403 at the Stadium. The previous high was 63,263, set in 1947. Cleveland won, 35-28, with two TDs coming after interceptions by defensive backs Junior Wren and Bobby Freeman. Another score came after Wren recovered a fumble by Cards HB Ollie Matson, who led Chicago rushers with 62 yards. Starting Cardinal QB Lamar McHan was replaced in the second half by rookie QB M. C. Reynolds. Reynolds, who completed eight of 11 for 198 yards, threw three of the Cards' four TDs, one coming on a 91-yard pass play to rookie HB John David Crow.

(Left) Browns FB Jim Brown eludes DB Jim Hill (41), DE Leo Sugar (84), and DE Dick Lane (81), after getting the ball from Browns QB Milt Plum (16). Brown led all rushers with 182 yards and three TDs on 34 carries, a team record. Plum completed 7 of 15 for 122 yards. **(Below left)** Guard Gene Hickerson (66), leads the blocking for rookie HB Bobby Mitchell who made his Stadium debut a success by rushing for 147 yards on 11 carries and scoring on a spectacular 63-yard dash. No. 66 is DE Ed Husmann. **(Below)** Over 12,000 Boy Scouts watched the game from the Stadium bleachers.

INDIVIDUAL RUSHING		
BROWNS	Att.	Yds.
Brown	34	182
P. Carpenter	2	12
Mitchell	11	142
Plum	4	-22
L. Carpenter	2	1

October 19, 1958
Cleveland-27, Pittsburgh-10

After beating the Chicago Cardinals, 35-28, in the home opener the previous week, the Cleveland Browns (3-0), returned to the Stadium on Sunday, October 19, 1958, to face the last-place Pittsburgh Steelers. 66,852 turned out to see Cleveland play its second game against the Steelers in 15 days. The Browns pounded out 409 yards in total offense, while the Steelers managed only 259 yards in total offense, 87 yards coming on the ground. Leading Cleveland to a 27-10 win was FB Jim Brown, who gained 153 yards on 19 carries and connected with QB Milt Plum on a 52-yard pass play for six points. Plum, who completed eight passes for 138 yards, passed for TDs to RH Ray Renfro and rookie HB Bobby Mitchell, who rushed thirteen times for 108 yards. The Steelers scored their only TD on a halfback pass from Tom Tracy to Ray Matthews, who raced 64 yards for the score. After two Cleveland touchdowns, the extra points were kicked by Plum, not starting kicker Lou Groza, who spent half the game on the bench with an ice pack after being knocked out in the second quarter. DT Bob Gain kicked off in Groza's absence. During the game, Cleveland lost the services of starting OT Mike McCormack who suffered torn cartilage in his right knee.

(Left) QB Bobby Layne, making his first appearance at the Stadium in a Steelers uniform, drops back to pass as Browns defenders DT Bob Gain (79), and DE Bill Quinlan (84), close in. Layne completed 14 out of 26 pass attempts for 133 yards, but none for TDs as the Cleveland defensive front line of Gain, Quinlan, DE Paul Wiggin and RT Don Colo kept constant pressure on the veteran passer. Six Layne passes went to FB Tank Younger for 39 yards.

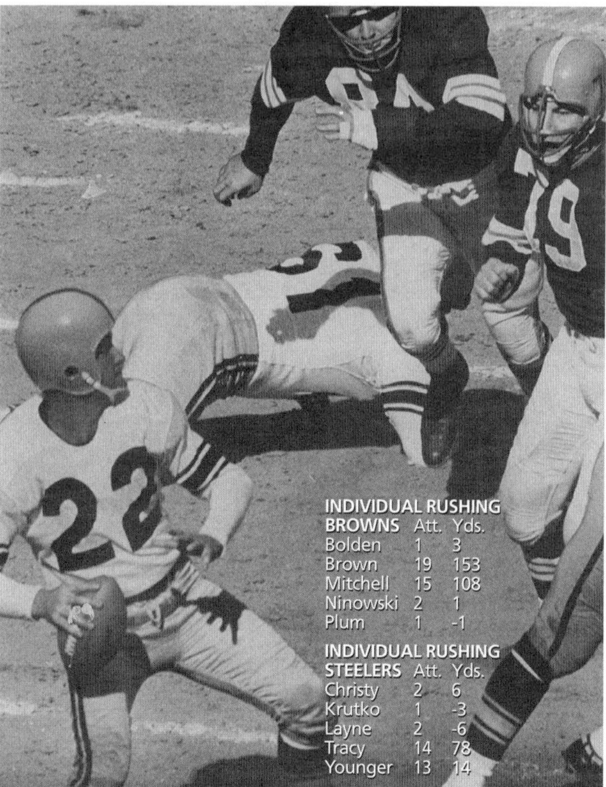

INDIVIDUAL RUSHING		
BROWNS	Att.	Yds.
Bolden	1	3
Brown	19	153
Mitchell	15	108
Ninowski	2	1
Plum	1	-1

INDIVIDUAL RUSHING		
STEELERS	Att.	Yds.
Christy	2	6
Krutko	1	-3
Layne	2	-6
Tracy	14	78
Younger	13	14

November 23, 1958 / Cleveland-28, Philadelphia-14

The Eastern Conference-leading Cleveland Browns (6-2), battled the Philadelphia Eagles (2-5-1), on November 23, 1958, before 51,319 at the Stadium. The Browns led, 7-0, before many fans reached their seats, when Bobby Mitchell, who was starting at halfback for the first time in several weeks, returned the opening kickoff 98 yards for a TD behind a wedge formed by Lew Carpenter, Jim Ray Smith, Chuck Noll and Ed Modzelewski. Mitchell scored again minutes later, returning a punt by the Eagles' Norm Van Brocklin 68 yards for six points. In the second period, Browns HB Lew Carpenter scored on a one-yard plunge to give the Browns a 21-7 halftime lead. In the final period, WR Ray Renfro scored on a 34-yard pass from QB Milt Plum, who completed 8 of 10 for 143 yards, to give Cleveland a 28-14 victory. Van Brocklin completed 18 of 29 for 210 yards at quarterback. Mitchell's kickoff return was the second longest in team history.

(Right) QB Milt Plum (16), runs around end on a power sweep. The play was used twice for gains of 15 and 12 yards. In the play are Marion Campbell (78), OG Vince Costello (50), DT Don Owens (70), OG Jim Ray Smith (64), Plum (16), HB Bobby Mitchell (in the air), E Pete Brewster (88, on ground), and DHB Tom Brookshier (right).

INDIVIDUAL RUSHING		
BROWNS	Att.	Yds.
Brown	23	123
Mitchell	26	45
Plum	1	1

October 18, 1959 / Groza's New Record

The Cleveland Browns' first TD in their 17-7 win over the Chicago Cardinals on Sunday, October 18, 1959, came on a seven-yard pass from QB Milt Plum (12-22, 126 yards), to HB Bobby Mitchell. Lou "The Toe" Groza kicked the PAT for his 317th National Football League extra point, erasing the NFL record set by Bob Waterfield from 1945 to 1952. Groza also kicked a 19-yard field goal. Played at the Stadium before 46,422, the win put Cleveland in a four-way tie for second place with a 2-2 record. Chicago's John David Crow, playing fullback, gained 71 yards on 18 carries.

(Left) Browns FB Jim Brown (32), starts around left end for a short gain in the fourth quarter as the Cardinals' Dick Lane (in foreground), fights off end Billy Howton's attempted block. Brown led all rushers with 123 yards on 23 carries.

November 8, 1959 / The Eagles

The Cleveland Browns, tied for second place behind the New York Giants with the Philadelphia Eagles, played the QB Norm Van Brocklin-led Eagles on Sunday, November 8, 1959, before 58,275 at the Stadium. Led by HB Bobby Mitchell and FB Jim Brown, who ran 29 times for 125 yards, Cleveland rolled to a 21-0 halftime lead. The Browns scored again in the final minutes to win, 28-7, when Mitchell sprinted 65 yards for the team's final score. QB Milt Plum threw for 146 yards, but was outgunned by the Eagle's Van Brocklin, who completed 23 of 40 passes for 260 yards in the loss.

(Right) Browns HB Bobby Mitchell breaks lose on his 65-yard TD run after getting the ball from Plum, who faked first to FB Jim Brown. In the play are Browns center Art Hunter (56), OT Willie Davis (behind Mitchell), and OG Gene Hickerson (far right), who blocked Eagle DB Tom Brookshier to spring Mitchell.

Notre Dame vs. Navy

On Monday, January 26, 1931, legendary Notre Dame football coach Knute Rockne was in Cleveland to address a Chamber of Commerce luncheon at Hotel Cleveland. Before he spoke, Rockne was interviewed by Cleveland Press reporter Omar Ranney. During the interview, Rockne said he thought Cleveland would have a hard time attracting colleges to play at its new stadium under construction. "Why, for instance, should Notre Dame leave its wonderful stadium in South Bend (opened in 1930), to come here for a game," he asked Ranney. "The only time I could see us doing that is when we play a team like Navy, whose home grounds are the United States." After the conclusion of the 1931 football season, The Cleveland Press reported on Friday, December 4, 1931, that Stadium Commissioner George H. Bender had secured a game between the Fighting Irish and the Midshipmen of Navy for the Stadium in 1932. The next week, Bender traveled to South Bend, Indiana, where he met with Notre Dame Athletic Director Jess C. Harper to finalize the details. On Saturday, November 19, 1932, 61,122 (over 70,000 with free admissions,) turned out for the debut of big time football at the Stadium. Coach Heartley "Hunk" Anderson's Notre Dame squad beat Navy, 12-0, on two second quarter scores by HB Joe Sheeketski. The gate receipts totaled over $150,000, with 10% of the gross returned to the city treasury. Rockne, who played a role in bringing the game to Cleveland, never got the chance to see his Fighting Irish play at the Stadium. Rockne died tragically in a plane crash on Tuesday, March 31, 1931, barely two months after his Cleveland speaking engagement.

November 19, 1932
Irish-12, Navy-0

(Top left) Notre Dame head coach Hunk Anderson is greeted by Mayor Ray T. Miller after arriving here with the team for the 1932 Notre Dame-Navy Game.

(Above left) The 82-piece Notre Dame Marching Band marches from Union Depot after arriving in Cleveland for the big game. Joining the band on "migration day," were over 1,000 Notre Dame students and boosters who came in for the game from South Bend, Indiana.

(Left) Some of the over 70,000 fans attending the first major football contest held at the Stadium on November 19, 1932. Led by HB Mike Koken, who rushed 15 times for 62 yards, Notre Dame gained 272 yards on the ground. The Fighting Irish completed only two of seven passes attempted.

October 21, 1939 / Irish-14, Navy-7

(Far right) Local attorney Don Miller (right), joins Notre Dame head coach Elmer Layden before the 1939 game. Miller and Layden were teammates as two of Notre Dame's famous "Four Horsemen." Layden starred at fullback and Miller at right halfback in coach Knute Rockne's talented 1924 backfield. Over 81,000 (including free admissions,) attended the 1939 Notre Dame-Navy game, making it, at the time, the largest crowd to watch a football game at the Stadium. Led by the rushing four-some of Benjamin Sheridan, Lou Zontini, who led his team with 127

yards on 16 carries, Milt Piepul and Bob Saggau, the Fighting Irish beat Navy, 14-7. Sheridan and Piepul rushed for the two Notre Dame TDs. The Fighting Irish outgained Navy in total yardage, 419 to 155, racking up 22 first downs to six by Navy, with all yardage gained on the ground. Notre Dame failed to complete any of the seven pass-es attempted. Navy's score came when QB Bob Leonard connect-ed with RH Ulmont Whitehead on a 64-yard pass play.

(Right) Mrs. Knute Rockne was one of the spectators at the 1939 Notre Dame-Navy game. Her husband was responsible for organizing the Notre Dame-Navy series in 1927.

November 1, 1952 / Irish-17, Navy-6

(Right) During their halftime presentation, the Notre Dame Marching Band formed the word "Navy" in tribute to the 25th anniversary meeting of the two teams and spelled out "Ike" and "Adlai" as part of a "Get Out The Vote," plea. Navy was represented by the Lakewood High School band.

(Below right) Notre Dame FB Neil Worden scores the second of his two TDs on a two-yard run. 61,928, 10,000 less than expected, watched coach Frank Leahy's Fighting Irish battle Navy in their ninth Stadium meeting. Led by Ralph Guglielmi at quarterback, Notre Dame beat Navy, 17-6, on a safety, Worden's two TDs and a field goal by Bob Arrix. Navy's only score came on a fourth-quarter pass from QB Steve Schoderbek to LE Jim Byron.

NOTRE DAME-NAVY FOOTBALL
at Municipal Stadium

STADIUM RECORD
Notre Dame- 9-1-1 / Navy 1-9-1

NOTRE DAME HEAD COACHES
Heartley "Hunk" Anderson ('32); Elmer Layden ('34, '39); Frank Leahy ('42, '43, '45, '47, '50, '52); Dan Devine ('76, '78)

Date:	ND	Navy	Attend
Nov. 19, 1932	Irish-12	Navy-0	61,122
Nov. 10, 1934	Irish-6	Navy-10	54,571
Oct. 21, 1939	Irish-14	Navy-7	78,257
Oct. 3, 1942	Irish-9	Navy-0	66,699
Oct. 30, 1943	Irish-33	Navy-6	77,900
Nov. 3, 1945	Irish-6	Navy-6	82,020
Nov. 1, 1947	Irish-27	Navy-0	84,070
Nov. 4, 1950	Irish-19	Navy-10	71,074
Nov. 1, 1952	Irish-17	Navy-6	61,927
Oct. 30, 1976	Irish-27	Navy-21	61,172
Nov. 4, 1978	Irish-27	Navy-7	63,780

Baseball at the Stadium

April 17, 1960 / "The Trade"

On Sunday, April 17, 1960, Cleveland Indians general manager "Trader" Frank Lane made the trade he will forever be remembered for. Only 48 hours before the Indians opened the regular season, Lane finalized the deal that sent 26-year-old Tribe outfielder Rocco Domenico (Rocky) Colavito to the Detroit Tigers for 29-year-old outfielder Harvey Kuenn, the American League's batting leader in 1959. Colavito, arguably one of the most popular players to put on a Cleveland uniform, batted only .257 to Kuenn's .353 in 1959, but hit 42 home runs with 111 runs-batted-in and 141 hits. Kuenn hit nine homers with 71 runs-batted-in and 191 hits. The next day, Lane traded popular southpaw Herb Score (and close friend of Colavito,) to the Chicago White Sox for 23-year-old hurler Barry Latman.

(Left) Rocky Colavito (right), with Indians GM Frank Lane during contract talks in February of 1960. Colavito learned of the trade during the Tribe's 2-1 exhibition win over the Chicago White Sox in Memphis Tennessee. After getting the news, he told reporters, "I hate to leave Cleveland because the fans have been so good to me."

(Left) Rocky Colavito (left), and Harvey Kuenn sported their new uniforms on Tuesday, April 19, 1960, as the Indians opened the season against the Detroit Tigers before 52,756 at the Stadium. The Tigers won, 4-2, in a 15-inning contest. The four-hour, 54-minute marathon was the longest opening-day game played in major league history at the time. Center fielder Al Kaline hit a bases-loaded, two-run single off reliever Bob Tiefenauer for the win. Colavito struck out four times, hit into a double play and flied out in six at bats. Rocky also misplayed two balls in right field. Kuenn got a double and single in seven at bats, but pulled a leg muscle during the game and was replaced the next day in center field by Jimmy Piersall. Reliever Pete Burnside got the win for Detroit. Jim (Mudcat) Grant, the third of five Indian pitchers, took the loss. The trades by GM Frank Lane came so quickly that printers couldn't change the scorecard in time for the home opener.

The Fans React

One newspaper reported that local fan reaction was 9 to 1 against the Kuenn for Colavito trade. Below are some of the angry fans protesting the trade outside the Stadium. Lower left is one of the banners inside the Stadium on Opening Day.

THE OPENING DAY LINEUPS

CLEVELAND INDIANS

Johnny Temple 2b
Harvey Kuenn cf
Walt Bond rf
Tito Francona lf
Russ Nixon c
George Strickland ss
Vic Power 1b
Bubba Phillips 3b
Gary Bell p

DETROIT TIGERS

Eddie Yost 3b
Frank Bolling 2b
Red Wilson c
Charlie Maxwell lf
Al Kaline cf
Rocky Colavito rf
Steve Bilko 1b
Chico Fernandez ss
Frank Lary p

April 20, 1960
The Rock Homers

The Cleveland Indians faced the Detroit Tigers in the second game of their two-game, season-opening series on Wednesday, April 20, 1960, before 4,836 at the Stadium. Pinch-hitter Norm Cash, a former Indian, homered in the eighth inning to tie the score at 4-4, and set the stage for center fielder Al Kaline, who homered in the ninth inning to break the deadlock. The Tigers won, 6-4, handing Cleveland its second straight defeat.

(Right) In the fourth inning, Detroit's Rocky Colavito hit his first homer as a Tiger, a three-run, upper-deck blast off Tribe starter Jim Perry that tied the score at 3-3. With Colavito are second baseman Casey Wise (left), and Al Kaline. After hitting 42 homers for the Indians in 1959, Colavito hit 35 home runs for the Tigers in 1960.

May 22, 1960
Baltimore-7
Cleveland-6

With second place at stake, the third-place Cleveland Indians faced the second-place Baltimore Orioles, only a half game ahead, on Sunday, May 22, 1960, before 12,268 at the Stadium. Tribe starter Gary Bell got hammered for four runs in the first inning, as the Orioles won the rain-shortened contest, 7-6. One of the few bright spots for the Indians was first baseman Vic Power's third-inning grand slam, which scored center fielder Jimmy Piersall, at right, who jumped for joy as he reached home plate. Rounding third is Tribe second baseman Ken Aspromonte. Shortstop Woodie Held also homered for the Indians. Jackie Brandt hit two-run homer for the Orioles.

April 13, 1962 /

The Home Opener
Washington-5, Cleveland-2

After splitting their first two games to open the season, the Cleveland Indians played their home opener against the Washington Senators on Friday, April 13, 1962, before 17,543 at the Stadium. Barry Latman went to the mound for Cleveland against Senator starter Pete Burnside, who pitched a four-hitter for the win. The Senators took a two-run lead in the first inning, scored again in the third inning, and then scored twice more in the fifth inning on right fielder Gene Woodling's two-run homer off reliever Bob Allen. The Indians managed to score twice, but lost the rain-shortened contest, 5-2.

(Right) Ex-Indian Gene Woodling, who went 2 for 2, is congratulated by his teammates after hitting a two-run homer in the fifth inning. Second from left is center fielder Jimmy Piersall, another ex-Indian. Coming up to bat is first baseman Dale Long (25).

July 24, 1963 / Gabe Paul & Branch Rickey

It was "Sandusky, Ohio Night" at the Stadium on Wednesday, July 24, 1963, as the sixth-place Cleveland Indians played the Minnesota Twins in a twi-night doubleheader. One of the guests of honor that night was reigning Miss America Jackie Mayer, a Sandusky native, who was introduced at home plate before the game and appeared between games with 22 Miss Ohio hopefuls. Another guest among the 11,347 in the stands was 81-year-old Branch Rickey (right, at left), who was working as a special consultant for the St. Louis Cardinals. Rickey was the guest of Tribe President Gabe Paul (left). Twins left-handers Dick Stigman and Jim Kaat shut out the Indians, 9-0, 5-0, striking out 19 Tribe batters. In the nightcap, Kaat and Tribe starter Dick Donovan had a scoreless game going until two outs in the ninth, when Minnesota outfielder Jimmy Hall homered to break the tie. Other Twins homers were hit by third baseman Rich Rollins, first baseman Don Mincher (2), and infielder Johnny Goryl, who knocked in four runs.

May 11, 1964 / Cleveland-11, Boston-7

With third place at stake, manager George Strickland's Cleveland Indians hosted the Boston Red Sox before 3,405 at the Stadium in a night game on Monday, May 11, 1964. On the mound for Cleveland was rookie southpaw Tommy John, who was looking for his second win of the season. The Indians scored first in the second inning, on a two-run, bases-loaded single by third baseman Max Alvis, who went 3 for 3. In the fifth inning, first baseman Fred Whitfield hit a grand slam over the center field fence to put the Indians ahead, 6-1. Cleveland scored again in the eighth inning, when shortstop Dick Howser's squeeze bunt scored center fielder Woodie Held and second baseman Larry Brown hit a three-run homer. In the ninth inning, with Cleveland ahead, 11-1, the Red Sox scored six runs off relievers Gary Bell and Ted Abernathy, closing the score to 11-7, before the last out. John compiled a 2-9 record in 25 games. In 1965, John won 14 games for the Chicago White Sox.

(Left) Tribe infielder Fred Whitfield (15), at left with teammate Larry Brown (16), displays the number of runs driven in by their two home runs.

June 1, 1964 / Cleveland-3, Chicago-0

The Cleveland Indians started right-hander Jack Kralick against the league-leading Chicago White Sox on Monday, June 1, 1964. Kralick celebrated his 28th birthday by pitching a complete-game, four-hitter to beat the White Sox, 3-0. Cleveland scored its first run in the fourth inning, when left fielder Leon "Daddy" Wagner hit his 11th homer of the year off Chicago starter Juan Pizarro. Cleveland's final two runs came on a bases loaded single by second baseman Larry Brown. Among the 5,005 at the Stadium was Hall of Fame pitcher Lefty Grove, who won the first major league game played at the Stadium in 1932.

(Left) Kralick (31), is joined after the game by right fielder Tito Francona (left), outfielder Al Smith, Leon Wagner, who got his 40th RBI, pitcher Dick Donovan, catcher John Romano (at right) and first baseman Bob Chance. Kralick raised his record to 5-1 with the win.

August 23, 1964 / John Romano Day

Over 10,000 Little Leaguers were among the 24,200 at the Stadium on August 23, 1964, as the 58-66 Cleveland Indians played a Sunday doubleheader with the 63-64 Los Angeles Angels on "John Romano Day." Cleveland won the first game, 6-4, on a six-hit, complete-game by 23-year-old rookie Luis Tiant. Rookie first baseman Bob Chance led the Tribe's 11-hit attack in the opener, with two doubles and a single. Cleveland also won the second game, 3-2, with starter Jack Kralick getting the win. Romano aided Kralick's effort with a game-winning two-run single in the third inning.

(Right) Between games, Tribe catcher John Romano (right), was honored by the Indians on his 30th birthday. Among the gifts he received was the oil painting at right, gift certificates from downtown stores, a radio and $250 Kennedy Bonds for his two sons. Romano was joined by his parents who came in from Hoboken, N. J.

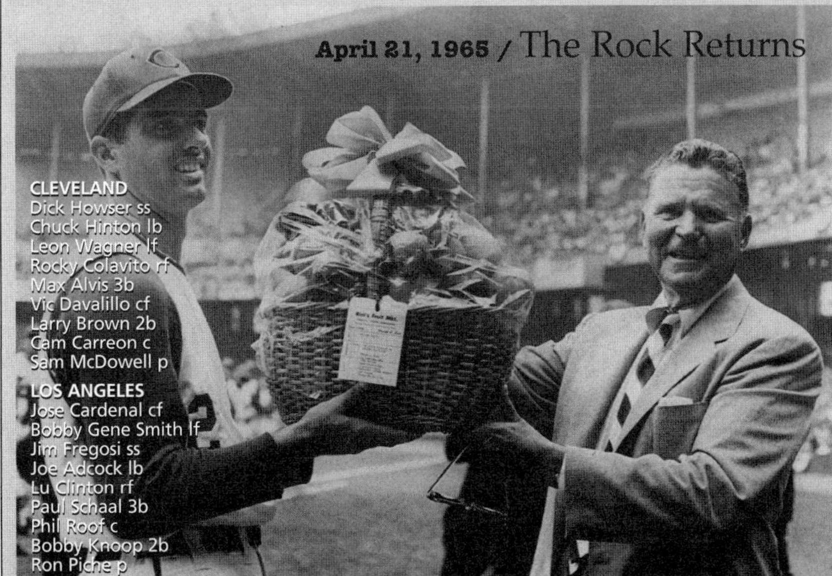

Played before 44,325, the largest home opening crowd in the majors that season, manager Birdie Tebbetts' Cleveland Indians faced the Los Angeles Angels at the Stadium on Wednesday, April 21, 1965. Part of the attraction that day was the return of popular 31-year-old right fielder Rocky Colavito to the Indians lineup. In 1960, former Tribe general manager Frank Lane traded Colavito to the Detroit Tigers for Harvey Kuenn. Southpaw Sam McDowell started for the Indians, striking out 10 in 8 2/3 innings. In the ninth inning, catcher Joe Azcue singled home center fielder Vic Davalillo to tie the game at 5-5. Cleveland won, 6-5, in the 10th inning, when left fielder Leon Wagner, the Tribe's lead-off batter, hit his second homer of the day. Colavito also homered, hitting a two-run, 400-foot blast in the sixth-inning that drew a dramatic standing ovation from the fans. Reliever Sonny Siebert got credit for the win.

(Above) Before the game, Cleveland fans gave a fruit basket to former Indians GM Frank Lane, then an executive with the Baltimore Orioles, who had allegedly called the Tribe's Rocky Colavito (left), "a handsome fruit peddler." Lane (right), passed the fruit along to Colavito as a Press photographer captured the scene. Colavito was traded to the Indians by the Chicago White Sox on January 20, 1965.

June 2, 1967
Boston-2, Cleveland-1

Tribe hurler Sonny Siebert threw a five-hitter against the Boston Red Sox in the Friday night contest on June 2, 1967, but lost the game to Boston right-hander Jim Longborg, 2-1, before 8,809 at the Stadium. Longborg, who won 22 games in 1967, had a no-hitter going until the 8th inning, when Tribe catcher Duke Sims hit a ground rule double. Sims went on to score the Tribe's only run. Longborg finished with a three-hitter. Siebert pitched a solid game except for one pitch. In the sixth inning, Siebert gave up a two-run homer to Red Sox left fielder Carl Yastrzemski.

(Right) Tribe catcher Duke Sims looks on as Boston's Carl Yastrzemski heads to the dugout after hitting his 11th homer of the year. Yastrzemski won baseball's triple crown for the American League-champion Red Sox in 1967, with 44 home runs, 121 runs-batted-in and a .326 batting average.

August 25, 1967
Dean Chance's No-Hitter

In the second game of a double-header between the Minnesota Twins and the Cleveland Indians on Friday, August 25, 1967, Wooster, Ohio's Wilmer Dean Chance pitched his way into baseball's Hall of Fame with a no-hitter for the first-place Twins. A crowd of 10,519 watched the Twins win the first game, 6-5, in 10 innings and the nightcap, 2-1. Cleveland right-hander Sonny Siebert, who pitched a no-hitter at the Stadium in 1966, took the loss in the second game. The Indian's only run off Chance came in the first inning on two walks, an error and a wild pitch. In the fifth inning, Tribe manager Joe Adcock had plate umpire Larry Napp check Chance's hands and glove for "a sticky substance." In the ninth inning, rookie second baseman Rod Carew helped secure the win for Chance by fielding grounders for two of the outs. Chance raised his record to 17-9 with the win.

(Left) Infielders Zoio Versailles (2), and Cesar Tovar congratulate Chance after his no-hitter. Behind Chance is first baseman Harmon Killebrew.

May 19, 1968 / Cleveland-2, Baltimore-0

The second-place Cleveland Indians hosted the Baltimore Orioles in a Sunday doubleheader before 15,363 at the Stadium on May 19, 1968. Cleveland won the first game, 11-5, as right-hander Steve Hargan got the win with help from Tribe catcher Duke Sims, who hit his sixth home run of the year, a three-run blast in the first inning, and right fielder Lee Maye, who went 3 for 3 with a double. In the second game, Indians right-hander Sonny Siebert took the mound for Cleveland against Baltimore left-hander Dave McNally. Siebert, who had already pitched an Opening Day two-hitter, a three-hitter against the Orioles on May 10th and a seven-inning one-hitter against the Minnesota Twins on May 5th, beat the Orioles 2-0, raising his record to 5-2, on a one-hit masterpiece. Siebert struck out six and walked only three Orioles. Baltimore's lone hit came off the bat of right fielder Curt Blefary, who rapped an opposite-field double. Left fielder Tommy Harper accounted for Cleveland's first run with a fourth-inning homer. The Indians scored their final run in the eighth inning, when first baseman Tony Horton doubled in second baseman Chico Salmon. Siebert's shutout was the 11th already recorded that season by Cleveland's five-man starting rotation of Sam McDowell, Luis Tiant, Stan Williams, Siebert and Hargan. The two wins moved Cleveland within two games of the first-place Detroit Tigers. Siebert finished the 1968 season with a 12-10 record and 146 strikeouts. The Indians finished in third place, sixteen and a half games behind the World Champion Detroit Tigers.

(Right) Indians right-hander Sonny Siebert (42), on the mound during the middle innings of his one-hitter.

CLEVELAND
Jose Cardenal cf
Chico Salmon 2b
Max Alvis 3b
Tony Horton 1b
Joe Azcue c
Tommy Harper lf
Vic Davalillo rf
Larry Brown ss
Sonny Siebert p

BALTIMORE
Dave May cf
Dave Johnson 2b
Frank Robinson lf
Boog Powell 1b
Brooks Robinson 3b
Curt Blefary rf
Andy Etchebarren c
Mark Belanger ss
Dave McNally p

Time of Game: 2:12

CLEVELAND
Max Alvis 3b
Larry Brown ss
Lou Johnson lf
Joe Azcue c
Jose Cardenal cf
Duke Sims 1b
Tommy Harper rf
Vern Fuller 2b
Luis Tiant p

Manager: Alvin Dark

MINNESOTA
Caesar Tovar 3b
Jim Holt lf
Ted Uhlaender cf
Tony Oliva rf
Rich Reese 1b
Frank Quilici 2b
Johnny Roseboro c
Jackie Hernandez ss
Jim Merritt p

Manager: Cal Ermer
Time of Game: 2:15

July 3, 1968 / Cleveland-1, Minnesota-0

The Cleveland Indians were fighting to stay in second place on Wednesday, July 3, 1968, when they hosted the Minnesota Twins before 21,135 at the Stadium. On the mound for Cleveland was 27-year-old Luis Tiant (at left). Pitching against Tiant for the Twins was right-hander Jim Merritt, who held the Indians scoreless until the tenth inning, when a single by catcher Joe Azcue drove home left fielder Lou Johnson for a 1-0 Tribe victory. It was one of only four hits Merritt surrendered. Of the 135 pitches Tiant threw during the ten-inning contest, 101 were strikes, as the Tribe ace fanned 19 of the 33 Twins he faced. Tiant struck out sixteen Twins in the first nine innings, two short of the American League night game record. His 19 strikeouts fell two short of the American League extra-inning mark set over 16 innings. In the 10th, one of the Twins Tiant fanned was former local sandlot star Rich Rollins, who entered the game as a pinch-hitter. The win raised Tiant's record to 13-5 before the All-Star break and dropped his league-leading earned-run-average to 1.11. It was his seventh straight shutout and eighth shutout in his last nine starts. Tiant ended the year with a 21-9 record, 264 strikeouts, 19 complete games and a league-leading 1.68 earned-run-average.

Pelé Comes to the Stadium

Led by Pelé, the 27-year-old soccer superstar called by most at the time, the greatest soccer star alive, the World Cup-champion Santos of Brazil faced the Cleveland Stokers of the North American Soccer League in an exhibition contest at the Stadium on Wednesday, July 10, 1968. The game was played before an announced crowd of 16,205, the largest turnout at the time to see a professional soccer game at the Stadium. Playing brilliant defense throughout the match, manager Norman Low's Cleveland squad stunned the soccer world by defeating the veteran Brazilian team, 2-1. It was the first loss handed Santos in eight games on its American tour. As the match entered the final minutes of the second half, an offsides call nullified a game-tying goal by Santos forward Toninho. Santos team members were so enraged by the call, that while some Santos players stormed the referee in protest, others began challenging fans in stands, throwing sand and verbal barbs at the spectators as time expired. Even Pelé was so disgusted by the call, that he reportedly spit on fans in the lower seats. After winning the Lakes Division of the NASL in 1968, the Stokers lost in overtime to the host Atlanta Chiefs in the Eastern Conference championships.

(Above) Pelé displays his ball handling skills against Stokers fullback John Best from Britain. The Brazilian superman took ten shots on goal, but failed to connect on any of the attempts. The Stokers scored first at 26:30 of the first half, when Enrique Mateos, the 31-year-old Spaniard who played inside left for the Stokers, drove a penalty kick past Santos goalie Laercio into the upper left corner of the net. Santos scored with 5:55 gone in the second half, when Pelé made a perfect pass to teammate Colavido, who flipped the ball to Toninho. Toninho controlled the pass with his chest and then slid the ball past Stoker goalie Paul Shardlow.

(Right) During a pre-game news conference at the Pick Carter Hotel, Pelé (right), said through his interpreter, "In one or two years, it (soccer) should be a very big success here." Pelé was impressed by Cleveland enough to say, "This is my first time to Cleveland, but I want to come back as a tourist." Tickets for the exhibition match were set at $5.00- upper boxes; $4.00- upper reserved; $3.00- lower deck seating and $1.00- bleacher seats.

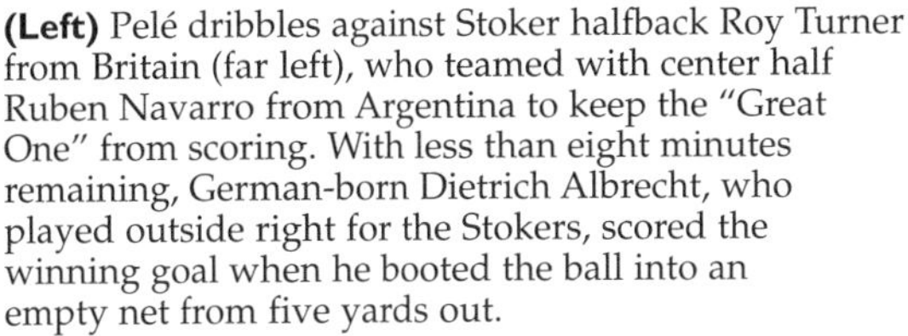

(Left) Pelé dribbles against Stoker halfback Roy Turner from Britain (far left), who teamed with center half Ruben Navarro from Argentina to keep the "Great One" from scoring. With less than eight minutes remaining, German-born Dietrich Albrecht, who played outside right for the Stokers, scored the winning goal when he booted the ball into an empty net from five yards out.

(Above) Ruben Navarro of the Stokers (in striped shirt above), steps between members of the Santos team and game fans after the disputed offside call caused tempers to flare between the Stadium crowd and the Brazilian team. One Santos player, who had climbed onto the third base tarp, had to be restrained from going after a heckler in the stands.

(Left) Pelé gestures his displeasure at the offside call that wiped out the game-tying score by Toninho. The superstar later said in his native Portuguese, "Cleveland's the best team we've played in the U. S., but the officials spoiled the game." Linesman Jack Connor, who made the offside call, said he had never seen a more perfect offside. "It was at least a yard," he declared, "The flag went up immediately." When asked what the Santos players said after the call, Connor, who got kicked by a Santos player after his decision, replied, "All I could understand was that they kept saying, 'a goal, a goal, a goal.' "So I said, 'No goal. No goal.' Then they said some things in Portuguese which I think I'm glad I couldn't understand."

The 1960's
Football at the Stadium

October 2, 1960
The Home Opener

The Cleveland Browns hosted their division rivals, the Pittsburgh Steelers, on Sunday, October 2, 1960, before a record home opening crowd of 67,692 at the Stadium. The Browns won, 28-20, as QB Milt Plum (16), threw for 308 yards, primarily to receivers Gern Nagler and Rich Kreitling. Cleveland scored three times to lead, 21-0, at halftime. Cleveland's final score came in the fourth quarter when FB Jim Brown, who led all rushers with 87 yards, scored from the one-yard line. Steelers QB Bobby Layne completed 14 of 21 for 296 yards in the loss.

(Right) Browns QB Milt Plum (16), hands off to HB Bobby Mitchell (49), as OG Jim Ray Smith (64), and C Art Hunter (56), lead the blocking. Mitchell ran for 52 yards, caught three passes for 72 yards and scored Cleveland's second TD. No. 32 at left is FB Jim Brown. Plum scored Cleveland's first TD on a one-yard plunge and connected with WR Rich Kreitling on a 69-yard TD pass.

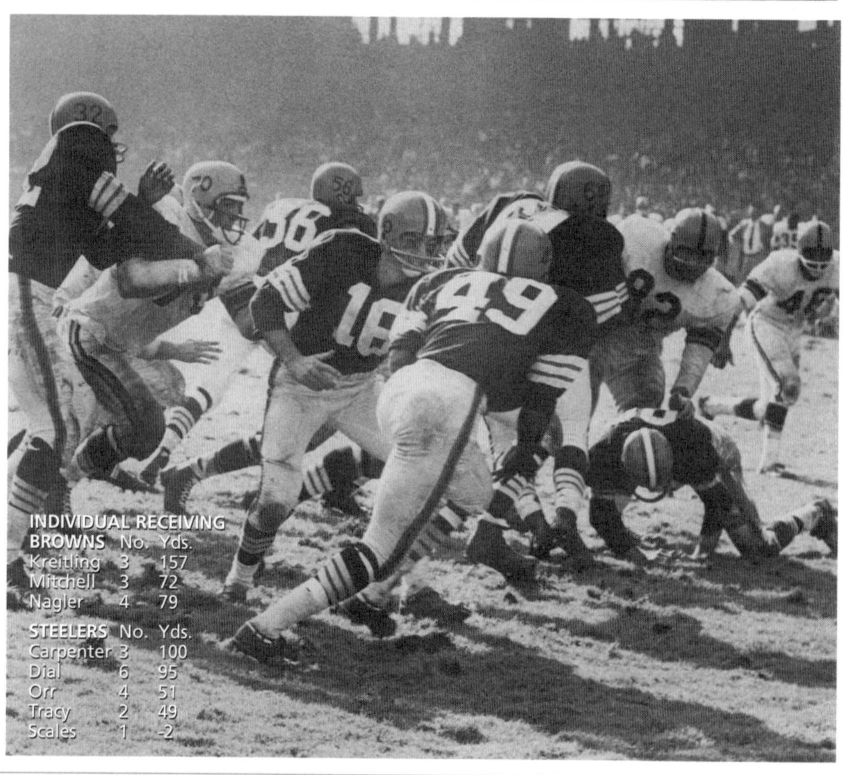

INDIVIDUAL RECEIVING

BROWNS	No.	Yds.
Kreitling	3	157
Mitchell	3	72
Nagler	4	79

STEELERS	No.	Yds.
Carpenter	3	100
Dial	6	95
Orr	4	51
Tracy	2	49
Scales	1	-2

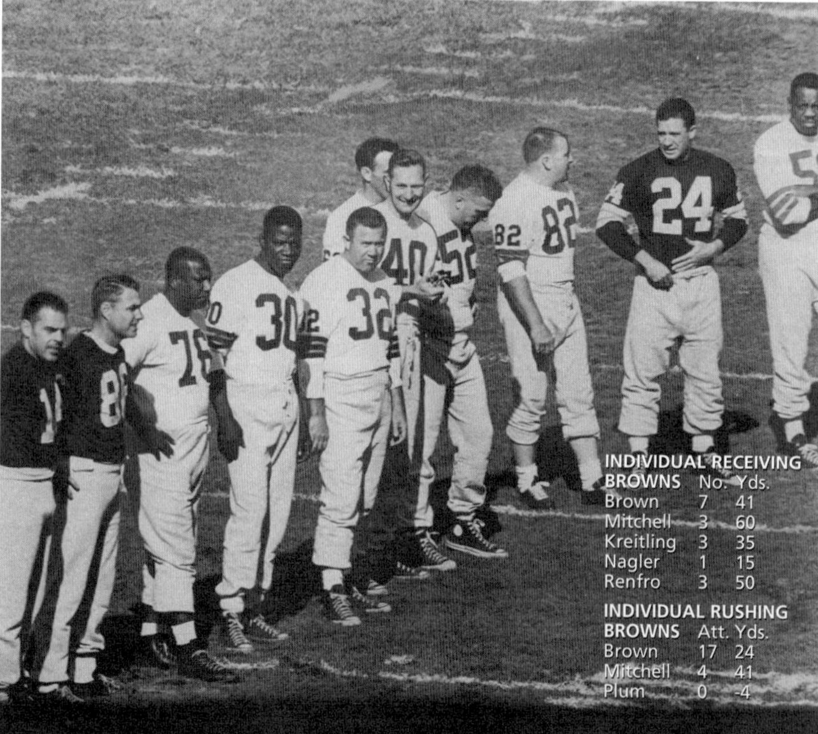

October 8, 1961
Cleveland-31, Washington-7

The Cleveland Browns played the Washington Redskins on Sunday, October 8, 1961, before 46,186 at the Stadium. The Browns won, 31-7, led by HB Bobby Mitchell, who caught three passes for 60 yards and scored three times on a 52-yard pass from QB Milt Plum, a 64-yard punt return and a 31-yard run. Plum completed 17 passes for 194 net yards. Cleveland's final TD came on a 17-yard pass from QB Len Dawson to WR Ray Renfro. Rookie Redskins QB Sam Snead completed 13 of 27 for 200 yards and a TD in the loss.

INDIVIDUAL RECEIVING

BROWNS	No.	Yds.
Brown	7	41
Mitchell	3	60
Kreitling	3	35
Nagler	1	15
Renfro	3	50

INDIVIDUAL RUSHING

BROWNS	Att.	Yds.
Brown	17	24
Mitchell	4	41
Plum	0	-4

(Left) At halftime, former members of the Cleveland Browns got together for a touch football game. From left to right are: Otto Graham, Dante Lavelli, Marion Motley, Bill Willis, Lin Houston, Cliff Lewis (partially hidden), Dub Jones, George Young, Tommy James, Warren Lahr and Horace Gillom. During the game, Lavelli made a spectacular catch, grabbing a 40-yard aerial from Graham between two defenders.

September 16, 1962 / Opening Day

A record Opening Day crowd of 81,115 watched the Cleveland Browns battle the New York Giants at the Stadium on Sunday, September 16, 1962. Cleveland scored first on a nine-yard run by FB Jim Brown, who rushed for 134 yards. In the second half, QB Jim Ninowski threw for six points to WR Rich Kreitling, who caught four passes for 92 yards. A Lou Groza field goal gave Cleveland a 17-7 win. In the fourth quarter, Browns HB Tom Wilson and Giants DB Erich Barnes were ejected when the two began fighting after Wilson, who thought Barnes had twisted his ankle during a tackle, tossed the ball in Barnes' face. Groza said after the game, "When you beat the Giants, its like two victories in the standings." The win was the Browns' second over New York in the last 10 meetings.

(Right) Giants QB Y. A. Tittle, (14), is about to be hit by Browns DE Bill Glass (80). Tittle completed 16 of 27 passes for 106 yards, but had three passes intercepted.

INDIVIDUAL RUSHING		
BROWNS	**Att.**	**Yds.**
Brown	17	134
Ninowski	3	5
Wilson	18	76
Green	1	1
Scales	1	0
GIANTS	**Att.**	**Yds.**
Tittle	1	-7
Gaiters	7	35
Webster	12	37
Counts	6	23
Guglielmi	1	-15

October 7, 1962
Cleveland-19, Dallas-10

Rookie Ernie Green made his regular season debut at left half for the Browns on Sunday, October 7, 1962, as Cleveland played coach Tom Landry's Dallas Cowboys before 44,041 at the Stadium. The Browns first scored in their 19-10 win, when FB Jim Brown turned a fumbled punt recovered by Green into a TD on two-yard run. Six Browns points came on field goals by Lou "The Toe" Groza, who was honored at halftime with his family. His last field goal gave Groza back the NFL's all time scoring record with 850 points.

(Right) Cleveland scored in the fourth quarter when QB Jim Ninowski (15), hit FB Jim Brown on a 50-yard pass off "No. 19 rollout, fullback up the gut." Brown first stopped to block before connecting with Ninowski, who rolled out to pass. Dallas defenders are DE Bob Lilly (74), and DT John Meyers (78). Ninowski completed 15 of 25 for 169 yards.

INDIVIDUAL RECEIVING		
BROWNS	**No.**	**Yds.**
Kreitling	3	62
Brown	4	55
L. Clarke	2	29
Brewer	2	11
Renfro	2	17
Green	2	-5

November 25, 1962
Cleveland-35, Pittsburgh-14

The Cleveland Browns (5-1), faced the Pittsburgh Steelers (6-4), on Sunday, November 25, 1962, before 53,601 at the Stadium. The Browns won, 35-14, scoring twice in the first half, on a 34-yard TD pass from QB Frank Ryan to FB Jim Brown and a 12-yard Ryan TD pass to rookie flanker Gary Collins. Ryan, who completed 21 of 33 for 284 yards, also hit HB Ray Renfro on a 31-yard second half TD. Cleveland also scored on two one-yard fourth quarter runs by Brown.

(Right) Browns FB Jim Brown scores on one of his two fourth quarter TDs. Blocking for Brown are HB Ernie Green (48), OG Gene Hickerson (66), OG Jim Ray Smith (64), and OT Dick Schafrath (77). No. 13 is QB Frank Ryan. Brown ran for 110 yards and caught five passes for 56 yards. Brown's three TDs gave the All-Pro fullback 15 for the year, three short of the NFL record.

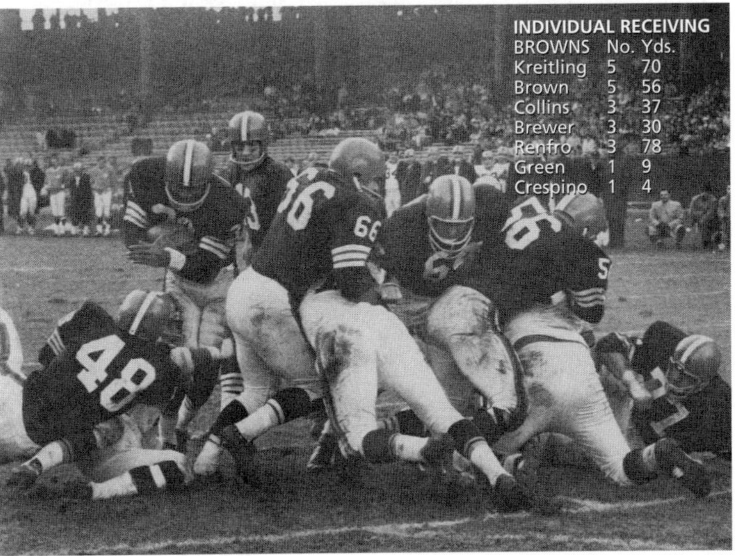

INDIVIDUAL RECEIVING		
BROWNS	**No.**	**Yds.**
Kreitling	5	70
Brown	5	56
Collins	3	37
Brewer	3	30
Renfro	3	78
Green	1	9
Crespino	1	4

1964- A Championship Season

INDIVIDUAL RUSHING

BROWNS	Att.	Yds.
Brown	21	79
Green	5	19
Kelly	1	1
Ryan	3	16

CARDINALS	Att.	Yds.
Johnson	1	0
Crow	11	58
Childress	14	52
Gautt	1	4

INDIVIDUAL RECEIVING

BROWNS	No.	Yds.
Collins	6	105
Brown	2	14
Warfield	3	63
Hutchinson	1	7

CARDINALS	No.	Yds.
Randle	4	121
Anderson	1	10
Conrad	3	50
Crow	3	29

September 20, 1964
Cleveland-33, St. Louis-33

The Home Opener

After beating the Washington Redskins, 27-13, in Washington to open the season, the Cleveland Browns opened at home against the St. Louis Cardinals on Sunday, September 20, 1964. Played before a capacity crowd of 76,954, the Browns led, 16-13, at halftime on three Lou Groza field goals and a 40-yard TD pass from QB Frank Ryan to rookie WR Paul Warfield. In the third period, Cleveland scored on a seven-yard TD pass from Ryan to flanker Gary Collins, but St. Louis rallied with 10 points to tie the game at 23-23. Cleveland led, 33-30, late in the fourth quarter after a one-yard TD run by FB Jim Brown, who led all rushers with 79 yards, but Cardinal QB Charley Johnson, with 48 seconds remaining, put St. Louis place-kicker Jim Bakken in position to kick a 28-yard field goal with only 11 seconds to go. Bakken's fourth field goal gave the Cardinals a 33-33 tie. An earlier 51-yard field goal by Bakken set a Cardinal distance record, breaking 50-yard marks set by Pat Summerall in 1954 and Paddy Driscoll, who scored on a 50-yard drop kick in 1924.

(Left) Rookie WR Paul Warfield is about to score his first regular season TD on a 40-yard pass from QB Frank Ryan. Warfield caught three passes for 63 yards. Ryan completed 12 of 26 for 189 yards.

October 4, 1964 / Cleveland-27, Dallas-6

The Cleveland Browns hosted their Eastern Division rivals, the Dallas Cowboys, on Sunday, October 4, 1964, before 72,062, the largest crowd at the time to watch Dallas play at the Stadium. The Browns scored on five of the first eight times they touched the ball, en route to a 27-6 rout of the Cowboys. Leading Cleveland on offense were FB Jim Brown, who rushed for 89 yards on 23 carries, and QB Frank Ryan, who completed 13 passes for 236 yards and three TDs. Ryan threw five passes to rookie WR Paul Warfield for 123 yards, three to WR Gary Collins for 62 yards, two to HB Ernie Green for 47 yards and two to Brown for 24 yards. With the win, Cleveland remained tied with the St. Louis Cardinals for first place in the NFL's Eastern Division at 3-0-1 record. Dallas QB John Roach was pressured all afternoon by the Browns defense who lost starting DT Bob Gain for the season with a broken leg.

INDIVIDUAL RUSHING

BROWNS	Att.	Yds.
Ryan	2	7
Brown	23	89
Green	5	20

COWBOYS	Att.	Yds.
Roach	3	0
Marsh	10	43
Perkins	18	80
Clarke	2	9

(Far left) Browns QB Frank Ryan (13), is hit by Dallas LB Chuck Howley after getting the pass away. No. 66 is DE George Andrie.

(Left) Browns FB Jim Brown avoids Howley for a 10-yard gain. No. 83 is RE Johnny Brewer.

November 15, 1964 / Cleveland-37, Detroit-21

The Cleveland Browns' first regular season win over
the Detroit Lions in franchise history came on Sunday,
November 15, 1964, when they beat the Lions, 37-21, before
83,064 at the Stadium. Leading the Cleveland attack was
FB Jim Brown, who rushed for 147 yards on 24 attempts.
Brown raised his season total to 1,081 yards, giving the All-
Pro runner his sixth 1,000-yard season. Brown also scored
two of the Browns' four TDs. QB Frank Ryan completed
15 passes for 178 yards, including an eight-yard TD strike
to WR Paul Warfield. Cleveland place-kicker Lou "The Toe"
Groza added thirteen points with three field goals and four
extra points. For Detroit, QB Milt Plum completed 15 of 27
for 236 yards. The game ball was given to CB Walter Beach,
who returned the first of his two interceptions 65 yards for
a TD.

(Right) Browns rookie WR Paul Warfield hauls down a 31-
yard fourth quarter pass from QB Frank Ryan as Detroit DB
Dick LeBeau hangs on. Warfield led all receivers with five
catches for 92 yards and a third quarter TD.

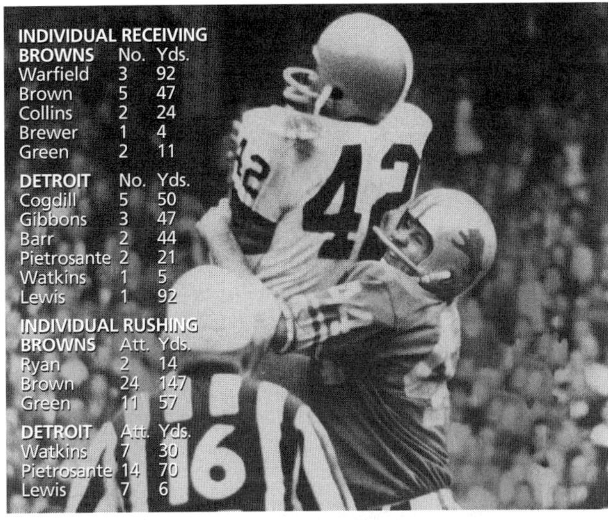

INDIVIDUAL RECEIVING

BROWNS	No.	Yds.
Warfield	3	92
Brown	5	47
Collins	2	24
Brewer	1	4
Green	2	11

DETROIT	No.	Yds.
Cogdill	5	50
Gibbons	3	47
Barr	2	44
Pietrosante	2	21
Watkins	1	5
Lewis	1	92

INDIVIDUAL RUSHING

BROWNS	Att.	Yds.
Ryan	2	14
Brown	24	147
Green	11	57

DETROIT	Att.	Yds.
Watkins	7	30
Pietrosante	14	70
Lewis	7	6

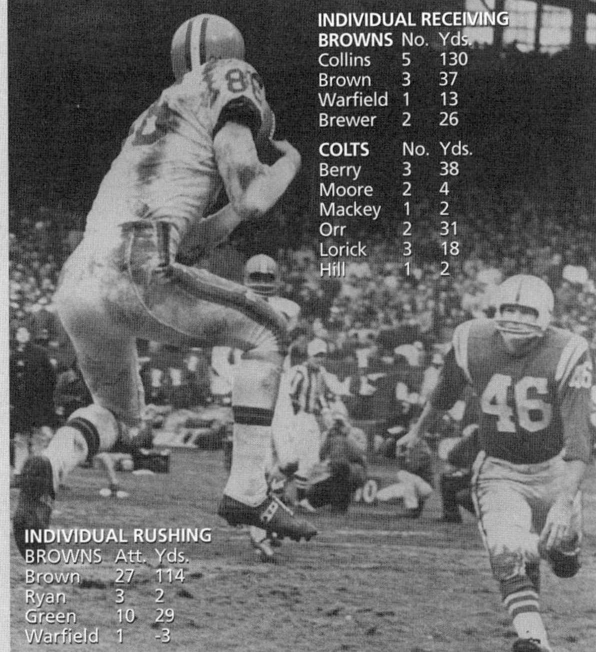

INDIVIDUAL RECEIVING

BROWNS	No.	Yds.
Collins	5	130
Brown	3	37
Warfield	1	13
Brewer	2	26

COLTS	No.	Yds.
Berry	3	38
Moore	2	4
Mackey	1	2
Orr	2	31
Lorick	3	18
Hill	1	2

INDIVIDUAL RUSHING

BROWNS	Att.	Yds.
Brown	27	114
Ryan	3	2
Green	10	29
Warfield	1	-3

The NFL Championship Game

December 27, 1964 / Browns-27, Colts-0

Determination was the word Browns DT Dick
Modzelewski used to describe the Cleveland Browns'
stunning 27-0 upset victory over the Baltimore Colts on
Sunday, December 27, 1964. The win gave the underdog
Browns, playing in their first NFL title game since 1957,
their first NFL title win since 1955, and first at the
Stadium since 1954. Played before 79,544, Cleveland QB
Frank Ryan completed 11 of 18 for 296 yards, including
three second-half TD passes of 18, 42 and 51 yards to
flanker Gary Collins. Collins led all receivers with five
catches for 130 yards. The three TDs scored by Collins
tied an NFL record set by Browns QB Otto Graham in
1954. Place-kicker Lou "The Toe" Groza added to his own
career playoff records, by kicking two field goals and
three extra points. FB Jim Brown led all rushers with 114
yards, while his teammates on defense held Baltimore to
only 171 yards of total offense. Colts QB Johnny Unitas
completed 12 of 20, but picked up only 95 yards in the air,
and had two passes intercepted. Browns players received
approximately $8,000 each from the winners' pool.

(Left) Gary Collins grabs the first of his three TD passes
from QB Frank Ryan. No. 46 is Colts safety Jim Welch.

(Left) Browns QB Frank Ryan leaves
the field after leading Cleveland to
the upset win over Baltimore.

1964 CLEVELAND BROWNS

OT	Brown, Clark, Schafrath, Shoals
G	Hickerson, Memmelaar, Wooten
C	Morrow
DE	Glass, Wiggin, Williams
DT	Gain, Kanicki, Modzelewski, Parker
LB	Costello, Fiss, Houston, Lucci, Sczurek
DB	Beach, Benz, Caylor, Fichtner, Franklin, Parrish, Raimey
QB	Ninowski, Ryan
HB	Green, Kelly
FB	Brown, Scales
FL	Collins, McNeil, Roberts
WR	Brewer, Hutchinson, Warfield
K	Groza

December 5, 1965
Jim Brown's Last Home Game
Cleveland-24, Washington-16

With the division title already under wraps, the Cleveland Browns were seeking their 10th win in 12 games, when they battled the Washington Redskins on Sunday, December 5, 1965, in the final home game of the season. Played at the Stadium before 77,765, Washington led 16-7 at the half, scoring on a two-yard run by HB Charley Taylor, a six-yard pass from Redskin QB Sonny Jurgensen to WR Pat Richter and a field goal by Bob Jencks. Cleveland battled back, scoring in the second half, on a third-quarter field goal by Lou Groza, a 14-yard TD pass from QB Frank Ryan to WR Tom Hutchinson- his first regular season TD catch- and a four-yard, fourth-quarter run by FB Jim Brown to win, 24-16. Brown's TD gave him 20 for the year, tying an NFL record. Brown rushed for 141 yards on 27 carries, raising his total yardage for the year to 1,450. It was his eighth game that season of 100 yards or more rushing and his 58th 100-yard plus game over his nine-year career.

The win over Washington marked Brown's last home game as a member of the Browns. The All-Pro fullback announced his retirement just before training camp began the following year.

INDIVIDUAL RUSHING

BROWNS	Att.	Yds.
Brown	27	141
Ryan	2	0
Green	8	43
Collins	1	16

REDSKINS	Att.	Yds.
Jurgensen	1	-17
Taylor	16	70
Lewis	2	5
Hughley	4	5

(Above left) Redskins HB Charley Taylor scores from the 2-yard line in the first period. No. 9 is QB Sonny Jurgensen. Taylor rushed for 70 yards.

(Left) Browns FB Jim Brown is greeted by Abe Abraham, affectionately known as "the man in the brown suit," after scoring in the fourth quarter. It would be Brown's last score at the Stadium.

September 18, 1966
Green Bay-21, Cleveland-20

The Cleveland Browns opened the 1966 season on Sunday, September 18th, before a record home-opening crowd of 83,943 at the Stadium. Their opponent was coach Vince Lombardi's Green Bay Packers, the same team that had beaten Cleveland in the NFL title game on January 2, 1966. Cleveland led, 17-7, at halftime, with Browns QB Frank Ryan completing 10 of 13 first half passes, two for TDs to flanker Gary Collins. The Browns led, 20-14, until Green Bay moved to the Browns' nine-yard line with three minutes remaining. On fourth down, Packer QB Bart Starr passed to FB Jim Taylor for six points. Don Chandler's extra point gave Green Bay a 21-20 win. The Packers' other scores came on a run by Taylor and a Starr pass to HB Paul Hornung, who led all receivers with three catches for 69 yards.

(Left) Browns flanker Gary Collins (86), pulls down one of his two TD catches from QB Frank Ryan (13). Packer defenders include DE Lionel Aldridge (82), DB Tom Brown (40) and DT Ron Kostelnik (77).

INDIVIDUAL RECEIVING

BROWNS	No.	Yds.
Kelly	3	27
Collins	4	70
Warfield	3	54
Green	5	33

PACKERS	No.	Yds.
Taylor	8	64
Hornung	3	69
Dale	2	23
Dowler	4	61
Fleming	2	15
Anderson	1	6

With the retirement of All-Pro FB Jim Brown on July 13, 1966, the Cleveland Browns turned to HB Leroy Kelly. On Sunday, December 4, 1966, the third-year back from Morgan State rushed for three TDs as the Browns rallied before 61,651 to beat the New York Giants, 49-40, on the icy Stadium turf. The winning TD came when FB Ernie Green took a flare pass from QB Frank Ryan 31 yards for the TD. Ryan completed 16 of 27 for 326 yards. Kelly, who broke the 1,000-yard mark with 126 yards rushing, became only the 12th player to rush for over 1,000 yards in a season. Kelly finished second to Chicago HB Gale Sayers for the NFL rushing title with 1,141 yards, but led the league in scoring with 16 touchdowns.

(Below) Browns HB Leroy Kelly (44), runs for 12 yards. In the play with Kelly are center Fred Hoaglin (54), TE Ralph Smith (41), OG John Wooten (60), E Gary Collins (86), DB Carl Lockhart (43), LB Mike Ciccolella (58), and DE Jim Katcavage (75).

INDIVIDUAL RUSHING BROWNS	Att.	Yds.
Ryan	1	1
Brown	13	126
Green	4	5

INDIVIDUAL RECEIVING BROWNS	No.	Yds.
Kelly	4	71
Smith	3	67
Green	4	68
Collins	5	120

GIANTS	No.	Yds.
Jacobs	2	21
Morrison	5	75
Crespino	1	4
Thomas	1	20
Jones	1	13

November 26, 1967
Cleveland-42, Washington-37

Game balls went to QB Frank Ryan, who completed 11 of 17 for 233 yards and one TD; HB Leroy Kelly, who scored twice; and rookie DB Carl Ward, who scored on a club-record 104-yard kickoff return; after the first-place Browns (7-4), beat the Washington Redskins (4-7), on Sunday, November 26, 1967 before 72,798 at the Stadium. Also scoring for the Browns were FB Ernie Green, WR Paul Warfield and LB Johnny Brewer who returned a tipped pass from QB Sonny Jurgensen 70 yards for six points. Jurgensen completed 32 of 50 passes for 418 yards and 3 TDs.

(Right) Browns HB Leroy Kelly, who enjoyed his best day as a pro, eludes Redskin defenders. Kelly led all rushers with 163 yards on 20 carries, putting him over the 1,000-yard mark for the second straight year.

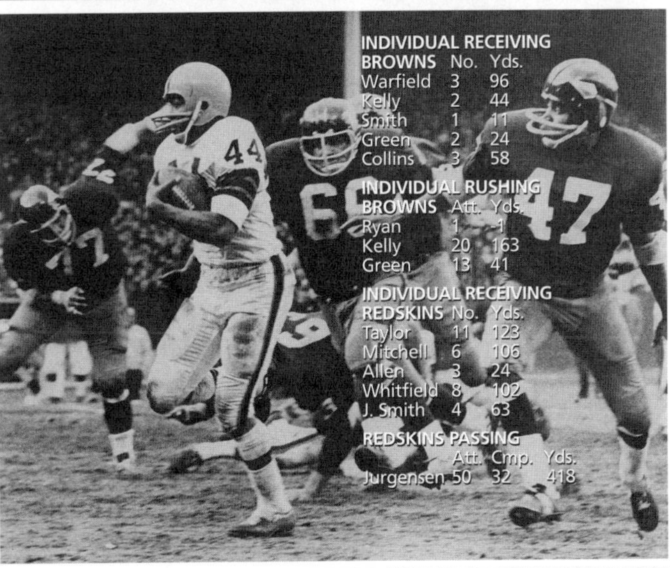

INDIVIDUAL RECEIVING BROWNS	No.	Yds.
Warfield	3	96
Kelly	2	44
Smith	1	11
Green	2	24
Collins	3	58

INDIVIDUAL RUSHING BROWNS	Att.	Yds.
Ryan	1	-1
Kelly	20	163
Green	13	41

INDIVIDUAL RECEIVING REDSKINS	No.	Yds.
Taylor	11	123
Mitchell	6	106
Allen	3	24
Whitfield	8	102
J. Smith	4	63

REDSKINS PASSING	Att.	Cmp.	Yds.
Jurgensen	50	32	418

December 3, 1967 / Cleveland-24, New York-14

After beating the Washington Redskins at home the previous week, the first-place Cleveland Browns battled their Century Division rivals, coach Allie Reynolds' New York Giants (6-5), on Sunday December 3, 1967, before 78,594 at the Stadium. Cleveland scored first in their 24-14 win over New York on a Lou "The Toe" Groza field goal, coming after LB Jim Houston blocked a field goal by New York's Charley Gogolak. HB Leroy Kelly scored from the one and QB Frank Ryan tossed a 24-yard pass to flanker Gary Collins to give Cleveland a 17-0 halftime lead. Ryan completed 6 of 13 for 67 yards.

(Left) Giants QB Fran Tarkenton (10), is about to be sacked by Browns DT Paul Wiggin. No. 80 is DE Bill Glass. Cleveland's final score came when LB Jim Houston intercepted a Tarkenton pass late in the fourth period and returned it 79 yards for a TD. It was one of two interceptions thrown by Tarkenton, who was pressured all day by the Browns' defense. Tarkenton completed 23 of 43 for 218 yards.

1968- Heading to the Championship

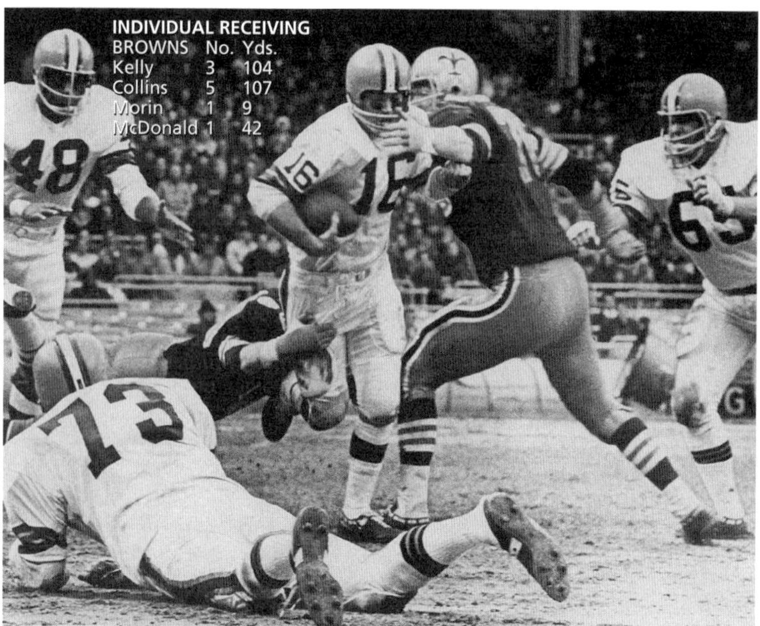

November 10, 1968
Cleveland-35, New Orleans-17

In a battle of division rivals, the Cleveland Browns (5-3), hosted the New Orleans Saints (3-5), on Sunday, November 10, 1968, before 71,025 at the Stadium. Browns QB Bill Nelsen completed 10 of 24 passes for 262 yards, throwing touchdowns to HB Leroy Kelly, who caught five-yard and 68-yard TD strikes, WR Paul Warfield, and TE Milt Morin. The Browns won the contest, 35-17, scoring a final TD on a fourth quarter run by Kelly, who led all rushers with 127 yards on 17 carries. Browns FB Charley Harraway added 79 yards on nine carries. Saints second-string QB Karl Sweetan, replacing injured starter Billy Kilmer, who was out with a broken ankle, completed only 10 of 27 for 103 yards. The win gave Cleveland sole possession of first place in the Century Division.

(Left) Browns QB Bill Nelsen (16), runs for a short gain against the Saints. Other Browns in the play are OG John Demarie (65), FB Ernie Green (48), and OT Monte Clark (73).

December 1, 1968
No. 76 Is Retired

Before the Cleveland Browns took the field against the New York Giants on Sunday, December 1, 1968, the Cleveland Browns retired the No. 76 jersey worn by former lineman and place-kicker Lou "The Toe" Groza, one of the original members of the Cleveland Browns. With Groza at left, is his wife, Jackie. First-place Cleveland (9-3), rolled over the Giants, 45-10, led by HB Leroy Kelly, who scored four times, all on the ground. Cleveland's last TD came on a twelve-yard pass from Frank Ryan to Tommy McDonald. Browns QB Bill Nelsen completed 13 of 25 for 204 yards. Place-kicker Don Cockroft added a field goal and 6 PATs.

(Right) Among the 83,193 at the Stadium on December 1st, was Ohio State University head football coach Woody Hayes (left, at right), joined before the game by Browns WR Paul Warfield, who played for Woody at Ohio State. Groza also played briefly at Ohio State under Paul Brown before entering the service during World War II. Hayes was at the Stadium to accept a check from the Browns to start a scholarship in Groza's name at Ohio State. Warfield led Cleveland receivers with six catches for 137 yards and a TD. It was the 7th-straight win for the Century Division-leading Cleveland Browns.

1968- The Playoffs

Winning the Eastern Conference

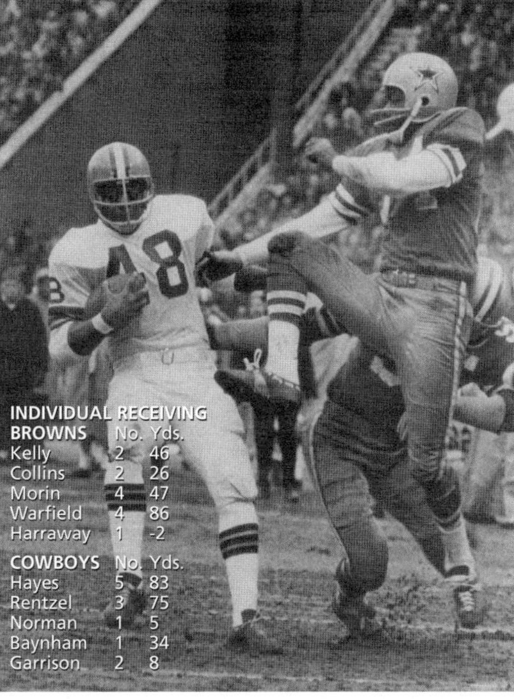

INDIVIDUAL RECEIVING

BROWNS	No.	Yds.
Kelly	2	46
Collins	2	26
Morin	4	47
Warfield	4	86
Harraway	1	-2

COWBOYS	No.	Yds.
Hayes	5	83
Rentzel	3	75
Norman	1	5
Baynham	1	34
Garrison	2	8

After clinching the Century Division title with a 10-4 record, the Cleveland Browns faced the Dallas Cowboys for the Eastern Conference title before 81,497 at the Stadium on Sunday, December 22, 1968. With the scored tied, 10-10, at halftime, the Browns scored 21 points in the second half on a 27-yard interception by LB Dale Lindsey, a 35-yard run by HB Leroy Kelly and a two-yard TD run by FB Ernie Green, to capture the playoff contest, 31-20. Less than twelve hours after the Browns clinched the title, fans began lining up at the Stadium to purchase championship game tickets priced at $12, $10, $8 and $6.

(Far left) Pressured throughout the game by the Browns' tenacious defense, starting Dallas QB Don Meredith, at far left, was replaced in the third quarter by Craig Morton after completing only three passes for 42 yards and throwing three interceptions.

(Left) FB Ernie Green scores Cleveland's final TD on a two-yard run.

The NFL Championship Game

December 29, 1968

An overflow crowd of 80,628 filled Municipal Stadium on Sunday, December 29, 1968, as coach Blanton Collier's Cleveland Browns battled coach Don Shula's Baltimore Colts for the National Football League championship. At stake was the chance to face the Joe Namath-led New York Jets in Super Bowl III. Baltimore overpowered the Browns in every category including the score, beating the home heroes, 34-0. Three Colts TDs were scored by HB Tom Matte, who led all rushers with 88 yards on 17 carries. HB Tim Brown scored the Colts final TD. Each Colts player received nearly $10,000 as their share of the winners' pool. It was the second time the two franchises met at the Stadium to decide the NFL title. In 1964, Cleveland upset the Colts, 27-0.

(Right) Colts HB Tom Matte (41), who played high school football at Cleveland's Shaw High, scores the second of three TDs after getting the ball from QB Earl Morrall (15). Defending on the play are DB Mike Howell (34), and DE Ron Snidow (88). Matte's three TDs tied an NFL playoff record set by Browns QB Otto Graham in 1954, and Browns flanker Gary Collins in 1964.

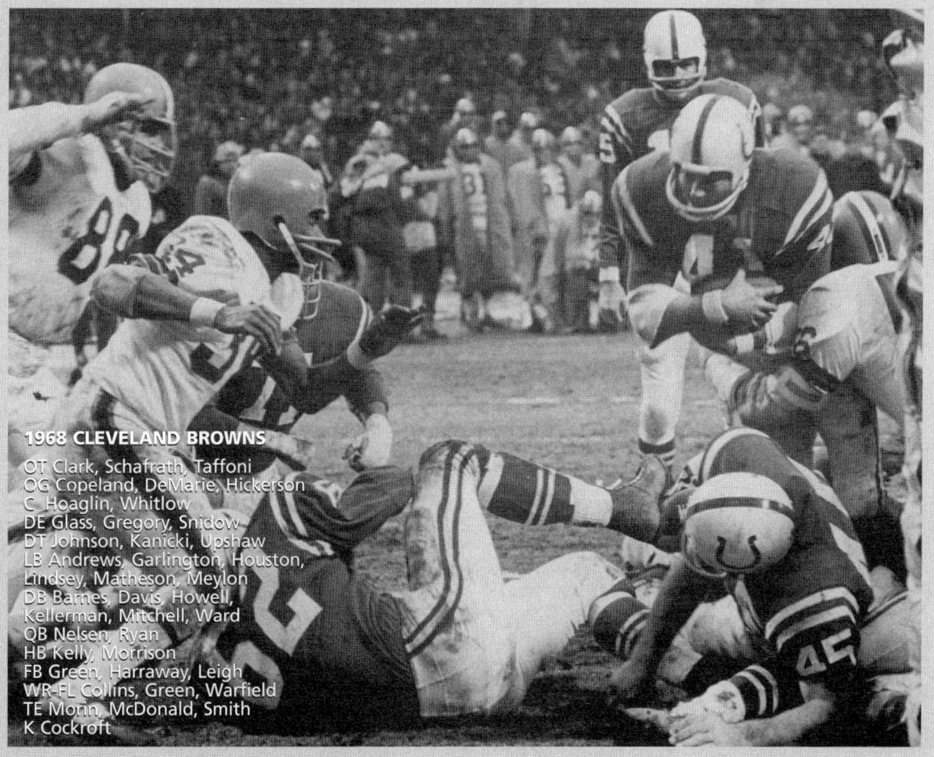

August 30, 1969 / The Doubleheader

(Far left) Rookie HB Ron Johnson (30), is introduced to the Stadium crowd. Johnson rushed for 20 yards, gained 30 yards receiving, and ran back kickoffs for another 60 yards in his home debut.

(Left) Veteran Chicago Bears HB Gale Sayers breaks through the Bills defense for six points in the second quarter.

An all-time Browns record crowd of 85,532 watched the eighth annual pro football exhibition doubleheader at the Stadium on Saturday, August 30, 1969 (SRO tickets were $4). The first game, billed as "the battle of the halfbacks," featured the Chicago Bears facing the Buffalo Bills. In the nightcap, the Cleveland Browns took on the QB Bart Starr-led Green Bay Packers. HB Gale Sayers, who scored a TD, and Mac Percival, who kicked five field goals, led Chicago to a 23-16 win over Buffalo, as Bills HB O. J. Simpson gained only 31 yards in total yardage. Cleveland, who scored both TDs in the first half, lost to Green Bay, 27-17. Packer TDs were scored by HB Travis Williams (2) and end Boyd Dowler on a pass from Starr.

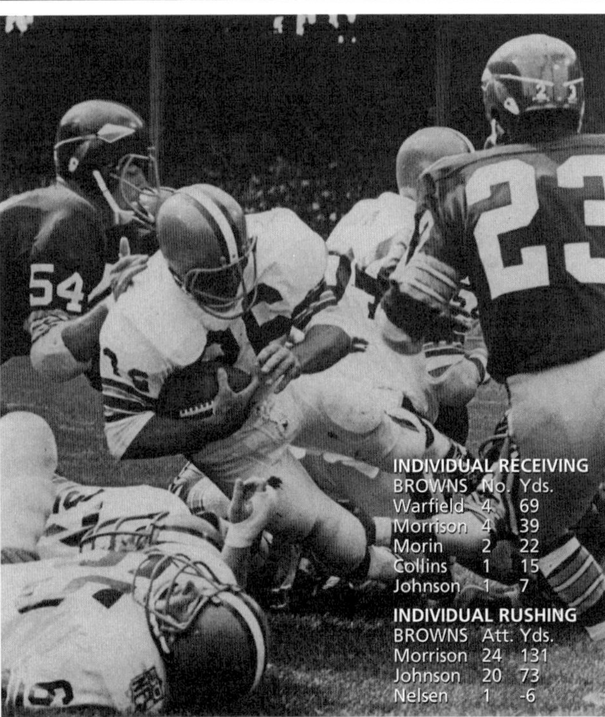

INDIVIDUAL RECEIVING		
BROWNS	No.	Yds.
Warfield	4	69
Morrison	4	39
Morin	2	22
Collins	1	15
Johnson	1	7

INDIVIDUAL RUSHING		
BROWNS	Att.	Yds.
Morrison	24	131
Johnson	20	73
Nelsen	1	-6

September 28, 1969 / Cleveland-27, Washington-23

The Cleveland Browns battled coach Vince Lombardi's Washington Redskins before a home opening crowd of 82,581 at the Stadium on September 28, 1969. Lombardi, in his first year as the Redskins' head coach, had beaten the Browns in six previous trips to the Stadium as coach of the Green Bay Packers. Trailing 23-20, the Browns got the ball on their own 26-yard line, with four minutes and 20 seconds left in the game. Seven plays later, QB Bill Nelsen had moved the ball to the Washington 15 yard line. With 1:24 to go and the ball at the fifteen, flanker Gary Collins broke loose on the first play to pull down a Nelsen pass for the winning TD. QB Sonny Jurgensen completed 14 of 21 for 121 yards and two TDs for the Redskins. On the Washington roster were ex-Browns FB Charley Harraway and QB Frank Ryan.

(Above left) Browns HB Reece Morrison, who led all rushers with 131 yards on 24 carries, is stopped after a short gain. Morrison also caught four passes for 39 yards. **(Above)** Browns head coach Blanton Collier talks with Browns center Fred Hoaglin. It was Collier's first home opening win at the Stadium since 1963, when he beat the Redskins in his head coaching debut.

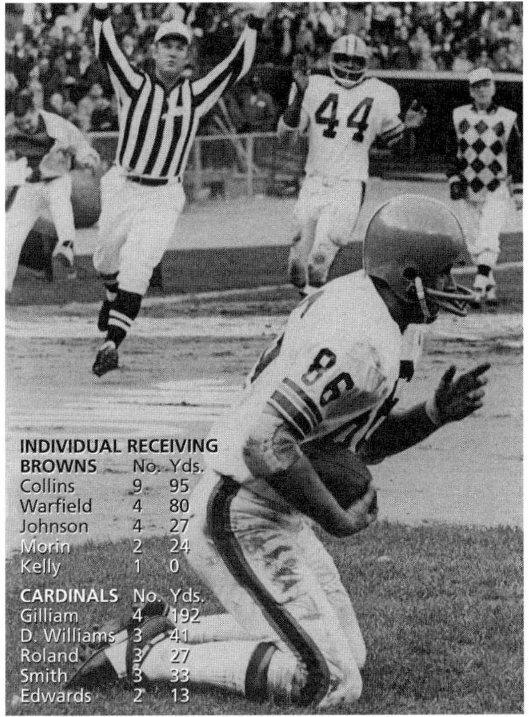

INDIVIDUAL RECEIVING

BROWNS	No.	Yds.
Collins	9	95
Warfield	4	80
Johnson	4	27
Morin	2	24
Kelly	1	0

CARDINALS	No.	Yds.
Gilliam	4	192
D. Williams	3	41
Roland	3	27
Smith	3	33
Edwards	2	13

October 26, 1969
Cleveland-21, St. Louis-21

With both teams expected to battle for the Century Division crown, the first-place Cleveland Browns (4-1), hosted coach Charley Winner's St. Louis Cardinals (2-2), on October 26, 1969, before 81,186 at the Stadium. The Browns were first to score, when HB Leroy Kelly connected with WR Paul Warfield on a 36-yard pass in the first quarter. St. Louis also tallied in the first quarter, when WR John Gilliam scored the first of his three TDs on an 84-yard pass from QB Charley Johnson. In the second half, St. Louis scored first, when Gilliam caught a 75-yard pass from Johnson for his second TD. Cleveland tied the score at 14-14 in the third quarter, when Kelly scored on a two-yard run. Cleveland broke the deadlock in the fourth quarter, when Nelsen connected with flanker Gary Collins on a 12-yard TD pass. With just over two minutes to go, Johnson got the ball back on the St. Louis 31-yard line. Johnson led the Cardinals to the Browns' 15-yard line, where he passed to Gilliam for a TD with eight seconds remaining. St. Louis place-kicker Jim Bakken, who missed on three field goal attempts earlier in the game, kicked the extra point, giving the Cardinals a 21-21 tie. Johnson connected on 15 of 30 passes, for 306 yards, several thrown in the direction of rookie cornerback Walt Sumner. Nelsen completed 19 of 28 for 198 yards.

(Left) Flanker Gary Collins (86), catches Cleveland's go-ahead TD in the fourth quarter as HB Leroy Kelly (44), watches in the background. Collins led Cleveland receivers with nine receptions for 95 yards. Kelly finished the game with 71 rushing yards on 16 attempts. Rookie FB Ron Johnson ran 13 times for 35 yards.

November 2, 1969 / Cleveland-42, Dallas-10

Browns QB Bill Nelsen threw five TD passes in leading the Cleveland Browns (4-1) to a 42-10 upset win over the Dallas Cowboys (6-0) on Sunday, November 2, 1969. The game was played before 84,450, the ninth straight Stadium sellout and largest crowd to watch a regular season game against the Cowboys. LB John Garlington recovered a fumble by Cowboy HB Walt Garrison to set up Nelsen's first TD, a 48-yard pass to WR Paul Warfield on the team's first play from scrimmage. An eight-yard pass from Nelsen to flanker Gary Collins, a one-yard run by rookie FB Ron Johnson and a 21-yard Nelsen pass to Warfield gave the Browns a 28-3 halftime lead. Cleveland scored twice in the fourth quarter, on a seven-yard Nelsen pass to Collins and a 10-yard Nelsen pass to TE Chip Glass. Nelsen completed 18 of 25 for 255 yards. The only Dallas TD came on a one-yard, fourth-quarter run by FB Calvin Hill, the NFL's leading rusher. Cowboy QBs Craig Morton and Roger Staubach completed only 17 of 33 for 221 yards and were intercepted three times, once by safety Mike Howell, who led the NFL in interceptions. TE Milt Morin, who joined the Browns' defensive line in receiving game balls, led Cleveland receivers with seven catches for 101 yards.

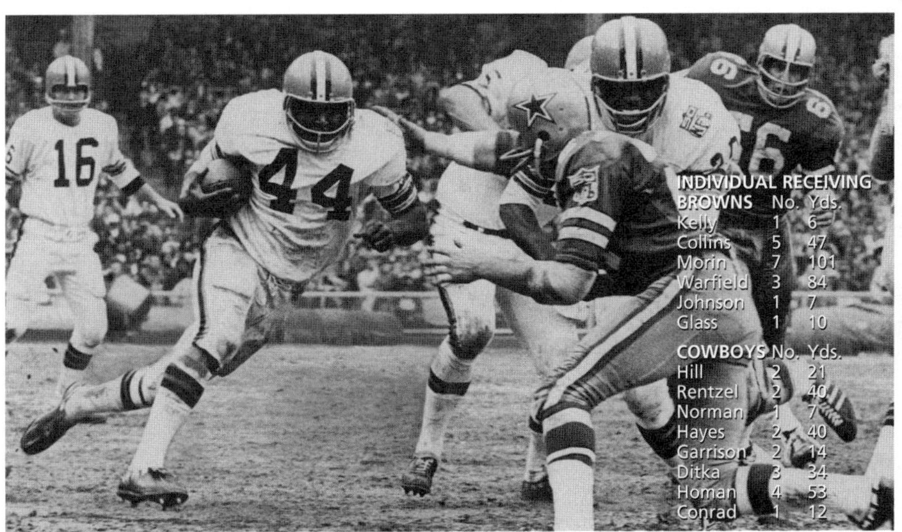

INDIVIDUAL RECEIVING

BROWNS	No.	Yds.
Kelly	1	6
Collins	5	47
Morin	7	101
Warfield	3	84
Johnson	1	7
Glass	1	10

COWBOYS	No.	Yds.
Hill	2	21
Rentzel	2	40
Norman	1	7
Hayes	2	40
Garrison	2	14
Ditka	3	34
Homan	4	53
Conrad	1	12

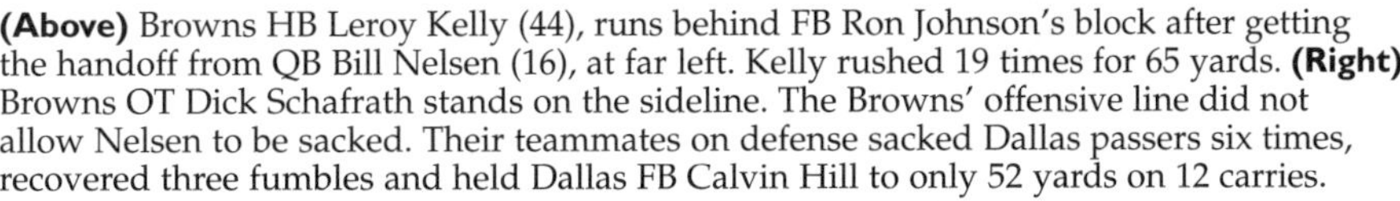

(Above) Browns HB Leroy Kelly (44), runs behind FB Ron Johnson's block after getting the handoff from QB Bill Nelsen (16), at far left. Kelly rushed 19 times for 65 yards. (Right) Browns OT Dick Schafrath stands on the sideline. The Browns' offensive line did not allow Nelsen to be sacked. Their teammates on defense sacked Dallas passers six times, recovered three fumbles and held Dallas FB Calvin Hill to only 52 yards on 12 carries.

The First Pro Football Doubleheader

"It is wonderful to see this many fans so interested in pro football here in August," remarked NFL commissioner Pete Rozelle after attending the National Football League's first exhibition doubleheader at the Stadium on Saturday, August 18, 1962. The inaugural contest attracted a record pre-season crowd of 77,683, who paid from $3 to $5 to witness the five-hour spectacle. In the first contest, the Dallas Cowboys battled the Detroit Lions. In the nightcap, the Cleveland Browns of coach Paul Brown were pitted against coach Buddy Young's Pittsburgh Steelers.

The First Game / Detroit-35, Dallas-24

Nearly 50,000 fans where in their seats when the first game pitting coach George Wilson's Detroit Lions against coach Tom Landry's Dallas Cowboys kicked off at 6:30 P.M. The Cowboys scored first on a 24-yard TD pass from QB Don Meredith to WR Amos Marsh. The Lions scored next on a one-yard plunge by starting QB Milt Plum. A 49-yard field goal by Dallas place-kicker Sam Baker gave the Cowboys a 10-7 lead. Both teams scored in the second quarter, when Plum connected with FB Ken Webb on a five-yard pass for the Lions, and rookie WR Pettis Norman scored for the Cowboys on a 10-yard pass from Meredith. In the second half, Detroit scored first, when QB Earl Morrall, who replaced Plum at halftime, connected with WR Pat Studstill on a 50-yard pass play. Dallas scored a final time in the fourth quarter, when Meredith connected with Bill Howton on a 51-yard TD pass to lead, 24-21, but the Lions rallied to defeat the Cowboys, 35-24, as Morrall connected with Detroit receivers Dan Lewis and Terry Barr on TD passes of 11 and 39 yards.

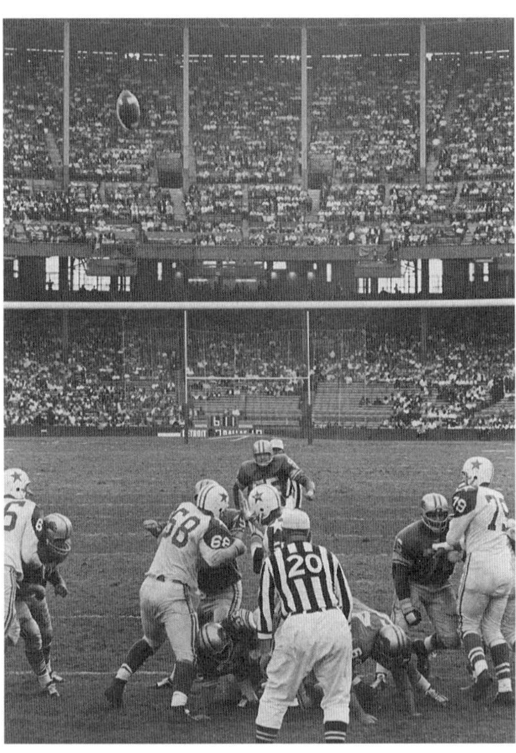

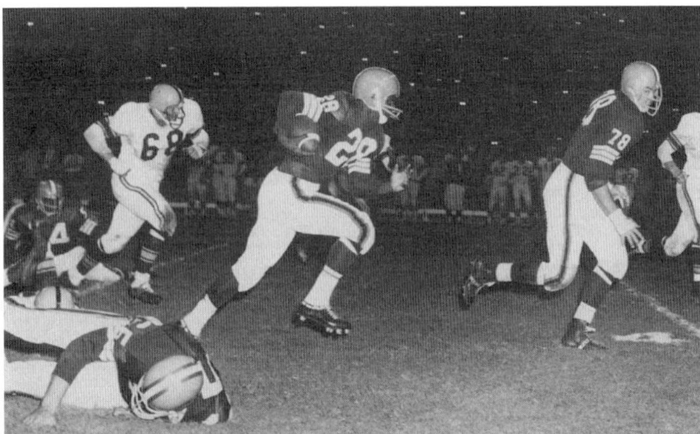

The Nightcap / Browns-33, Steelers-10

(Left) HB Ernie Green (28), returns a punt 54 yards to set up Cleveland's final TD. Green, who was obtained earlier in the week in a trade with the Green Bay Packers, turned out to be one of the pleasant surprises for the Browns in their win over Pittsburgh.

(Left) Cleveland's goal-line defense stops Pittsburgh, setting up a 12-yard Steelers field goal by Walt Michaels. The Steelers were held to 52 yards passing and 163 yards of total offense. Steelers QB Ed Brown completed 10 of 21 passes before being replaced by Terry Nofsinger. Cleveland tested a number of rookies including LB Mike Lucci and former Ohio State basketball star John Havlicek, who played briefly in the Browns backfield. A twist block off the right corner by Havlicek helped set up Cleveland's second TD by springing FB Jim Brown for a 45-yard gain. QB Jim Ninowski then passed to rookie flanker Gary Collins for the score. Ninowski completed 11 passes for 159 yards in the first half, including TD passes to WR Ray Renfro, Collins and HB Pete Brewster. In the second half, veteran QB Frank Ryan led the Browns to scores on field goals by Lou "The Toe" Groza and rookie Fred Cox, and a six-yard TD run by RB Charlie Scales.

October 31, 1965- Filming "The Fortune Cookie"

Municipal Stadium served as center stage on Sunday, October 31, 1965, to both a professional football contest between the Minnesota Vikings and the first-place Cleveland Browns, and the Hollywood film crew of producer-director Billy Wilder. Wilder, who was at the game filming scenes for "The Fortune Cookie," a feature film starring Jack Lemmon and Walter Matthau, used six cameras to capture the action around the Stadium. One camera was positioned in the end zone, one in the parking lot, another behind the Browns bench and two on the Stadium roof. A portable camera was used to capture sideline scenes. As the cameras rolled, 83,505 watched Cleveland lose 27-17 to the QB Fran Tarkenton-led Vikings, who held Browns FB Jim Brown to only 39 yards on 18 carries. On November 1st and 2nd, Wilder used the Stadium to shoot additional crowd scenes, using over 10,000 Clevelanders as extras each day.

(Top) Film director Billy Wilder (left), confers with actor Jack Lemmon between takes. **(Above)** Filming scenes at the Stadium on November 3rd. **(Top right)** Over 10,000 Clevelanders were in the stands during the filming of scenes from "The Fortune Cookie" on November 1st. **(Right center)** Wilder signs autographs on November 2nd. **(Right)** "Extras" waiting outside the Stadium.

Baseball at the Stadium

CLEVELAND
Eddie Leon 2b
Graig Nettles 3b
Duke Sims rf
Ray Fosse c
Vada Pinson cf
Tony Horton lb
Roy Foster lf
Jack Heideman ss
Rick Austin p

WASHINGTON
Eddie Brinkman ss
Tom Grieve lf
Frank Howard lb
Rich Reichardt rf
Aurelio Rodriguez 3b
Paul Casanova c
Ed Stroud cf
Tim Cullen 2b
Casey Cox p

July 9, 1970
Lou Boudreau Is Honored

It was "Lou Boudreau Night" at the Stadium on Thursday, July 9, 1970, as the Cleveland Indians honored the man who wore No. 5 as the youngest manager in major league history in 1942, and as player-manager of the World Series-winning Indians in 1948. In recognition of his recent induction into baseball's Hall of Fame, the Indians retired Boudreau's uniform number before battling the Washington Senators. Boudreau finished his thank-you remarks by stating, "Please don't forget me ever... because I'll never forget you all." Tribe catcher Ray Fosse, who was named to the American League All-Star team that

day, hit his 16th homer of the season, but the Indians, who had won four straight, lost to the Senators, 9-3. Grieve, Casanova and Reichardt all homered for Washington.

(Far left) Boudreau (left), who was working as a broadcaster covering Chicago Cubs games for WGN radio, was joined during the pre-game ceremony by Washington Senators manager Ted Williams.

(Left) Tribe manager Alvin Dark (left), wore No. 5 until switching his jersey number to No. 1 that evening.

April 8, 1971 / Opening Day

Tickets prices were up 50¢ to $4.00 for box seats and $3.50 for general admission seats, when the Cleveland Indians faced the Boston Red Sox at the Stadium on Thursday, April 8, 1971. Played before 40,442, the largest Opening Day crowd since 1965, the Indians won, 3-2, when with two outs in the ninth inning, 27-year-old rookie Harold (Gomer) Hodge, who entered the game as a pinch-hitter in the eighth inning, lined reliever Ken Tatum's first pitch to center field, scoring catcher Ray Fosse and rookie infielder Lou Camilli for the winning runs. Reliever Vince Colbert got the win, combining with starter Sam McDowell on a 3-hitter. Two Red Sox hits off McDowell were home runs by Luis Aparicio and starter Sonny Siebert.

BOSTON
Luis Aparicio ss
Reggie Smith rf
Carl Yastrzemski lf
Rico Petrocelli 3b
George Scott lb
Duane Josephson c
Tony Conigliaro cf
Doug Griffin 2b
Sonny Siebert p

CLEVELAND
ss Larry Brown
3b Graig Nettles
rf Vada Pinson
c Ray Fosse
lb Ken Harrelson
lf Roy Foster
2b Eddie Leon
cf Buddy Bradford
p Sam McDowell

(Far left) Ohio Gov. John J. Gilligan (left), jokes with American League President Joe Cronin and Indians general manager Gabe Paul (right), before throwing out the first pitch. **(Left)** Gilligan receives some batting tips from the Indians' Ken (The Hawk) Harrelson who went 0 for 3. Gilligan sat in a special box near the dugout with local notables including TV personality Dorothy Fuldheim.

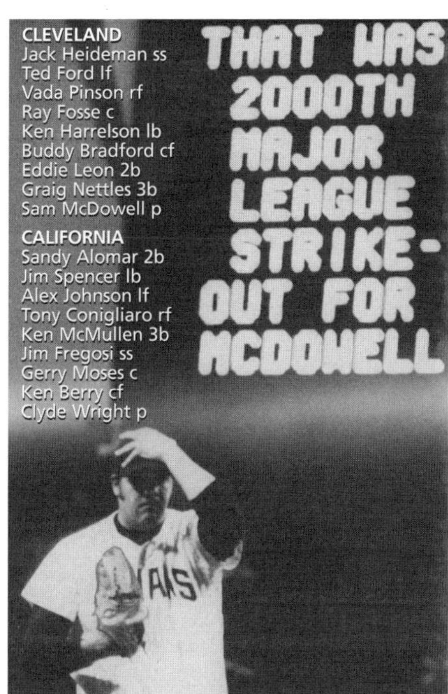

May 5, 1971 / California-4, Cleveland-2

The Cleveland Indians (8-18), faced the California Angels (15-14), before 4,602 at the Stadium on Friday, May 5, 1971. Pitching for Cleveland was left-hander Sam McDowell, a twenty-game winner in 1970, who went eight innings before being relieved by Vince Colbert. In the fourth inning, McDowell (at left), struck out Angel outfielder Alex Johnson, the 1970 AL batting champion, for his 2,000th career strikeout. McDowell, who fanned five, left the game with the Tribe losing, 2-0, after allowing a run in the eighth when Johnson singled to score Angel second baseman Sandy Alomar, who went 1 for 4. The Indians tied the game in the eighth inning on runs by outfielders Vada Pinson and Ted Ford, but lost to California, 4-2, when shortstop Syd O'Brien hit a two-run homer in the 11th inning. Angels starter Clyde Wright, who posted a 22-12 record with a 2.83 ERA in 1970, pitched 7 2/3 innings, striking out nine.

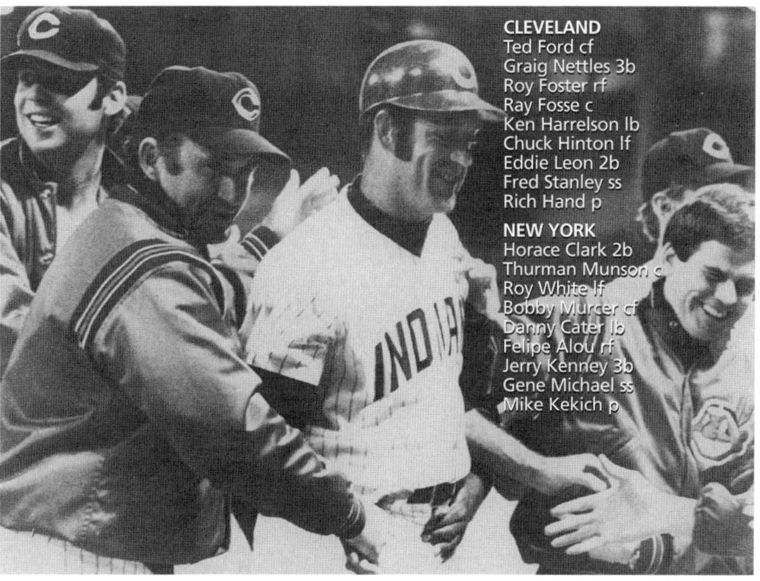

(Right)
May 21, 1971 / Indians-8, Yankees-7

The Cleveland Indians (14-22), were battling for fifth-place when they played the fourth-place New York Yankees before 6,981 at the Stadium on Friday, May 21, 1971. Down 7-6, the Indians started the ninth inning with singles to center by catcher Ray Fosse and first baseman Ken Harrelson, who raised his average to .207 with three hits, including a two-run homer. The next batter, second baseman Eddie Leon, singled to right scoring Fosse. Tribe manager Alvin Dark then sent rookie Gomer Hodge in to pinch-hit for rookie shortstop Fred Stanley. Hodge responded by hitting a single to center that drove in pitcher Steve Dunning who was pinch-running for Harrelson. The next day, Hodge, who had become a local folk hero, was honored at the Stadium with a special "Day" for his newly-organized 2,200-member fan club.

(Above) Indians manager Alvin Dark (left), and trainer Jim Warfield (right), congratulate pinch-hitter Gomer Hodge after his game-winning hit.

April 15, 1972 / Opening Day

Rookie manager Ken Aspromonte's Cleveland Indians opened the 1972 season, delayed six games by a players' strike, on Saturday, April 15, 1972, against the Milwaukee Brewers before 22,831 at the Stadium. The Indians' Opening Day roster found rookie Buddy Bell in right field, Alex Johnson in left field and Del Unser in center field. Eddie Leon was at second base, Frank Duffy at shortstop and Graig Nettles at third base. Ray Fosse was behind the plate and Chris Chambliss, the American League's Rookie of the Year in 1971, at first. On the mound was Tribe right-hander Gaylord Perry, who was making his American League debut. The Indians lost, 5-1, with Perry, who gave up nine hits, taking the loss. The Indians finished the year in fifth place with a 72-84 record, 14 games behind the Detroit Tigers.

(Right) Starter Gaylord Perry gives new owner Nick Mileti tips on throwing a baseball before the game. Mileti joined an investor group that bought the team on March 22, 1972 from local businessman Vernon Stouffer, who had been in control of the Cleveland franchise since 1966. 1972 turned out to be a career year for Perry, who tied for the American League lead in wins with 24, finished first in complete games with 29, finished second in innings pitched with 342.2 and third in strikeouts with 324. Perry beat Jim Palmer, Nolan Ryan, Sparky Lyle, Luis Tiant, Mickey Lolich, Catfish Hunter and runner-up Wilbur Wood to win the American League's Cy Young Award.

July 9, 1972 / Early Wynn's Inducted

It was "Hall of Fame" Day at the Stadium on Sunday, July 9, 1972, as former Cleveland Indians pitcher and 300-game winner Early Wynn was inducted into the Indians' Hall of Fame between games of a doubleheader between Cleveland and manager Bob Lemon's Kansas City Royals. Wynn was being honored in recognition of being voted into baseball's Hall of Fame earlier in the year. Tribe third baseman Graig Nettles hit homers in both games, but it wasn't enough to stop the Royals from taking both games, 6-4, 8-5, before 15,327 at the Stadium. In the opener, A's center fielder Amos Otis, who also made a sensational catch in the second game, homered, doubled and singled in five at bats, driving in four runs. In the second game, six of Kansas City's eight runs were scored by center fielder Richie Scheinblum, who drove in four runs, and left fielder Lou Piniella, who doubled in a run and homered. At the time, Scheinblum led the A. L. with a .333 average. Second was Piniella, who was batting .320.

(Above) Early Wynn waives to fans as he circles the field.

(Left) Kansas City manager Bob Lemon (far left), shakes hands with former teammate Mike Garcia, as guest of honor Early Wynn (second from right), and Indians general manager Gabe Paul look on. The three right-handers, Wynn, Garcia and Lemon, combined to win 513 games for the Indians from 1946 to 1963. Wynn was also joined at home plate by former teammates George Strickland and Luke Easter. Among the gifts the former Cleveland hurler received was a portrait from Gabe Paul.

August 24, 1973
John Adams

On Friday, August 24, 1973, 21-year-old John Adams of Parma began his new 'career' as "Chief Boom Boom," rallying Cleveland Indians fans at the Stadium with his bass drum from the 50¢ bleacher seats. "I do it for selfish reasons. I love it. My drum and the Indians," Adams told Cleveland Press reporter Bob Sudyk. "It's my way of drumming up enthusiasm for the team." On the field, manager Ken Aspromonte's 52-75 last-place Indians hosted the Texas Rangers before 5,736. Cleveland beat the Rangers, 11-5, behind shortstop Frank Duffy, who raised his average to .272 by driving in four runs with back-to-back homers, and left fielder Walt Williams, who went 4 for 4. Tom Timmerman (7-4), pitched a complete game for the win.

(Right) John Adams, at far right with friend Mark Chahulski on snare drums, got permission to bring his drum to home games from Indians publicist Dino Lucarelli. Lucarelli agreed to let Adams drum away as long as nobody complained.

(Above) April 10, 1974 / The Home Opener

When a blanket of snow covered the Stadium on Tuesday, April 9, 1974, the Cleveland Indians' home opener was delayed a day for the first time since 1961. The game-time temperature was 42° on Wednesday, April 10th, as pre-game activities began with Juanita Gamble singing the national anthem and human cannonball Hugo Zacchini (above), being shot through the air before 22,036 die-hard fans. Jim Perry started for manager Ken Aspromonte's squad, wearing their new bright red tops, against the Milwaukee Brewers. Perry, charged with halting the team's three-game losing streak, had a six-hitter going until the 9th inning, when Cecil Upshaw relieved the veteran with the score tied 2-2 and the bases loaded. Four pitches later, Upshaw gave up a grand slam to third baseman Don Money for a 6-2 Brewers lead. Cleveland scored twice in the ninth, with one run coming on catcher Dave Duncan's solo homer, but lost, 6-4. Milwaukee left-hander Clyde Wright gave up eight hits over eight innings, striking out three, for the win.

May 13, 1974
Jim, Ruby & Gaylord on Mother's Day

Tribe hurlers Jim and Gaylord Perry weren't the only members of the Perry family at the Stadium on Monday, May 13, 1974. Mother Ruby reigned as "Mother of the Day," as the Cleveland Indians battled the Boston Red Sox. The Indians celebrated Mother's Day a day late after their Sunday doubleheader with the Baltimore Orioles was rained out. At left, sons Jim (left), and Gaylord, join mother Ruby before the game. Ruby and her husband Evan were flown in from their home in Farm Life, North Carolina. 4,234 braved the spring chill to watch Cleveland move into a tie for first-place with a 4-1 victory. First baseman John Ellis cracked a three-run, first-inning homer off ex-Indian Luis Tiant to put the Tribe ahead for good. Brother Jim got his third win of the year and 197th career victory. Tom Buskey got the save. Brother Gaylord, sporting a 4-1 record, was in the midst of a 15-game winning streak. The younger Perry didn't lose a game until July 8th, when he lost a 10-inning contest, 4-3, to the Oakland Athletics before 47,582 in Oakland.

The Indians' 10¢ Beer Night

It was "10¢ Beer Night" at the Stadium on Tuesday, June 4, 1974, as manager Ken Aspromonte's third-place Cleveland Indians hosted manager Billy Martin's Texas Rangers (with rookie Texas first baseman Mike Hargrove hitting .358), before 25,134, who consumed an estimated 60,000 10-ounce 3.2% beers at the game. The crowd began getting out of hand in the fourth inning, when a few rowdies ran across the field. In the sixth inning, a fan disrobed and streaked across the outfield. In the seventh inning, fans began tossing fireworks at Texas players, forcing the Rangers to evacuate their bullpen. The Indians had rallied to tie the game at 5-5 in the ninth inning, with two outs and a runner on third base, when spectators leaped over the Stadium wall and tried to steal the cap of Texas right fielder Jeff Burroughs (above, center). As Burroughs fought back, both benches emptied with bats in hand to protect their teammates from the hundreds of hooligans, some with knives, that mobbed the field as fireworks rained from the upper deck. After umpire Nestor Chylak was hit on the head during the 10-minute melee, the game was called and the Tribe forced to absorb a 9-0 forfeit loss, the first forfeit in Indians history. Chylak told reporters, "They were uncontrollable beasts. The only other place you might experience this is a [expletive deleted] zoo."

CLEVELAND
John Lowenstein 3b
Jack Brohamer 2b
Leron Lee lf
Charlie Spikes rf
Oscar Gamble dh
George Hendrick cf
Ossie Blanco 1b
Dave Duncan c
Frank Duffy ss
Fritz Peterson p

TEXAS
Cesar Tovar cf
Lenny Randle 2b
Alex Johnson lf
Jeff Burroughs rf
Tom Grieve dh
Jim Fregosi 1b
Larry Brown 3b
Toby Harrah ss
Jim Sundberg c
Ferguson Jenkins p

(Above) Nestor Chylak leads the umpire crew off the field after calling the game. **(Right)** Tribe pitcher Tom Hilgendorf gets assistance after being hit by a steel folding chair during the riot.

Dick Bosman's No-Hitter

Reeling from six straight losses, manager Ken Aspromonte's Cleveland Indians faced the Oakland Athletics with Reggie Jackson at the Stadium on Friday, July 19, 1974. The Athletics were leading the American League West and riding a six-game win streak. It took 30-year-old Tribe right-hander Dick Bosman only 79 pitches to break Cleveland's losing ways by beating the World Champion Athletics, 4-0, with his first major league no-hitter. In the ninth inning, Bosman got Dick Green to ground out to third baseman Buddy Bell and pinch-hitter Jesus Alou to ground out to second baseman Jack Brohamer. The final out came when Bosman struck out Oakland lead-off hitter Bill North with a sailing fast-ball. A perfect game was prevented when Bosman, making his fifth start of the season, threw wildly to first base after fielding a two-out, fourth-inning infield chopper by Sal Bando. Bosman then struck out Jackson to strand Bando at second, one of four strikeouts Bosman recorded. Of the 79 pitches Bosman threw, sixty were strikes. Among the 24,304 who experienced the history-making performance were Bosman's wife, their four-year-old daughter, his youngest sister and his parents from Kenosha, Wisconsin. It was the Tribe's first no-hitter pitched since June 10, 1966, when Sonny Siebert beat the Washington Senators, 2-0, and only the 13th no-hitter in Cleveland Indians history. Bosman ended the year with a 7-5 record.

CLEVELAND
John Lowenstein lf
Frank Duffy ss
George Hendrick cf
Charlie Spikes rf
John Ellis c
Buddy Bell 3b
Tom McCraw 1b
Joe Lis dh
Jack Brohamer 2b
Dick Bosman p

Manager: Ken Aspromonte

OAKLAND
Bill North cf
Bert Campaneris ss
Sal Bando 3b
Reggie Jackson rf
Joe Rudi lf
Claudell Washington dh
Pat Bourque 1b
Dick Green 2b
Larry Haney c
Dave Hamilton p

Manager: Alvin Dark

Time of Game: 1:56

(Left) Tribe right-hander Dick Bosman is mobbed by batterymate, catcher John Ellis (center), and third baseman Buddy Bell (left), after pitching his first no-hitter. Bell, who went 2 for 3, drove in one run with a double and scored the Tribe's other run. Designated hitter Joe Lis helped Bosman's cause with what turned out to be the game-winning blast, a two-run homer in the third inning. Bell and Ellis, who was starting his first game in three weeks in relief of starting catcher Dave Duncan, scored the Tribe's two other runs in the fourth inning.

(Below) Bosman waves to the crowd after the no-hitter.

Manager Frank Robinson's Debut

The Cleveland Indians opened the 1975 baseball season at the Stadium on Tuesday, April 8th, with Mrs. Rachel Robinson, the widow of Jackie Robinson, the first black to break baseball's color barrier, throwing out the ceremonial first pitch. The reason for Mrs. Robinson's Opening Day appearance was the debut of 39-year-old Frank Robinson as the first black manager in major league baseball history. Robinson, starting his 20th major league season, was beginning his tenure as the Cleveland Indians' 28th manager and the team's third player-manager following in the footsteps of hall-of-famers Tris Speaker and Lou Boudreau. 56,715 hearty souls braved the 36° game-time temperature to experience the historic event. Playing in their bright red home uniforms, the Indians battled manager Bill Virdon's New York Yankees who opened with ex-Indians Graig Nettles, Chris Chambliss and Lou Piniella in the starting lineup. Cleveland beat the Yankees, 5-3, with Robinson hitting a home run in his first at bat to start the Tribe scoring. The first-inning blast was his 575th career homer and 2,901 career base hit. 36-year-old veteran right-hander Gaylord Perry pitched a complete game, striking out six, for his 199th career win. After the game Perry, who had challenged Robinson during spring training, gave the game ball to his new leader. Robinson's contract was reported to be a one-year deal worth $200,000.

(Above) Robinson, at the time, the only player to win Most Valuable Player Awards in both the American and National Leagues, tips his cap after being introduced to the crowd. The charged audience responded with a minute-long standing ovation when the Tribe's new manager was introduced. Robinson received a second ovation after hitting his first-inning home run. Cleveland finished the year in fourth place, fifteen and a half games behind the pennant-winning Boston Red Sox.

(Above right) Baseball commissioner Bowie Kuhn (at the microphone,) called it "a historic day for baseball," while addressing the Opening Day crowd before the game. At Kuhn's right is Mayor Ralph J. Perk. **(Right)** After throwing out the first pitch, Rachael Robinson, at right, told the crowd, "Cleveland fans and owners, I am proud, proud, proud to be here and I want to congratulate you on honoring yourself by being the first to take this important step."

(Left) New Tribe skipper Frank Robinson (right), is greeted by Tribe infielder John Lowenstein after hitting his first-inning homer. Robinson, the second batter to face Yankee starter George (Doc) Medich, drove Medich's eighth pitch, a 2-2 fast ball, over the left field fence 360 feet away, for the home run. Cleveland Press sports reporter Bob Sudyk wrote, "It was one of the most dramatic home runs in baseball history." Robinson finished the 1975 season with a .237 average and nine homers in 118 at bats.

(Right) Six foot-four, 250-pound first baseman John Wesley (Boog) Powell (left), traded by the Baltimore Orioles to the Indians with pitcher Don Hood for catcher Dave Duncan and a minor leaguer on February 25, 1975, made his debut in a Cleveland uniform on April 8th. The 33-year-old slugger called it his greatest opening day after scoring three runs and driving in two with a walk, single, double and home run. Congratulating Powell after his fourth-inning homer is Tribe outfielder Oscar Gamble. Powell played in 134 games for Cleveland in 1975, batting .297 with 27 homers in 435 at bats. Gamble, who played in 121 games, batted .261 for the season with 91 hits, including fifteen homers, in 348 times at the plate.

(Far left) Second baseman Duane Kuiper got his first major league hit, but the fifth-place Cleveland Indians still lost to the Milwaukee Brewers, 4-3, on September 24, 1974. The Indians finished the year in fourth place with a 77-85 record. **(Center left)** The fifth-place Cleveland Indians lost to the Milwaukee Brewers, 10-3, on September 24, 1975. The Indians finished 1975 in fourth place with a 79-80 record. **(Left)** The Cleveland Indians finished the 1976 season in fourth place with a 81-78 record.

Welcome Back, Bill Veeck Night

The Stadium clock was turned back thirty years on Friday, June 11, 1976, as the second-place Cleveland Indians hosted the Chicago White Sox on "Welcome Back, Bill Veeck" Night, held to honor 62-year-old Bill Veeck Jr., who was bringing his White Sox to town for a four-game weekend series. The special evening was scheduled ten days shy of when the Cleveland Indians were purchased by Veeck, who served as president of the team from 1946 to 1949. Among those paying tribute to Veeck were Joe Earley, the subject of a Veeck promotion in 1948 as "Mr. Average Fan," Rudie Schaffer, who served as the Indians' business manager during the Veeck regime, and Charley Lupica, a loyal fan who became a national celebrity when he perched atop a flagpole during the 1949 season. The game was played before a "Beer Night" crowd of only 11,984, in part because a media-hyped "feud" between Veeck and Indians player-manager Frank Robinson. The White Sox owner had reportedly upset Robinson the week before while the Indians played a weekend series in Chicago. Veeck had gone beyond the American League

time limit between games of a Sunday double-header at Comiskey Park to present, "A Salute to Mexico," one of his infamous promotions. Robinson wanted to get the second game underway without delay and head back to Cleveland. Robinson gained some measure of satisfaction over the former Tribe owner on "Veeck Night," when he drove his 584th career homer into the left field stands with second baseman Larvell Blanks on board, giving the Indians a dramatic, 5-4, thirteen-inning victory.

(Above) Veeck (left), was presented a number of gag gifts before the game. Among the presents were the huge tie and a leisure suit inside the gift-wrapped box he received from former Cleveland Indians first-baseman Luke Easter (right).

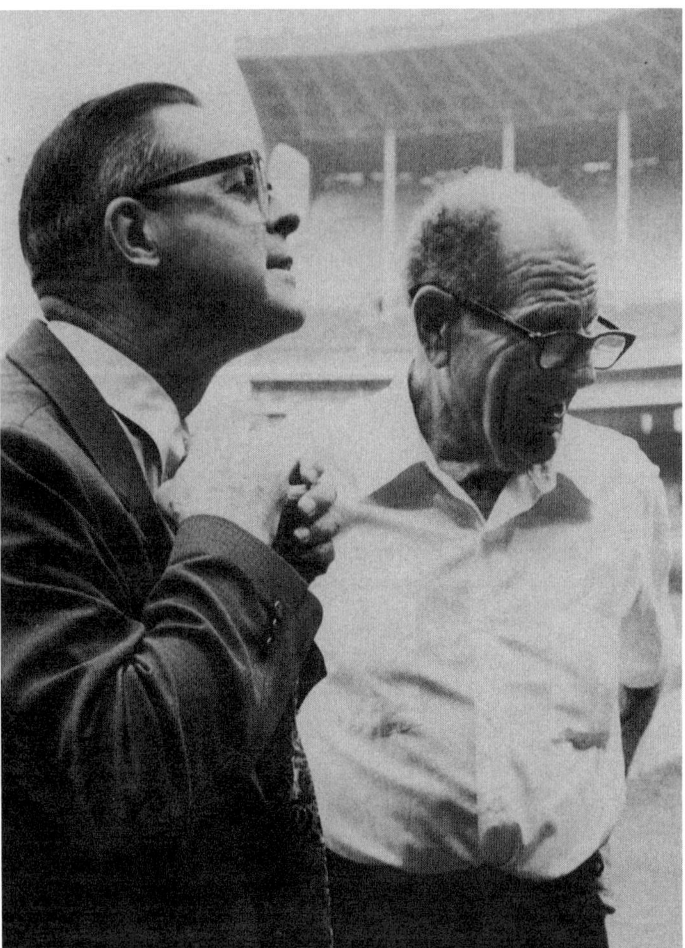

(Left) Veeck joins Joe Earley (left), who was the featured honoree on 'Good Ole Joe Earley' Night at the Stadium in September of 1948. Earley was driven to home plate during pre-game festivities in a gray Rolls Royce.

(Above) After hitting his game-winning homer in the 13th inning off White Sox reliever Terry Forster, Indians player-manager Frank Robinson (center), was mobbed at home plate by his teammates, including catcher Ray Fosse (10), Duane Kuiper (18), third baseman Buddy Bell (second, right), and catcher Alan Ashby (far right). Bell, who raised his average to .309, homered earlier in the game to give Cleveland a one-run lead. Larvell Blanks went 4 for 6, including hitting a triple.

(Far left) Charley Lupica stands atop a specially-built flag pole during Bill Veeck Night. In 1949, Lupica became a national celebrity by living on a flag pole while he waited for the Indians to take over first place. On Sunday, September 25th, with the Tribe in third place, Lupica came down after an 118-day stay.

(Left) Veeck, signing an autograph, was the guest of honor at a pre-game picnic held behind the outfield fence. Such picnics were common during the Veeck era. Veeck was the last to leave the Stadium, departing hours after the game ended.

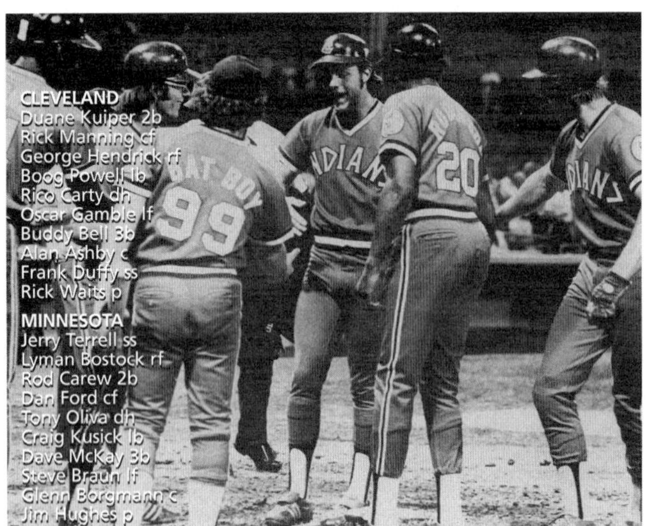

August 29, 1975 / Cleveland-9, Minnesota-6

The fourth-place Cleveland Indians, with a 61-67 record, hosted the fifth-place Minnesota Twins in a night game on Friday, August 29, 1975, before 6,520 at the Stadium. Cleveland was leading, 5-4, in the bottom of the eighth inning, when 20-year-old rookie center fielder Rick Manning, batting .285 with 2 homers, came up to bat with the bases loaded. Facing left-handed Twins reliever Vic Albury, Manning (center at left), hit his first major-league grand slam, driving a 1-0, waist-high fast ball 375 feet over the right-center field fence. The blast scored catcher Alan Ashby (far right), shortstop Frank Duffy (second from left), and pinch-hitter Frank Robinson (20). Credit for the Indians' 9-6 victory went to right-hander Don Hood, who relieved starter Rick Waits. After the game, Manning was reportedly fined $1 by the team's Kangaroo Court for being a "hot-dog" while rounding the bases after hitting his home run. Manning finished the year with a .285 average and 137 hits in 120 games. Twins second baseman Rod Carew went 2 for 2, raising his league-leading average to .370.

July 2, 1976 / Bob Lemon is Honored

Manager Billy Martin's league-leading New York Yankees played the second game of a four-game holiday weekend series against the second-place Cleveland Indians on Friday, July 2, 1976, before 35,000 at the Stadium. Yankee starter Catfish Hunter got the win, beating Cleveland, 7-1. Ex-Indians Lou Piniella and Chris Chambliss homered to lead the Yankee charge. Tribe starter Rick Waits, ousted in the first inning, saw his record fall to 2-3. The Indians lost again to the Yankees, 7-3, on Saturday, July 3rd before a "Bat Night" crowd of 64,500. On Sunday, the 4th, a bicentennial fireworks display followed the game.

(Right) New York Yankees coach Bob Lemon samples one of the 20 lemon pies he was presented before the game. Lemon, a former star hurler for the Cleveland Indians, received the pies in recognition of his recent election into baseball's Hall of Fame. Lemon compiled a 207-128 career record from 1947 to 1958 for Cleveland, winning 20 or more games seven times.

September 7, 1977 / New York-4, Cleveland-3

"Two Million Dollar Man" Wayne Garland started on the mound for Cleveland, as manager Jeff Torborg's Indians battled manager Billy Martin's first-place New York Yankees on Sunday, September 7, 1977, before 7,284 at the Stadium. The Indians led, 3-0, after eight innings, with Garland pitching a five-hitter. But in the ninth inning, New York scored three runs off Garland to tie the score. Yankee catcher Thurman Munson led off the 10th inning with a single. The next batter, right fielder Reggie Jackson, blooped a single toward Indians left fielder Bruce Bochte off reliever Jim Kern. Munson, who never stopped running, scored the winning run from first base. Yankee starter Ron Guidry pitched a complete game for the win, while Garland's record dropped to 10-18. Cleveland finished the year in fifth place with a 71-90 record. The Yankees went on to win the World Series, as Jackson earned the nickname "Mr. October."

(Right) Yankees president George Steinbrenner (center, with tie), celebrates from his box seat above the visitors dugout after Munson (15), scores the go-ahead run. Sitting with Steinbrenner is his wife (at left), and Yankees general manager Gabe Paul (next to George), who left the Cleveland Indians organization in 1973 to join Steinbrenner when George purchased the Yankees. Steinbrenner, no stranger to Cleveland sports, once owned the Cleveland Pipers of the old American Basketball League in the early 1960's.

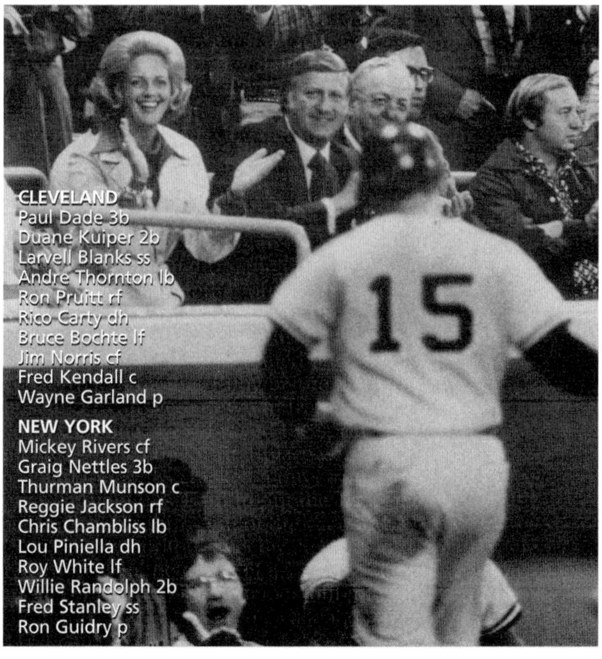

Dennis Eckersley's No-Hitter

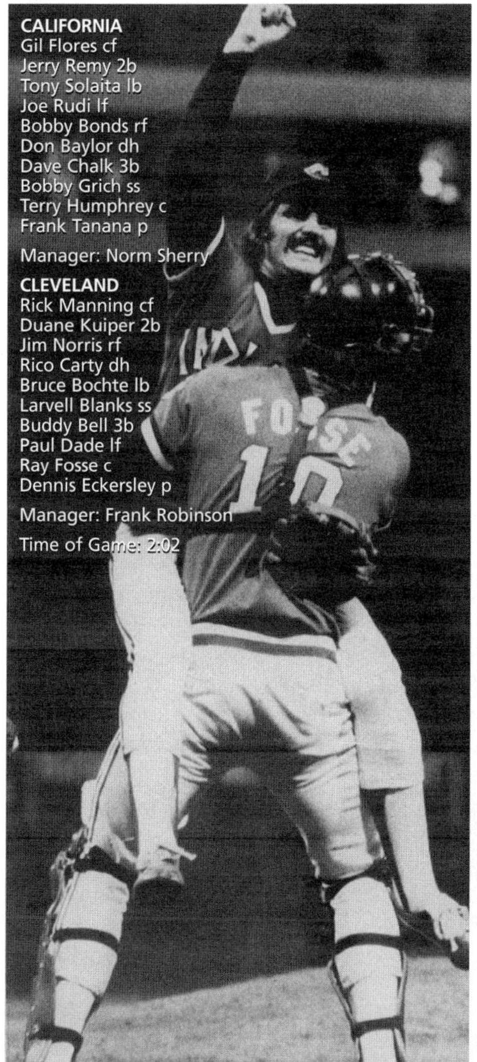

CALIFORNIA
Gil Flores cf
Jerry Remy 2b
Tony Solaita 1b
Joe Rudi lf
Bobby Bonds rf
Don Baylor dh
Dave Chalk 3b
Bobby Grich ss
Terry Humphrey c
Frank Tanana p

Manager: Norm Sherry

CLEVELAND
Rick Manning cf
Duane Kuiper 2b
Jim Norris rf
Rico Carty dh
Bruce Bochte 1b
Larvell Blanks ss
Buddy Bell 3b
Paul Dade lf
Ray Fosse c
Dennis Eckersley p

Manager: Frank Robinson

Time of Game: 2:02

After hurling seven and 2/3 innings of hitless ball in his last outing, on Monday, May 30, 1977, 22-year-old Cleveland Indians right-hander Dennis Eckersley entered the record books by pitching the 14th no-hitter in Indians history, beating starter Frank Tanana and the California Angels, 1-0, before 13,400 in the Stadium. Eckersley started the 9th inning by striking out shortstop Bobby Grich and rookie pinch-hitter Willie Aikens. The final out came when Eckersley struck out lead-off hitter Gil Flores on a checked-swing third strike. Eckersley walked only one batter, Tony Solaita, who was down 0-2, on a 3-2 pitch with two out in the first inning. Eckersley struck out twelve on 114 pitches (83 fastballs, 31 breaking pitches). The only other Angel to get on board was outfielder Bobby Bonds, who reached first on a third-strike wild pitch in the eighth inning. The no-hitter was the first recorded at the Stadium since July 19, 1974, when Tribe hurler Dick Bosman beat the Oakland Athletics. Tanana, who pitched a five-hitter, striking out six, saw his record fall to 8-2.

(Far left, left) Cleveland catcher Ray Fosse (10), celebrates with Eckersley following the final out. Tribe president Ted Bonda announced after the game that Eckersley would receive a $3,500 bonus for pitching the no-hitter and Fosse would receive a $1,500 bonus for calling the game. Eckersley, Cleveland's No. 3 pick in the June 1972 free-agent draft, joined the Indians in 1975 and was named rookie of the year by the Sporting News after compiling a 13-7 record with a 2.60 ERA. Eckersley, who raised his record to 5-3, finished the 1977 season with a 14-13 record and 191 strikeouts.

(Below) Eckersley closes out the 9th inning. Cleveland's lone run came in the first inning, when second baseman Duane Kuiper tripled and then scored on a suicide-sacrifice bunt by right fielder Jim Norris. The following year, Eckersley won 20 games for the Boston Red Sox.

The 64-59 Cleveland Indians hosted the 54-72 Minnesota Twins before 14,211 at the Stadium on Monday, August 25, 1980. On the mound for Cleveland was right-hander Dan Spillner, who won his 12th game of the year, beating the Twins, 4-3, with help from rookie "Super Joe" Charboneau. Charboneau (second from right), hit a three-run homer, his 18th, in the fourth inning scoring catcher Ron Hassey (right), and third baseman Toby Harrah. The Tribe win spoiled the debut of Johnny Goryl, who replaced Gene Mauch as manager of the Twins. Charboneau was named the American League's Rookie of the Year in 1980, after ending the season with 87 runs-batted-in, 23 home runs, 131 hits in 131 games, and a .289 average in 453 at bats.

CLEVELAND
Miguel Dilone lf
Jorge Orta rf
Mike Hargrove 1b
Ron Hassey c
Toby Harrah 3b
Jack Brohamer 2b
Joe Charboneau dh
Rick Manning cf
Tom Veryzer ss
Dan Spillner p

MINNESOTA
Hosken Powell rf
John Castino 3b
Roy Smalley ss
Glen Adams dh
Mike Cubbage 1b
Butch Wynegar c
Rick Sofield cf
Rob Wilfong 2b
Bombo Riviera lf
Fernando Arroyo p

Len Barker's Perfect Game   May 15, 1981

CLEVELAND
Rick Manning cf
Jorge Orta rf
Mike Hargrove 1b
Andre Thornton dh
Ron Hassey c
Toby Harrah 3b
Joe Charboneau lf
Duane Kuiper 2b
Tom Veryzer ss
Len Barker p

Manager: Dave Garcia

TORONTO
Alfredo Griffin ss
Lloyd Moseby rf
George Bell lf
John Mayberry 1b
Willie Upshaw dh
Damaso Garcia 2b
Rick Bosetti cf
Danny Ainge 3b
Buck Martinez c
Luis Leal p

Manager: Bobby Mattick

Last out:
Ernie Whitt ph

Home run: Orta

Time of Game: 2:09

"I had total command, I could throw anything, anywhere I wanted," declared 25-year-old Tribe right-hander Leonard Harold (Len) Barker on Friday, May 15, 1981, after hurling major league baseball's first perfect game since 1968, a 3-0 win over the Toronto Blue Jays before 7,290 at the Stadium. Pitching in a light mist with a game-time temperature of 49 degrees, Barker struck out 11 and allowed only four fly balls. Only one batter came close to getting a hit off Barker. In the first inning, Alfredo Griffin sent a ground ball up the middle. Shortstop Tom Veryzer made the difficult play to get Griffin at first base. Pitching coach Dave Duncan reported that 60 of the

103 pitches Barker threw were curveballs, with 45 thrown for strikes. Barker threw a total of 84 strikes and never threw more than five balls in any inning. The win raised the first-place Indians' record to 16-8 and Barker's record to 3-1. It was the 11th perfect game pitched in major league history and the only perfect game ever recorded at the Stadium. The only other perfect game thrown by a Cleveland pitcher came on October 2, 1908, when Cleveland Naps right-hander Adrian (Addie) Joss beat the Chicago White Sox, 1-0, at old League Park. Barker's ERA dropped to 1.06 with the win.

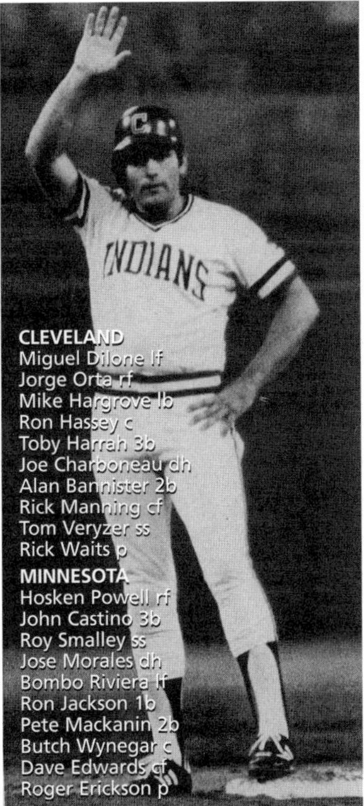

August 26, 1980
Mike Hargrove's 1,000th Hit

The 6th-place Cleveland Indians faced the Minnesota Twins on Tuesday, August 26, 1980, before 6,483 at the Stadium. In the fourth inning, Tribe first baseman Dudley Michael (Mike) Hargrove, batting in the third spot, rapped his only hit that evening, a double, for his 1,000th career hit. Catcher Ron Hassey, the next batter up, singled to drive in Hargrove for the Tribe's only run. Cleveland lost, 5-1, as starter Rick Waits suffered his tenth loss. **(Above)** Hargrove, who averaged 144 hits a year over his first six seasons, waves to the crowd after reaching second base.

July 14, 1981
The All-Star Game that Wasn't

Tuesday, July 14, 1981 turned out to be an open date on the Stadium events calendar, when baseball's All-Star Game scheduled for that evening, was postponed by a players' strike. In place of the baseball classic, WKYC Channel 3 news producers Jon Halpern and Jim Schaefer created their own "All-Star" game by setting up a Strat-O-Matic game board at home plate on the 14th. Halpern, playing the role of National League Manager Dallas Green, wore a Philadelphia Phillies jersey. Schaefer played his counterpart, American League Manager Jim Frey of the Kansas City Royals. The Baseball Bug was there. So was Hall of Famer Bob Feller and local tenor Rocco Scotti, who delivered stirring renditions of "Oh Canada" and "The Star Spangled Banner" to the accompaniment of an accordion player. WKYC sportscaster Jim Mueller even announced the starting lineups over the public address system. Before the final dice were rolled, the outcome had long been decided. The National League overpowered the American League, 15-2, with Pittsburgh Pirates outfielder Dave Parker named the game MVP. Time of Game-1:01. Attendance-58.

August 9, 1981
Rocco Elijah (Scotti) Biscotti

After a "Rally Around Rocco," campaign was launched in May of 1981 by Cleveland Press columnist Bob August, on June 29, 1981, Rocco Scotti, Cleveland's 'Mr. Star Spangled Banner,' received notice of his selection to sing the national anthem at the Stadium during the 1981 All-Star game. The game, first scheduled for July 14th, took place before a record crowd of 72,086 on Saturday, August 9th. Scotti's stirring renditions of "The Star Spangled Banner" and "O Canada," was followed by Vice-President George Bush throwing out the ceremonial first pitch to begin the game. The National League won, 5-4.

(Left) Local favorite Rocco Scotti sings the national anthem at the Stadium in June of 1980.

The Billy Graham Crusade

After preaching to an estimated 44 million people around the world during his 24-year career, evangelist Billy Graham brought his famous Crusade to Cleveland for a 10-night series of spiritual rallies beginning at the Stadium on Friday, July 14, 1972. Though Graham never reached his goal of filling the Stadium in his first trip here, 50,175 came out on Sunday, July, 23rd to hear Graham on the final night. His Northern Ohio Crusade attracted 372,440 visitors, many more than hoped for. Graham was most moved by the 19,609 who came forward during his stay, the third highest number reached during a 10-day Graham Crusade. Graham's next stop was Nagaland on the China-India border.

(Above) On Monday, July 17th, the fourth night of the Crusade, 2,722 came forward, filling the Stadium infield. The number of persons making the walk from their seats to the platform passed the 8,000 mark that evening. The next night Graham spoke during what he called, "One of the greatest thunderstorms I've ever seen at a Crusade."

(Left) 76-year-old singer Ethel Waters was among the featured performers on July 14th as evangelist Billy Graham opened his Northern Ohio Crusade at the Stadium.

(Right) Over 34,000 turned out on opening night to hear Graham speak on "God's Unchanging Word in a Revolutionary World." That night, a volunteer choir of 6,000 formed one of the largest choral groups ever assembled for a Graham Crusade. More than 1,600 came forward on the 14th.

World Series of Rock- Rolling Stones/Pink Floyd

June 14, 1975

The Rolling Stones

It was called the world's largest rock concert held in an outdoor stadium, as over 80,000 watched Mick Jagger and The Rolling Stones headline the World Series of Rock concert at the Stadium on Saturday, June 14, 1975. Vitale's Madmen began the day-long music fest at 2:30 P.M., followed by the Tower of Power and the J. Geils Band. The Rolling Stones took the stage at 7:12 P.M., leading off with "Honky Tonk Woman."

(Below, Right) Concert fans at the Stadium on June 14th. Concert promoter Jules Belkin told a reporter that 82,800 tickets were sold at $10 each.

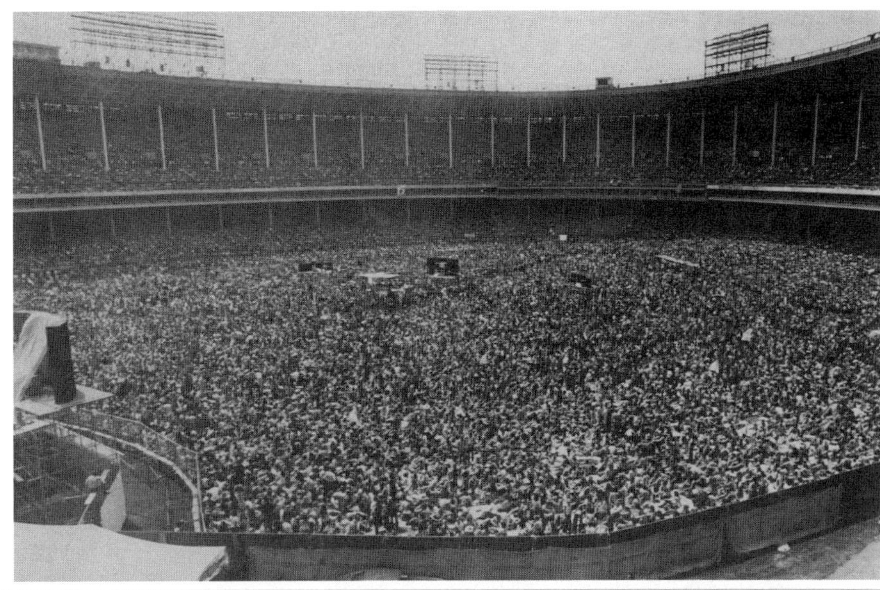

June 25, 1977 / Pink Floyd

A new record was set for concert attendance at the Stadium on Saturday, June 25, 1977, when 83,199 paid to see the second World Series of Rock concert of the season featuring British rockers Pink Floyd in their only Midwest appearance.

(Above) A giant 50' pink balloon pig hangs above the Stadium infield during the Pink Floyd concert. It was one of the inflatable animals pulled above the crowd as Pink Floyd performed songs from their new "Animals" album.

(Left) Pink Floyd fans wait for the doors to open at 6 P.M. Rain delayed the concert start by a half hour. General admission tickets were $10.50 before the show and $12.50 on the day of the concert.

Football at the Stadium

October 11, 1970 / Cleveland 30, Cincinnati-27

The Cleveland Browns (2-1), faced new Central Division rivals, the Cincinnati Bengals (1-2), who were making their first appearance at the Stadium on Sunday, October 11, 1970. The game, played before 83,250, also marked the first appearance of Cincinnati head coach Paul Brown in the Stadium since being fired as head coach of the Browns in 1962. Cleveland scored on TD passes from QB Bill Nelsen to HB Leroy Kelly and TE Milt Morin, and when DT Walter Johnson sacked Bengal QB Virgil Carter for a safety, but trailed at halftime, 17-16. In the second half, the Browns scored 14 points on one-yard runs by Kelly and FB Bo Scott to win 30-27. One drive was kept alive when veteran Browns OT Dick Schafrath, touching the ball for the first time, rambled 27 yards after picking up a Kelly fumble.

(Right) Forty-five minutes before the game, and before most fans had arrived, Browns head coach Blanton Collier (left), met with Bengals head coach Paul Brown near the 50-yard line. Collier worked as an assistant coach under Brown beginning in 1946, when Brown served as head coach of the Cleveland Browns, and succeeded Brown as Browns head coach after Brown was fired after the 1962 season.

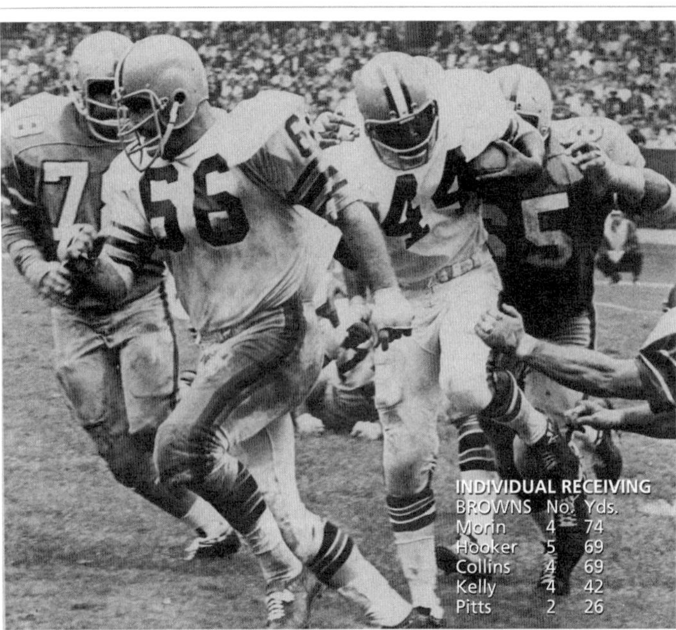

INDIVIDUAL RECEIVING		
BROWNS	No.	Yds.
Morin	4	74
Hooker	5	69
Collins	4	69
Kelly	4	42
Pitts	2	26

September 19, 1971 / The Home Opener

"Now they're gamblers," said Houston Oilers QB Charley Johnson of Cleveland's veteran 'rubber band' defense, after completing only 9 of 19 for 109 yards with five interceptions in the Oilers' 31-0 loss to the Browns on Sunday, September 19, 1971. Rookie DB Clarence Scott intercepted two Johnson passes. The game, played before 73,387 at the Stadium, was both a win for Nick Skorich, in his debut as head coach of the Browns, and Cleveland's first Opening Day shutout since 1953. Browns QB Bill Nelsen led the charge, completing 17 of 31 for 254 yards, including TD passes to flanker Gary Collins and WR Frank Pitts. Oilers RB Earl Campbell was held to only 22 yards on 11 carries.

(Left) Browns guard Gene Hickerson (66), leads the way for HB Leroy Kelly (44). The Browns' first two TDs came on one-yard runs by Kelly, who led all rushers with 60 yards on 17 carries.

October 15, 1972 / Chicago-17, Cleveland-0

On Sunday, October 15, 1972, the Cleveland Browns (2-2), faced the Chicago Bears (0-3-1), before 72,339 at the Stadium. Leading Chicago at quarterback was fleet-footed Bobby Douglass, who completed only two of nine passes, but carried the ball 11 times for 117 yards and six points, as the "Monsters of the Midway" flattened the Browns, 17-0. One of his two completions went to TE Earl Thomas for Chicago's other TD. Mac Percival added a field goal and the extra points. Frustrated by the Bears' fierce linebacker blitz led by MLB Dick Butkus, the Cleveland offense gained only 37 yards on the ground. Browns QBs Mike Phipps and Bill Nelsen threw for only 126 more. After the win, Douglass presented the game ball to first year Bears coach Abe Gibron, a former guard for the Browns, in celebration of his first victory as head coach and Chicago's first shutout since 1965.

(Left) Bears QB Bobby Douglass (10), takes off on third down against Browns defender DE Rich Jackson (87). No. 61 is Bears OG Glen Holloway.

(**Below**) The photograph appeared on the front page of The Cleveland Press on October 14, 1974, after Cleveland lost to the Cincinnati Bengals, 34-24. (**Below center**) At the Stadium on December 14, 1975. The Cleveland Browns beat the Kansas City Chiefs, 40-14, in the last home game of the season. Cleveland finished the year at 3-11. (**Below right**) At the Stadium on August 25, 1977. Former Browns QB Mike Phipps returned to lead the Chicago Bears against the Browns in a pre-season contest. Phipps completed only 3 of 13 and was sacked five times in Chicago's 14-7 loss to the Browns.

December 11, 1977 / 42's Last Home Game

Veteran WR Paul Warfield played his last game before the home crowd on Sunday, December 11, 1977, as the Cleveland Browns faced the Houston Oilers before only 30,898 at the Stadium. David Mays started at QB for the Browns, but was replaced with Cleveland down, 7-0, by rookie Terry Luck. Luck, who threw to TE Gary Parris in the fourth quarter for the team's only TD, completed 16 of 27 for 188 yards. The Browns led in total yardage, 400-167, and first downs, 22-10, but lost, 19-15. Two Browns points came on a safety by DT Jerry Sherk, who registered eight unassisted tackles. The Oilers scored on a 72-yard punt return by Billy "White Shoes" Johnson and a three-yard run by HB Ronnie Coleman. Oilers QB Dan Pastorini completed 7 of 12 for 74 yards. Browns HB Greg Pruitt, who rushed for 92 yards, needed only 41 more to reach his third straight 1,000 yard season. The next day, Forrest Gregg announced he was stepping down as head coach of the Browns.

(**Right**) WR Paul Warfield is greeted by fans after playing in his last home game. Warfield, who announced his retirement after playing 14 seasons in the National Football League, caught two Luck passes for 24 yards.

INDIVIDUAL RUSHING

BROWNS	Att.	Yds.
G. Pruitt	23	92
Poole	1	5
C. Miller	15	84
Luck	2	-3

INDIVIDUAL RECEIVING

BROWNS	No.	Yds.
Rucker	7	101
G. Pruitt	5	42
Logan	1	21
C. Miller	2	20
Parris	2	14
Warfield	2	24

INDIVIDUAL RUSHING

BROWNS	Att.	Yds.
G. Pruitt	22	106
Newsome	1	33
Sipe	4	32
C. Miller	10	31
M. Pruitt	2	6
T. Sullivan	2	5

INDIVIDUAL RECEIVING

BROWNS	No.	Yds.
Rucker	3	113
G. Pruitt	3	25
Logan	1	24
C. Miller	3	15
M. Pruitt	1	7
Newsome	1	6

September 3, 1978
The Season Opener

After finishing the 1977 season with a 6-8-0 record under coach Forrest Gregg, new head coach Sam Rutigliano's Cleveland Browns opened the 1978 season on Sunday, September 3rd against the San Francisco 49ers before 68,973 at the Stadium. Cleveland scored twice in the first half on a 2-yard run by HB Greg Pruitt and a 33-yard run by rookie TE Ozzie Newsome to lead, 14-7. Two more scores in the fourth quarter on a 69-yard TD pass from QB Brian Sipe to WR Reggie Rucker and a Don Cockroft field goal gave Cleveland a 24-7 victory. Sipe completed 12 of 25 for 190 yards. Pruitt gained 106 yards on 22 carries. The 49ers' only TD came on a seven-yard pass from QB Steve DeBerg to TE Ken MacAfee.

(**Left**) OG Robert E. Jackson (68), leads the way for rookie TE Ozzie Newsome (82), who scored his first regular season touchdown. After sprinting 33 yards for the score, Newsome celebrated by spiking the ball.

The First Monday Night Football Game

Trivia quiz: Who were the three sportscasters who worked the broadcast booth during the first Monday Night Football game? The answer: Howard Cosell, Don Meredith and Keith Jackson were the men wearing the headphones at 9 P.M. on September 21, 1970, when coach Blanton Collier's Cleveland Browns faced the Super Bowl Champion New York Jets at the Stadium in the first ABC-TV Monday Night Football contest. Led by "Broadway Joe" Namath at quarterback, the Jets were making their National Football League debut after playing in the old American Football League. The game was played before a record home opening crowd of 85,703, the thirteenth straight turnout of over 80,000 for a home Browns contest. Cleveland was outgained in total offense, 455 to 221 yards, but capitalized on Jets mistakes to win the Monday night battle, 31-21. The Browns scored twice in the first quarter on an eight-yard pass from QB Bill Nelsen to flanker Gary Collins and a two-yard run by FB Bo Scott to lead 14-0. New York narrowed the score before the half to 14-7, on a two-yard, second-period run by HB Emerson Boozer. Two scores by Cleveland on a 94-yard kickoff return by Homer Jones, and a 27-yard Don Cockroft field goal countered a second TD by Boozer on a 10-yard run, to give the Browns a 24-14 lead after three quarters. In the fourth quarter, a 33-yard TD pass from Namath to WR George Sauer narrowed the Browns' lead to 24-21. After getting the ball back, the Browns were forced to punt. Don Cockroft's kick sailed to the Jets' 30-yard line, where return man Mike Battle let it hit the ground, hoping the ball would bounce out of bounds. The ball took a Browns bounce, pinning the Jets on their own four-yard line with less than two minutes of play. A desperation pass by Namath was intercepted by Browns LB Billy Andrews, who returned the pass 25 yards for Cleveland's final score.

(Above) New York Jets QB "Broadway Joe" Namath (above), threw 32 times for 299 yards and a TD. Browns QB Bill Nelsen completed 12 passes for 145 yards and a TD.

(Right) Browns LB Jim Houston (82), heads upfield after intercepting a Namath pass meant for Jets receiver Don Maynard (13), in the second quarter. To Houston's right is Cleveland CB Erich Barnes (40). It was one of three key interceptions made by the Browns. In the second quarter, CB Walt Sumner picked off a Namath pass on the Browns' six yard line to protect a 14-7 lead. LB Billy Andrews added to Cleveland's margin of victory with a fourth quarter interception that he ran back for a TD.

	JETS					BROWNS		
RUSHING:	No.	Yds.					No.	Yds.
Shell	17	108				Scott	9	12
Boozer	14	58				Kelly	20	62
Nock	1	3				Nelsen	1	2
White	1	0						
PASSING:	Att.	Cm.	Yds.	TD	Int.			
Namath	32	19	299	1	3			
Woodall	2	1	7	0	0			
Nelsen	27	12	145	1	0			
RECEIVING:	No.	Yds.					No.	Yds.
Maynard	4	69				Morin	5	90
Boozer	3	38				Scott	4	21
Sauer	10	172				Collins	2	21
White	1	1				Hooker	1	13
Caster	1	19						
Stewart	1	7						

N. Y. JETS	0	7	7	7	**21**
CLEVELAND	14	0	10	7	**31**

FIRST QUARTER
Cle- Collins, 8-yard pass from Nelsen (Cockroft kick)
Cle- Scott, 2-yard run (Cockroft kick)

SECOND QUARTER
NY- Boozer, 2-yard run (Turner kick)

THIRD QUARTER
Cle- Homer Jones, 94-yard kickoff return (Cockroft kick)
NY- Boozer, 10-yard run (Turner kick)
Cle- FG, Cockroft, 27 yards

FOURTH QUARTER
NY- Sauer, 33-yard pass from Namath (Turner kick)
Cle- Andrews, 25-yard interception return (Cockroft kick)

(Right) Cleveland HB Leroy Kelly (44 with ball), led Browns rushers with 62 yards on 20 carries. Jets FB Matt Snell, a former Ohio State University standout, led all rushers with 108 yards on 17 attempts. Coach Weeb Ewbank's Jets outgained the Browns in rushing yardage, 169 to 76 yards. With Namath at quarterback, the Jets picked up 31 first downs to Cleveland's 20, but much of that yardage was negated by 13 Jet penalties for a team record 161 yards. The Browns were penalized eight times for 101 yards.

(Left) Browns WR Gary Collins prepares to catch a pass from QB Bill Nelsen for the game's first score, one of only two passes the veteran receiver caught before being knocked out of the game. Browns TE Milt Morin led Cleveland receivers with five catches for 90 yards. WR George Sauer led the Jets with 10 catches for 172 yards and a TD. The Jets outgained the Browns in passing, 286 yards to 145. In the fourth quarter, the Browns got a break when DE Jack Gregory recovered the fumble by FB Matt Snell at the Browns' seven yard line. Gregory also sacked Namath. Though the game was televised nationally, the broadcast was blacked out locally. WEWS-TV offered the movie "Garden of Evil."

1970 CLEVELAND BROWNS

OT	Jenkins, McKay, Schafrath, Taffoni
G	Copeland, Demarie, Hickerson
C	Hoaglin, Reynolds
DE	Gregory, J. Jones, Snidow
DT	Johnson, Righetti, Sherk
LB	Andrews, Beutler, Garlington, Houston, Lindsey, Matheson
DB	Barnes, Howell, Kellerman, Stevenson, Summers, Sumner
QB	Gault, Nelsen, Phipps
HB	Kelly, Morrison
FB	Engel, Scott
WR	Collins, Hooker, D. Jones, H. Jones
TE	Glass, Morin
K	Cockroft

Cleveland vs. Pittsburgh

October 3, 1970
Cleveland-15, Pittsburgh-7

After losing to the San Francisco 49ers, 34-31, in San Francisco the previous week, the Cleveland Browns (1-1), returned home to face second-year head coach Chuck Noll's Pittsburgh Steelers (0-2), in a Saturday night contest on October 3, 1970, before 84,329 at the Stadium. With starting Browns QB Bill Nelsen sidelined by an injury, the game was billed as "the battle of the rookie quarterbacks," with Don Gault starting for head coach Blanton Collier's Browns against Terry Bradshaw, the Steelers' highly touted first round draft choice. Cleveland scored first when Bradshaw was sacked for a first quarter safety by DE Ron Snidow. Gault connected on only one of 16 passes, a 44-yard strike to TE Chip Glass, before being replaced in the third quarter by rookie teammate Mike Phipps, who was making his first pro appearance. With the Browns down, 7-2, Phipps led Cleveland on a 90-yard, come-from-behind scoring drive, sparked by three long third down pass completions. The quarterback's final toss was a 53-yard pass to

HB Reece Morrison for six points. Three plays later, Browns DB Erich Barnes intercepted a Bradshaw pass and returned it 38 yards for the insurance touchdown. It was the seventh scoring return with an interception of Barnes's career, tying him with Herb Adderly of Dallas for the NFL record in career interception tallies. Barnes joined DB Walt Sumner and LB John Garlington in picking off Bradshaw passes. Pittsburgh's only TD came on a 22-yard second-quarter run by Bradshaw. The Steelers finished ahead in first downs, 17-8, total yardage, 263 to 199, and offensive plays, 62 to 55, but lost the contest, 15-7, falling to 0-3-0. It was Cleveland's seventh straight win over the Steelers dating back to 1966. With two rookies at quarterback, Browns offensive coach Nick Skorich called all the plays, alternating tight ends Chip Glass and Milt Morin as his messengers.

(Above) Cleveland Browns DE Ron Snidow sacks Pittsburgh QB Terry Bradshaw for a first quarter safety. Bradshaw connected on only 13 of 29 passes for 207 yards in his regular season debut at the Stadium. Browns QB Mike Phipps completed three of five passes for 86 yards.

(Left) Browns LB Billy Andrews (52), watches fellow linebacker Jim Houston upend Steelers RB Preston Pearson during Cleveland's 15-7 win. No. 66 is Steelers OG Bruce Van Dyke. No. 56 is Pittsburgh center Ray Mansfield.

October 10, 1971 / Cleveland-27, Pittsburgh-17

The Cleveland Browns and the Pittsburgh Steelers carried identical 2-1-0 AFC Central Division into their match before 83,891 at the Stadium on Sunday, October 10, 1971. It was the eighth straight turnout of over 80,000 at the Stadium, and 17th in the last 20 Browns home games (3,500 $5 standing room tickets went on sale at Gate A at 9 A.M.). Cleveland took a 20-7 halftime lead on a TD catch by 6-4, 236-pound TE Milt Morin, two Don Cockroft field goals and a 19-yard run by FB Bo Scott, who led all rushers with 73 yards on 22 carries. The Steelers' first half score came on a 22-yard pass from QB Terry Bradshaw to E Dave Smith. Pittsburgh rallied in the second half to score 10 points on a field goal and a TD pass, but the Browns countered with a third Cockroft field goal and a seven-yard run by HB Leroy Kelly to beat the Steelers, 27-17, giving the team a one-game lead in the AFC Central Division. Browns QB Bill Nelsen completed 18 of 27 for 236 yards, including seven in the first half to Morin. Bradshaw, who completed only 12 of 27 for 126 yards, was sacked three times.

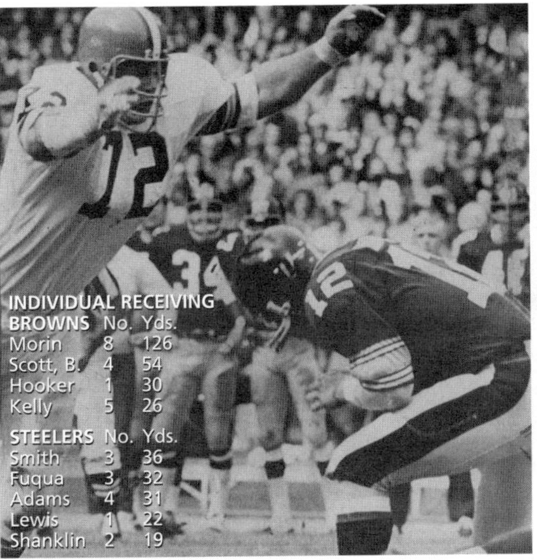

INDIVIDUAL RECEIVING

BROWNS	No.	Yds.
Morin	8	126
Scott, B.	4	54
Hooker	1	30
Kelly	5	26
STEELERS	No.	Yds.
Smith	3	36
Fuqua	3	32
Adams	4	31
Lewis	1	22
Shanklin	2	19

(Left) Browns DE Jerry Sherk (72), sacks Steelers QB Terry Bradshaw.
(Below) TE Milt Morin (89), catches a 19-yard TD pass for the Browns' first score. Morin, who led all receivers with eight receptions for 126 yards, beat rookie Steelers DB Mike Wagner (23), on the play. Five of Morin's first half catches came on third down situations.

INDIVIDUAL RUSHING

BROWNS	Att.	Yds.
Scott	22	73
Kelly	17	63
Nelsen	1	-5
STEELERS	Att.	Yds.
Pearson	7	73
Fuqua	10	22
Bradshaw	3	15

November 19, 1972 / Cleveland-26, Pittsburgh-24

The Cleveland Browns faced the Pittsburgh Steelers on Sunday, November 19, 1972, before 83,009 at the Stadium. The Browns led 20-10 at halftime on a one-yard run by QB Mike Phipps, two field goals by place-kicker Don Cockroft and a 17-yard pass from Phipps to WR Frank Pitts. In the second half, Cleveland scored again in the third quarter on a Cockroft field goal, but gave up two scores on a one-yard run by FB John (Frenchy) Fuqua, and a 75-yard run by rookie FB Franco Harris. With the Steelers leading, 24-23, Cleveland missed a chance to win with 1:58 left in the game, when Cockroft sliced a 27-yard field goal. Fortunately, Browns LB

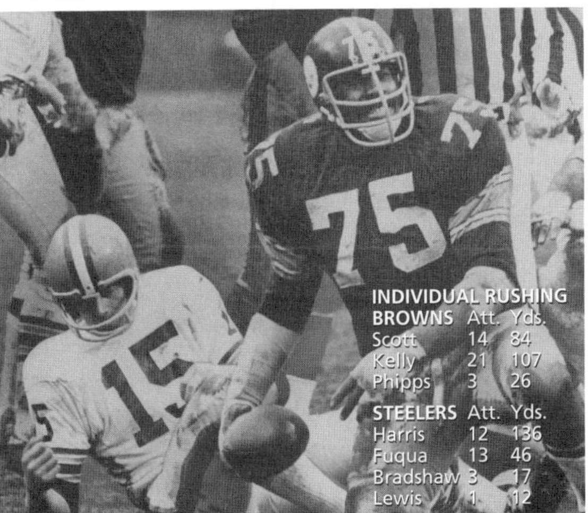

INDIVIDUAL RUSHING

BROWNS	Att.	Yds.
Scott	14	84
Kelly	21	107
Phipps	3	26
STEELERS	Att.	Yds.
Harris	12	136
Fuqua	13	46
Bradshaw	3	17
Lewis	1	12

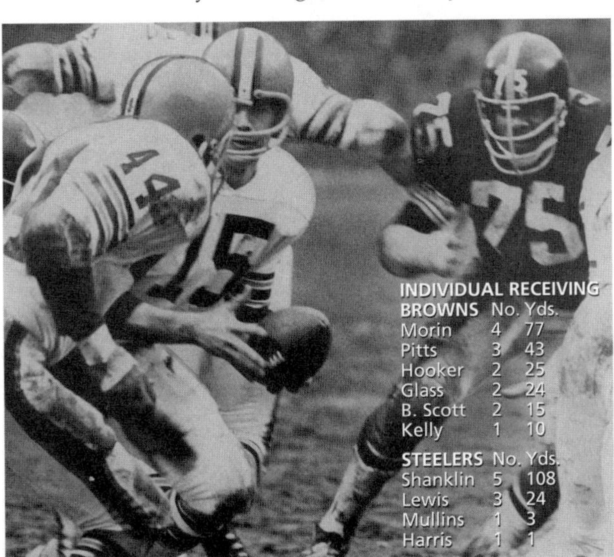

INDIVIDUAL RECEIVING

BROWNS	No.	Yds.
Morin	4	77
Pitts	3	43
Hooker	2	25
Glass	2	24
B. Scott	2	15
Kelly	1	10
STEELERS	No.	Yds.
Shanklin	5	108
Lewis	3	24
Mullins	1	3
Harris	1	1

Dale Lindsey stopped Steelers QB Terry Bradshaw short of a first down, forcing Pittsburgh to punt. With only 13 seconds remaining, Cockroft kicked a game-winning field goal from the 26-yard line. The 26-24 Cleveland win put the Browns in a first-place tie with Pittsburgh for the Central Division lead.

(Above) Pittsburgh DT Mean Joe Greene smiles after recovering a fumble by Mike Phipps (15), that was nullified by an offside call. Phipps completed 14 of 25 for 194 yards. Bradshaw completed 10 of 21 for 136 yards.

(Left) Browns QB Mike Phipps hands off to HB Leroy Kelly (44), who rushed for 107 yards on 21 carries. Pittsburgh's rookie FB Franco Harris led all rushers with 136 yards on 12 carries.

November 25, 1973 / Cleveland-21, Pittsburgh-16

Played at the Stadium before 67,773, (SRO tickets were $5,) the Browns (6-3-1), upset the Pittsburgh Steelers (8-2), 21-16, on Sunday, November 25, 1973, when a 42-yard third down pass to rookie HB Greg Pruitt with only two minutes remaining, set up the winning TD by Pruitt 59 seconds later. Terry Hanratty started at quarterback for Pittsburgh, but left the game early with a wrist injury. Hanratty was replaced by third-string quarterback Joe Gilliam, who led Pittsburgh to its first score, a nine-yard first quarter pass to WR Ron Shanklin. Cleveland scored in the first quarter on a quarterback sneak by QB Mike Phipps. Phipps, who completed only 5 of 17 for 146 yards, connected with Pruitt on a 15-yard TD pass to give the Browns a 14-10 halftime lead. Two Roy Gerela field goals moved Pittsburgh ahead, 16-14, in the fourth-quarter, but with the clock winding down, Phipps dodged the Steelers rush to hit Pruitt on the third down pass that moved the ball to the Steelers' 19-yard line. Two plays later, Pruitt scored on "29 sweep" for the win with Don Cockroft adding the PAT. It was the Steelers' ninth straight loss at the Stadium.

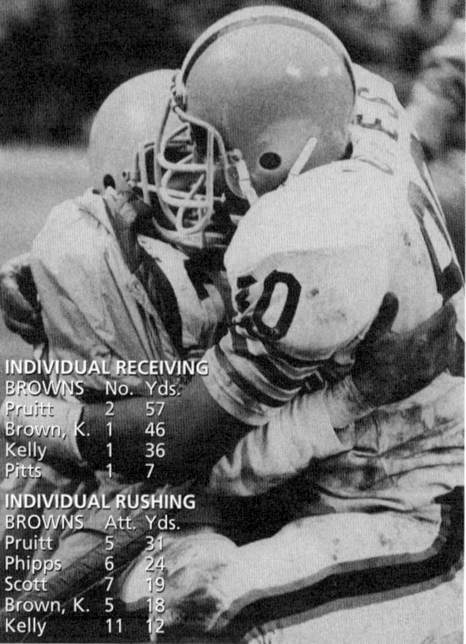

INDIVIDUAL RECEIVING

BROWNS	No.	Yds.
Pruitt	2	57
Brown, K.	1	46
Kelly	1	36
Pitts	1	7

INDIVIDUAL RUSHING

BROWNS	Att.	Yds.
Pruitt	5	31
Phipps	6	24
Scott	7	19
Brown, K.	5	18
Kelly	11	12

(Far left) Rookie HB Greg Pruitt (34), rests on the sidelines after scoring the game-winning TD. Game balls went to Pruitt, each member of the defensive unit, and OG Gene Hickerson, who announced his retirement before the game.

(Left) HB Greg Pruitt gets hugged by Browns DE Joe Jones (80), after scoring the winning TD.

October 5, 1975 / Pittsburgh-42, Cleveland-6

After losing to the Minnesota Vikings, 42-10, at the Stadium the previous week, the Cleveland Browns (0-2), faced the Pittsburgh Steelers on Sunday, October 5, 1975, before a soldout crowd of 73,595 at the Stadium. The Steelers won, 42-6, with Cleveland's only score coming on a seven-yard fourth quarter run by FB Hugh McKinnis. The Browns defense gave up 372 yards in the air to Pittsburgh QBs Terry Bradshaw and Joe Gilliam, allowing Steelers WR Lynn Swan to pick up 126 yards on five receptions and teammate John Stallworth to gain 109 yards on only four catches. The Steelers also gained 122 yards rushing, with FB Franco Harris and HB Rocky Bleier each gaining 37 yards. Browns QB Mike Phipps completed 16 of 31 for 136 yards. Cleveland ended 1975 with a 3-11 record under first-year head coach Forrest Gregg. Pittsburgh went on to beat the Dallas Cowboys in Super Bowl X.

(Right) In the 2nd quarter, a fight broke out when Steelers DT Mean Joe Greene (75), began kicking OG Bob McKay (78), in the groin and stomach. Center Tom DeLeone, who jumped in to help McKay, was ejected with Greene from the game. Other players in the melee were OT Gerry Sullivan (79), TE Garry Parris (84), HB Billy Pritchett (39), OG Chuck Hutchinson (67), DB Glen Edwards (27), and DE L. C. Greenwood (68).

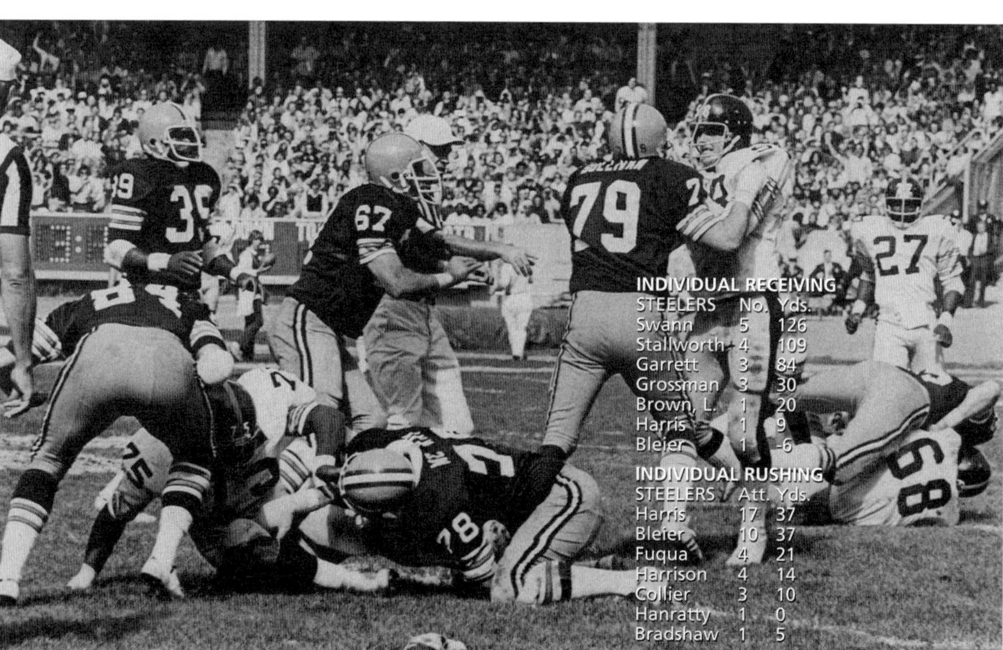

INDIVIDUAL RECEIVING

STEELERS	No.	Yds.
Swann	5	126
Stallworth	4	109
Garrett	3	84
Grossman	3	30
Brown, L.	1	20
Harris	1	9
Bleier	1	-6

INDIVIDUAL RUSHING

STEELERS	Att.	Yds.
Harris	17	37
Bleier	10	37
Fuqua	4	21
Harrison	4	14
Collier	3	10
Hanratty	1	0
Bradshaw	1	5

October 10, 1976
Cleveland-18, Pittsburgh-16

After losing the previous week to the visiting Cincinnati Bengals, 45-24, the Cleveland Browns (1-3), faced their division rivals, the Pittsburgh Steelers (1-3), on Sunday, October 10, 1976, before 76,411 at the Stadium. When starting QB Brian Sipe was knocked out of the game, 27-year-old third string QB David Mays, playing in his first pro game, stepped in to lead the Browns to an 18-16 win over the Steelers. Mays completed five passes for 70 yards and ran three times for 14 yards in the win. Place-kicker Don Cockroft's twelve points on four field goals led the scoring for Cleveland. FB Cleo Miller, who rushed 23 times for 57 yards, scored the Browns' lone TD on a one-yard run. Browns HB Greg Pruitt led all rushers with 76 yards on 22 attempts.

(Right) Steelers QB Terry Bradshaw (12), was sacked four times. The last sack came in the fourth quarter, when Browns DE Joe Jones (64), tackled Bradshaw as the whistle blew. Bradshaw, who complete 10 of 18 for 75 yards, was carried off on a stretcher. Jones was penalized 15 yards for unnecessary roughness.

INDIVIDUAL RECEIVING

BROWNS	No.	Yds.
G. Pruitt	4	55
Rucker	3	77
Warfield	2	36
C. Miller	1	8

INDIVIDUAL RUSHING

BROWNS	Att.	Yds.
C. Miller	23	57
G. Pruitt	22	76
Mays	3	14

INDIVIDUAL RECEIVING

STEELERS	No.	Yds.
Swann	3	74
Harris	6	13
Grossman	3	41
Lewis	1	6

INDIVIDUAL RUSHING

STEELERS	Att.	Yds.
Harris	13	39
Bleier	8	25
Bradshaw	2	17
Kruczek	2	30

October 15, 1978
Pittsburgh-34, Cleveland-14

Played before 81,302 at the Stadium on Sunday, October 15, 1978, coach Sam Rutigliano's Cleveland Browns (3-3), turned over the football four times, twice on fumbles and twice on interceptions, in their 34-14 loss to the Steelers (6-0). Pittsburgh started the scoring with two first quarter field goals by Roy Gerela. Cleveland's first score came on a 17-yard second quarter pass from QB Brian Sipe to TE Dave Logan for six points. Logan's TD catch climaxed a 70-yard drive that began with a 25-yard pass from Sipe to WR Reggie Rucker for the veteran receiver's 300th career reception in the National Football League. On the ensuing kickoff, rookie kick returner Larry Anderson returned Don Cockroft's kickoff 95 yards for a TD, giving Pittsburgh a 13-7 halftime lead. Pittsburgh owned the second half, as the Steelers scored three times on a 28-yard pass from QB Terry Bradshaw to WR Lynn Swann, a one-yard run by HB Rocky Bleier and a 32-yard pass from Bradshaw to TE John Stallworth. Cleveland's lone second half score came on a 28-yard pass from Sipe to Rucker. Sipe finished with 17 completions in 30 attempts for 213 yards. Bradshaw completed 21 of 30 for 175 yards. Bleier led all rushers with 57 yards on 13 carries. FB Calvin Hill led Browns rushers with 42 yards on 10 attempts.

(Above left) Pittsburgh's Mean Joe Greene (75), and Browns HB Greg Pruitt exchange words after the game. Pruitt caught one pass for eight yards and gained only six yards on eight carries against the famed "Steel Curtain" defense.

(Left) Late in the second quarter, Pittsburgh Steelers All-Pro middle linebacker Jack Lambert was penalized for unnecessary roughness after a late hit on QB Brian Sipe. Lambert was ejected from the game after the melee at left broke out following the hit.

INDIVIDUAL RECEIVING

STEELERS	No.	Yds.
Swann	5	76
Stallworth	2	68
Grossman	2	25
Bell	1	6

INDIVIDUAL RUSHING

STEELERS	Att.	Yds.
Bleier	13	57
Harris	5	41
Thornton	5	38
Deloplaine	3	34
Bradshaw	1	0
Kruczek	1	-2

Cleveland vs. Cincinnati

October 1, 1972
Cleveland-27, Cincinnati-6

Coach Nick Skorich's Cleveland Browns (1-1), handed the Cincinnati Bengals (2-0), their third straight loss in three Stadium appearances, beating the Bengals, 27-6, on Sunday, October 1, 1972, before 81,564. At QB for Cleveland was third-year pro Mike Phipps, who completed 12 of 24 passes for 198 yards. The Browns led 10-3 at halftime, on a Don Cockroft field goal and a two-yard run by Browns HB Leroy Kelly. Following a 38-yard third-quarter field goal by Cockroft, Phipps broke the game open with a 68-yard TD bomb to WR Frank Pitts. Cleveland's final score came when DE Bob Briggs scooped up a Bengal fumble and ran eleven yards for a touchdown. The win put the Browns in a three-way tie for first place in the AFC Central Division with Cincinnati and the Pittsburgh Steelers, but cost Cleveland the services of starting DE Ron Snidow, who left in the fourth quarter with a broken leg. Snidow became the fourth Browns player, joining Joe Jones, Les Sims and Jim Copeland, to suffer a season-ending injury. Kelly, who gained 82 yards on 22 carries, moved into fifth place among all-time NFL rushers with 6,249 career yards.

(Right) Starting Bengal QB Ken Anderson (14), a second-year pro from Augustana College, confers with head coach Paul Brown during the game. After the game, Brown told reporters, "The contest has lost the personal feelings as far as I'm concerned," referring to the famous "feud" between Browns owner Art Modell and Brown, who had served as head coach of the Cleveland Browns from the team's inception in 1945 to after the 1962 season, when he was fired by Modell. Anderson completed 21 passes for 221 yards.

INDIVIDUAL RECEIVING

BROWNS	No.	Yds.
Pitts	4	105
Hooker	4	47
Morin	2	34
Brown K.	1	15
Kelly	1	-5

INDIVIDUAL RUSHING

BROWNS	Att.	Yds.
Kelly	27	83
Brown K.	11	28
Phipps	1	-2

October 7, 1973
Cleveland-17, Cincinnati-10

Two scores by 10-year veteran HB Leroy Kelly helped lead the Cleveland Browns (2-1), to a 17-10 win over the Cincinnati Bengals (2-1), on Sunday, October 7, 1973, before 70,805 at the Stadium. The first six-pointer scored by Kelly, a three-yard, second-quarter run, ended a 10-quarter stretch without a TD for the low-scoring Browns. As Cleveland's offense regained its scoring touch, the Browns defense shut down the Bengal attack, holding Cincinnati running backs HB Essex Johnson and FB Booby Clark, to only 96 net yards on the ground. The defense put constant pressure on Bengals QB Ken Anderson, who completed only 11 of 23 attempts for 177 yards. Anderson was sacked twice and had a pass intercepted by Browns CB Clarence Scott. Cincinnati's only TD came a 60-yard, fourth-quarter pass from Anderson to rookie Isaac Curtis, the receiver's first TD catch as a pro. Kelly, who gained 73 yards on 21 carries, received one of the two game balls awarded after the win. The other went to Browns FB Ken Brown, who rushed for 93 yards on 26 attempts. Browns QB Mike Phipps completed 9 of 18 passes, including four to TE Milt Morin for 32 yards.

INDIVIDUAL RECEIVING

BROWNS	No.	Yds.
Hooker	1	8
Morin	4	32
Brown K.	1	13
Kelly	1	34

INDIVIDUAL RUSHING

BROWNS	Att.	Yds.
Kelly	21	73
Brown K.	26	93
Phipps	4	52
Pruitt	1	-2

(Left) Bengal FB Boobie Clark (35), is brought down by Browns DE Walter Johnson (71). Clark was held to 44 yards on 12 carries.

October 13, 1974 / Cincinnati-34, Cleveland-24

Coach Nick Skorich's Cleveland Browns (1-3), faced the Central Division-leading Cincinnati Bengals (3-1), on October 13, 1974, before 70,897 at the Stadium. Giving up 452 yards in total offense, the Browns suffered their fourth defeat in five games, losing to the Bengals, 34-24. Cincinnati QB Ken Anderson completed 19 of 29 for 278 yards, including scoring passes to WR Charlie Joiner for 65 yards, HB Lenvil Elliott for 28 yards and WR Isaac Curtis for the game-breaker, an 18-yard fourth down pass in the fourth quarter. Anderson also ran for six points. After the game, the Cincinnati quarterback called it his best day ever. Cleveland scored on a nine-yard pass from QB Mike Phipps to TE Milt Morin, a 50-yard bomb from HB Greg Pruitt to WR Gloster Richardson and a 20-yard run by FB Ken Brown. The win gave the Cincinnati Bengals their first victory over the Browns at the Stadium. At halftime, former Browns All-Pro Lou "The Toe" Groza, who was recently elected to the Pro Football Hall of Fame, received his official Hall of Fame ring from Hall of Fame director Dick Gallagher.

(Left) TE Milt Morin (89), scores on a nine-yard pass from QB Mike Phipps, one of three passes Morin caught for 30 yards.

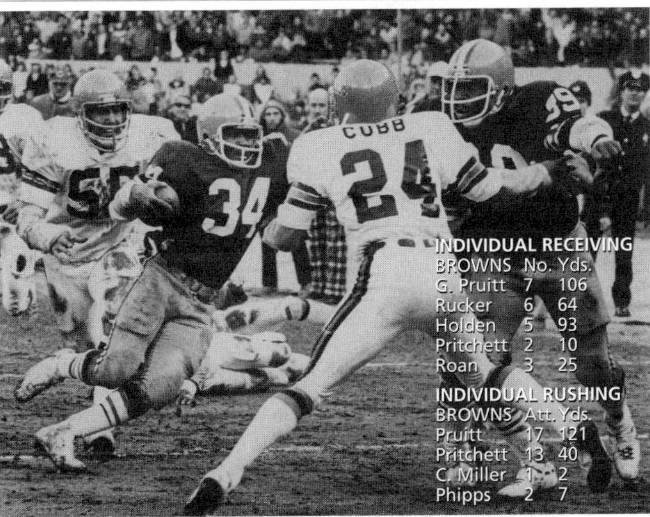

November 23, 1975
Cleveland-35, Cincinnati-23

Sunday, November 23, 1975 was a career day for Cleveland Browns QB Mike Phipps, who passed for over 200 yards for the first time in his pro career, while leading the Browns (0-9), to a 35-23 upset win over the Cincinnati Bengals (8-1). Played before 56,427 at the Stadium, Phipps hit on 23 of 36 attempts for 298 yards, with TD passes to TE Oscar Roan and HB Greg Pruitt. Browns place-kicker Don Cockroft added nine points with field goals of 27, 32 and 43 yards. Cleveland clinched the win in the final period, when safety Jim Hill returned an intercepted pass from Bengal QB John Reaves for a TD. After the game, the game ball was given to rookie head coach Forrest Gregg. It was Gregg's first win as the Browns' leader after nine straight losses.

(Left) HB Greg Pruitt (34), runs against the Bengals. Pruitt gained 121 yards rushing on 17 attempts, caught seven passes for 106 yards, ran back two punts for 41 yards and returned two kickoffs for 36 yards.

September 10, 1978 / Cleveland-13, Cincinnati-10

After beating the San Francisco 49ers, 24-7, in the home opener, the Cleveland Browns returned the next week to face the Cincinnati Bengals on Sunday, September 10, 1978, before 72,691 at the Stadium. Led by HB Greg Pruitt, who rushed 22 times for 120 yards and QB Brian Sipe, who completed 16 of 32 for 219 yards, the Browns rallied from a 10-0 halftime deficit to tie the game in the final period on Sipe's 13-yard TD pass to WR Reggie Rucker. Browns place-kicker Don Cockroft, who kicked an earlier field goal, booted the extra point to force the game into overtime. Cincinnati missed a chance to win as time ran out when Chris Bahr's 37-yard field goal hooked to the left. After winning the coin toss, Browns rookie Larry Collins returned the kickoff to near midfield, giving his team great field position. Sipe moved his club down to the Bengals' 28-yard line on runs by Pruitt, FB Mike Pruitt and an 18-yard sideline pass to rookie TE Ozzie Newsome, who had his face mask grabbed by the Bengals' Ken Riley. On third and five at Cincinnati's 13-yard line, Cockroft nailed a 27-yard field goal for a 13-10 win. HB Archie Griffin led Bengals receivers with six catches for 36 yards. Bengals FB Pete Johnson ran 21 times for 81 yards.

(Right) WR Reggie Rucker (33), hauls in the 13-yard fourth-quarter TD pass from QB Mike Phipps over rookie Bengals DB Louis Breeden. Rucker caught four passes for 77 yards.

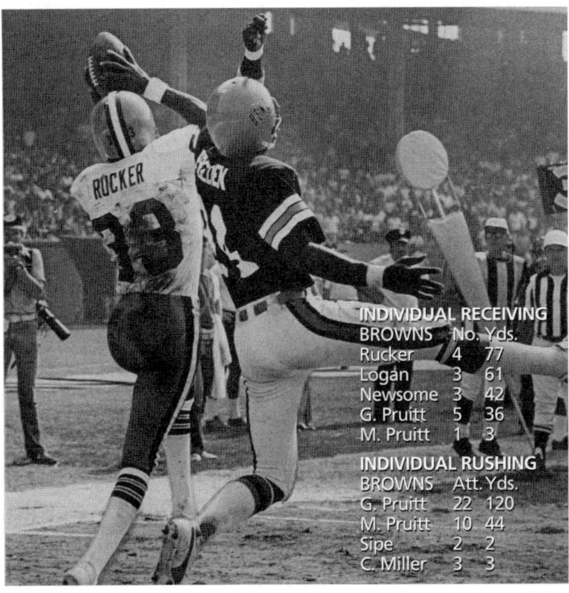

November 18, 1979 / Cleveland-30, Miami-24

The Cleveland Browns (7-4), battled coach Don Shula's Miami Dolphins (7-4), tops in NFL defense, on Sunday, November 18, 1979, before 80,374 at the Stadium. At the half, Cleveland led, 7-3, on a two-yard TD run by former Benedictine High star HB Pat Moriarity. In the third quarter, Miami scored its first TD on a nine-yard run by HB Delvin Williams to lead, 10-7. Cleveland regained the lead, 14-10, on a 14-yard pass from QB Brian Sipe to TE Ozzie Newsome, who made a sensational one-handed grab for the TD. A Don Cockroft field goal gave the Browns a 17-10 lead going into the fourth quarter. In the final period, Miami grabbed the lead, 24-17, on short passes from backup QB Don Strock to Williams and TE Bruce Hardy for scores. With less than four minutes to go, Sipe rallied the "Kardiac Kids" to victory, first throwing 34 yards to Newsome for a TD with only 1:29 left on the clock. Cockroft kicked the extra point to tie the score. After getting the kickoff in OT, Sipe moved his club to Miami's 39 yard line, where he threw to WR Reggie Rucker for a TD and a 30-24 win. Sipe, who broke the 10,000-yard mark in career passing, completed 23 of 42 attempts for 358 yards. Browns FB Mike Pruitt led all rushers with 93 yards on 19 carries. Miami QB Bob Griese completed only 10 of 21 for 115 yards before Strock stepped in.

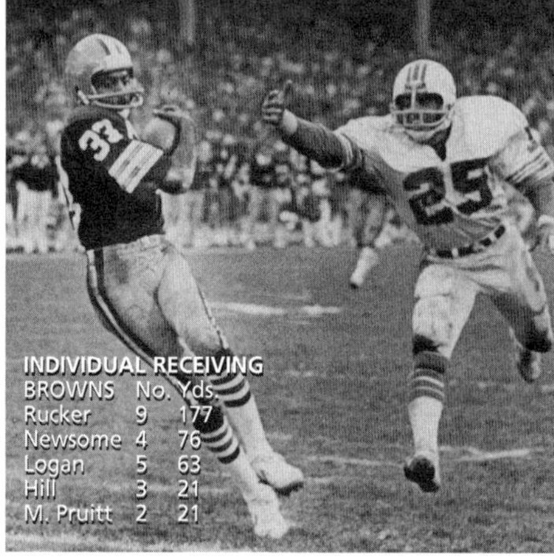

INDIVIDUAL RECEIVING

BROWNS	No.	Yds.
Rucker	9	177
Newsome	4	76
Logan	5	63
Hill	3	21
M. Pruitt	2	21

(Far left) DT Mickey Sims (78), and DT Rich Dimler (92), close in on Miami QB Rob Griese.

(Left) Browns WR Reggie Rucker (37), beats DB Tim Foley (25), on "80-dig," for the winning TD in OT. Rucker was Sipe's favorite receiver with nine catches for 177 yards, five yards short of tying Pete Brewster's team record of 182 yards on seven catches set in 1953.

December 7, 1980
Cleveland-17, N. Y.-14

Played before 78,454 at the Stadium, the Cleveland Browns, with a 9-4 record, faced the 3-11 New York Jets in the last home game of the regular season on December 7, 1980. It was the sixth Stadium sellout in eight home contests for Cleveland's "Kardiac Kids." Cleveland's first score came on a 34-yard second period field goal by Don Cockroft. Browns FB Mike Pruitt scored the next points on a nine-yard run in the third period. New York took a 14-10 lead in the second half on two TD passes by Jets QB Richard Todd. Cleveland rallied to win, 17-14, when QB Brian Sipe threw five yards to HB Greg Pruitt off "85 Option," for a TD. Pruitt, who rushed for 11 yards on three carries, led all receivers with 10 catches for 75 yards, one catch short of Mac Speedie's team record set 28 years before. Though sacked twice by the Jets' Mark Gastineau and Joe Klecko, Sipe set a team record with 30 completions in 41 attempts for 340 yards.

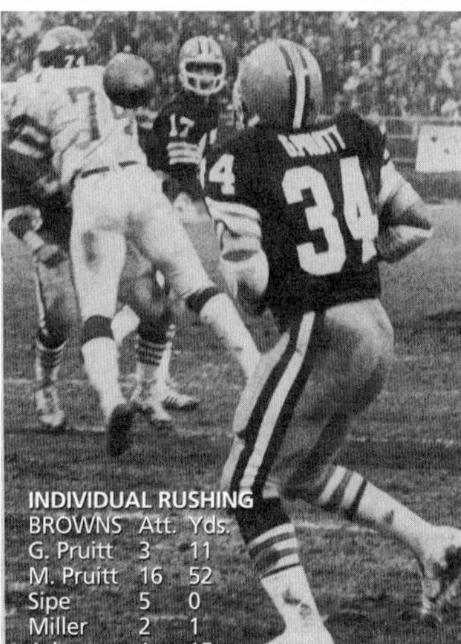

INDIVIDUAL RUSHING

BROWNS	Att.	Yds.
G. Pruitt	3	11
M. Pruitt	16	52
Sipe	5	0
Miller	2	1
Adams	1	15

INDIVIDUAL RECEIVING

BROWNS	No.	Yds.
Logan	6	87
Rucker	5	108
Newsome	3	28
M. Pruitt	6	42
G. Pruitt	10	75

(Above left) Browns LB Clay Matthews celebrates after sacking Jets QB Richard Todd.

(Above, far left) QB Brian Sipe (17), passes to HB Greg Pruitt (34), for the game-winning TD.

(Far left, left) Rooting on Cleveland's "Kardiac Kids."

January 4, 1981
Cleveland vs. Oakland

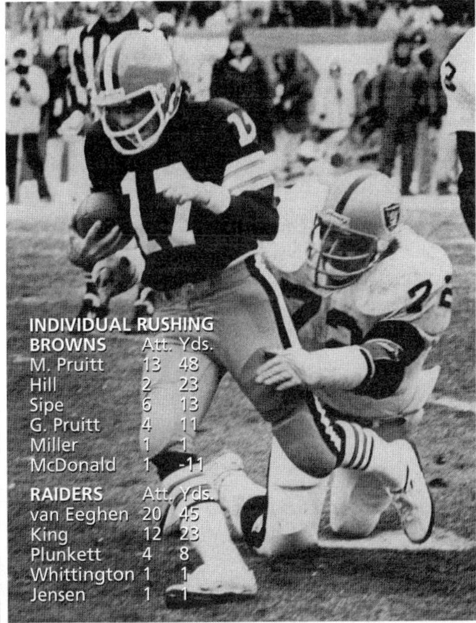

After beating the Cincinnati Bengals in Cincinnati to win their first division crown since 1971, the Cleveland Browns entered the playoffs against the wild-card Oakland Raiders on January 4, 1981, before a soldout crowd of 77,655 at the Stadium. Playing in the coldest playoff game on record since 1967, The Browns scored first to lead 6-0, when CB Ron Bolton returned a pass from Raider QB Jim Plunkett 42 yards for a TD. The extra point was blocked. Oakland countered with the first of two one-yard TD runs by FB Mark van Eeghen to lead, 7-6, at halftime. In the third quarter, two Don Cockroft field goals gave the Browns a 12-7 lead, but van Eeghen scored again in the fourth quarter, putting the Raiders ahead, 14-12, for the win. Plunkett completed 14 of 30 for 149 yards. Browns FB Mike Pruitt led all rushers with 48 yards on 13 carries.

INDIVIDUAL RUSHING

BROWNS	Att.	Yds.
M. Pruitt	13	48
Hill	2	23
Sipe	6	13
G. Pruitt	4	11
Miller	1	1
McDonald	1	-11

RAIDERS	Att.	Yds.
van Eeghen	20	45
King	12	23
Plunkett	4	8
Whittington	1	1
Jensen	1	1

(Top) Game-day nose warmers. **(Above)** Special benches were rented to combat the wind chill temperatures of minus 37°, generated by gusts reaching 28 miles an hour. **(Upper right)** Browns QB Brian Sipe (17), is tackled by Raider DE John Matuszak. Sipe, the NFL's top-rated passer in 1980, completed 13 of 40 attempts for 183 yards. HB Greg Pruitt led Browns receivers with 54 yards on three receptions. TE Ozzie Newsom caught four Sipe passes for 51 yards.

(Right) Browns CB Ron Bolton (28), celebrates with his teammates after scoring on his first quarter interception.

Red Right 88- "The Play"

With only 56 seconds remaining in the game, the Browns, trailing 14-12, had the ball on Oakland's 13-yard line. Head coach Sam Rutigliano chose not to go with a Don Cockroft field goal attempt for the win, but instead chose a pass play, "Red Right 88," designed to have QB Brian Sipe look for TE Dave Logan. But Logan was covered, forcing Sipe to throw toward TE Ozzie Newsome (82). As Sipe released the ball, Oakland safety Mike Davis (with ball), jumped in front of Newsome to intercept the pass, killing Cleveland's last chance for victory.

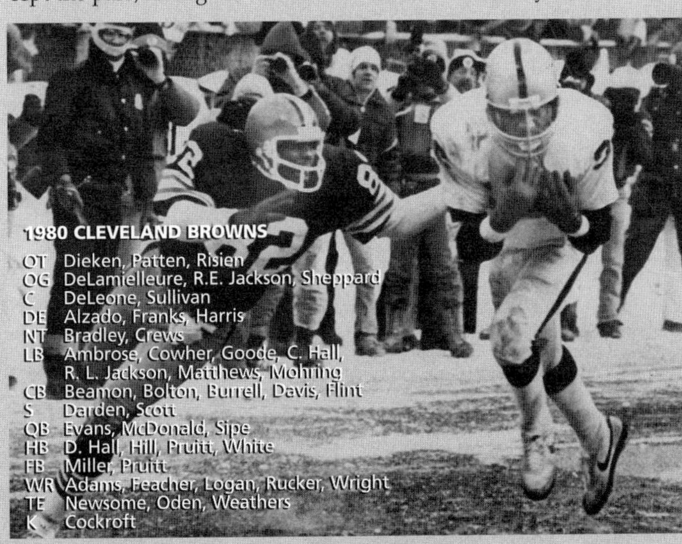

1980 CLEVELAND BROWNS

OT	Dieken, Patten, Risien
OG	DeLamielleure, R.E. Jackson, Sheppard
C	DeLeone, Sullivan
DE	Alzado, Franks, Harris
NT	Bradley, Crews
LB	Ambrose, Cowher, Goode, C. Hall, R. L. Jackson, Matthews, Mohring
CB	Beamon, Bolton, Burrell, Davis, Flint
S	Darden, Scott
QB	Evans, McDonald, Sipe
HB	D. Hall, Hill, Pruitt, White
FB	Miller, Pruitt
WR	Adams, Feacher, Logan, Rucker, Wright
TE	Newsome, Oden, Weathers
K	Cockroft

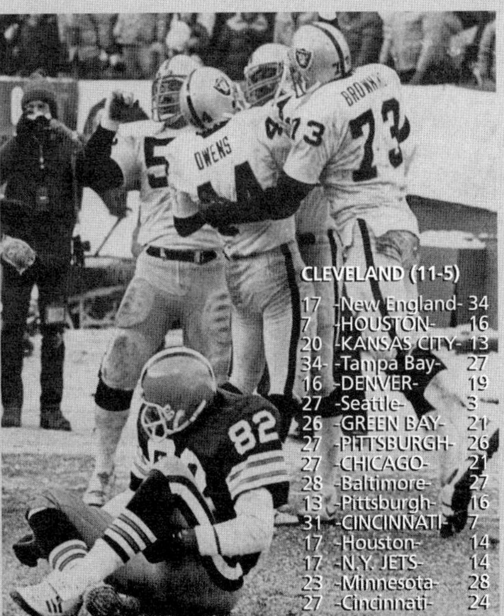

CLEVELAND (11-5)

17	New England-	34
7	HOUSTON-	16
20	KANSAS CITY-	13
34	Tampa Bay-	27
16	DENVER-	19
27	Seattle-	3
26	GREEN BAY-	21
27	PITTSBURGH-	26
27	CHICAGO-	21
28	Baltimore-	27
13	Pittsburgh-	16
31	CINCINNATI-	7
17	Houston-	14
17	N.Y. JETS-	14
23	Minnesota-	28
27	Cincinnati-	24

City High School Championship Football
1931-1970 / The Plain Dealer Charity Game

In 1931, a committee formed by President Herbert Hoover requested that all cities host a charity football game for relief purposes. The Cleveland Plain Dealer, responding to the challenge, announced on October 18, 1931, that a contract had been signed with Stadium Commissioner George H. Bender for such a game to played at the Stadium. On Saturday, November 28, 1931, coach Herb Eisele's Cathedral Latin High eleven, winners of the Catholic League, battled coach Frank Civeletto's Senate League-winning Central High squad for the city scholastic football title. Twelve area marching bands added to the pageantry of the first Charity Game, which was viewed by 19,304, a record scholastic game turnout. Cathedral Latin, gaining 140 yards rushing and 70 more passing, won, 18-0, on TDs by Eddie Mahon, Vince McDonough and Bob Dreamann. Among the spectators was Bishop Joseph Schrembs, head of the Cleveland Catholic Diocese, who saw his first football game. "When I went to school, everyone played rugby," Schrembs told reporters. Game proceeds, raised from the sale of $1 general admission tickets or $3 and $5 patrons' boxes, provided holiday meals for over 1,500 needy families through the newspaper's Give-A-Christmas Fund.

YEAR	DATE		CITY CHAMPION	OPPONENT	ATTENDANCE	GAME STAR (S)
1931	Nov. 28[1]		Cathedral Latin- 18	Central High- 0	19,304	Vince McDonough, Jimmy Farasey, Cath. Latin
1932	Nov. 26		Cathedral Latin- 13	Collinwood- 0	25,274	Johnny Koprowski, Cathedral Latin
1933	Dec. 2		South High- 7	Shaker Heights- 0	19,985	Dominic Di Santo; Leonard Janiak, South
1934	Dec. 1	(tie)	West High- 0	Shaker Heights- 0	25,235	Pat Brooks, Shaker; Elmer Gedeon, West
1935	Nov. 30		Collinwood- 21	Holy Name- 6	24,768	Paul Lundblad, Collinwood
1936	Nov. 28	(tie)	Cathedral Latin- 0	Cleveland Hts.- 0	19,000	Joe Prokop, Cath. Latin; Sam Greenwood, Hts.
1937	Nov. 27		John Adams- 19	West Tech- 6	47,315	Nick Barille, John Adams
1938	Nov. 26		Cathedral Latin- 7	West Tech- 0	54,164	Jim Fenton, Cathedral Latin
1939	Nov. 25		John Adams- 31	South High- 6	44,084	Angelo Consolo, John Adams
1940	Nov. 23		Cathedral Latin- 20	West Tech- 6	39,917	Jack Sague, Cathedral Latin
1941	Nov. 29	(tie)	Collinwood- 12	Lincoln High- 12	46,686	L. Romankowski, Lincoln, T. Adamle Collinwood
1942	Nov. 28		Lincoln High- 26	Collinwood- 0	28,077	Gene Slusarski, Lincoln
1943	Nov. 27		Cathedral Latin- 18	Lincoln High- 12	40,582	Ray Rakar, Cathedral Latin
1944	Nov. 25		Cathedral Latin- 33	Lincoln High- 0	52,888	Cliff Oliver, Cathedral Latin
1945	Nov. 24		Cathedral Latin- 13	St. Ignatius- 7	53,356	Tom Lobe, St. Ignatius, Len Lapka, Benedictine
1946	Nov. 23		Cathedral Latin- 35	Holy Name- 6	70,955[2]	Emery Csizma, Cathedral Latin
1947	Nov. 22		Cathedral Latin- 12	James F. Rhodes- 0	57,329	(MVP)[3] Marty Kiousis, Cathedral Latin
1948	Nov. 27		Benedictine- 7	South High- 0	45,117	(MVP) John Turk, South
1949	Nov. 26		St. Ignatius- 13	East Tech- 0	30,227	(MVP) Chuck McMillan, East Tech
1950	Dec. 9	(tie)	St. Ignatius- 14	Benedictine- 14	17,225	(MVP) Jack Siekar, Benedictine
1951	Nov. 24		James F. Rhodes- 21	Collinwood- 14	18,759	(MVP) Frank Guzik, Rhodes
1952	Nov. 14[4]		Benedictine- 26	St. Ignatius- 18	33,689	(MVP) Tom Forrestal, St. Ignatius
1953	Nov. 20		James F. Rhodes- 40	Benedictine- 14	38,058	(MVP) Al Karp, Rhodes
1954	Nov. 19		Cathedral Latin- 13	Holy Name- 0	33,146	(MVP) Jack Goodrich, Cathedral Latin
1955	Nov. 24[5]		Benedictine- 47	St. Ignatius- 6	21,029	(MVP) Tom Rini, Benedictine
1956	Nov. 22		Benedictine- 19	St. Ignatius- 7	21,703	(MVP) Paul Hrisko, Benedictine
1957	Nov. 28		Benedictine- 27	St. Ignatius- 3	31,644	(MVP) Gary Hansley, Benedictine
1958	Nov. 27		Cathedral Latin- 12	St. Ignatius- 6	21,079	(MVP) Mike Wasdovich, Cathedral Latin
1959	Nov. 26	(tie)	Benedictine- 12	John Marshall- 12	23,809	(MVP) Neil James, John Marshall
1960	Nov. 24		John Marshall- 6	Benedictine- 0	31,545	(MVP) Dick Kestner, Benedictine
1961	Nov. 23		Holy Name- 12	Cathedral Latin- 7	29,918	(MVP) Frank Solich, Holy Name
1962	Nov. 22		St. Ignatius- 6	Benedictine- 0	35,320	(MVP) Steve Huntz, St. Ignatius
1963	Nov. 28		Benedictine- 30	St. Ignatius- 16	37,673	(MVP) Jim Yacknow, Benedictine
1964	Nov. 26		St. Ignatius- 48[6]	Benedictine- 6	41,183	(MVP) Brian Dowling, St. Ignatius
1965	Nov. 25		Benedictine- 29	South High- 8	36,202	(MVP) Larry Zelina, Benedictine
1966	Nov. 24		Benedictine- 32	South High- 6	35,327	(MVP) Larry Zelina, Benedictine
1967	Nov. 23		St. Ignatius- 21	Collinwood- 0	27,651	(MVP) Frank Gusich, St. Ignatius
1968	Nov. 28	(tie)	St. Ignatius- 14	John F. Kennedy- 14	17,582	(MVP) Don Pfeil, St. Ignatius

THE CHAMPIONSHIP DOUBLEHEADERS (In 1969 and 1970, Municipal Stadium played host to two title matches on the same day. Following the annual contest between the East Senate and West Senate champions for the city title, the city's Crown Conference champion battled the conference runner-up. In 1971, the city championship game moved to John Marshall High.)

1969	Nov. 15	Benedictine- 18	St. Ignatius- 7	15,671	(MVP) Tim Tyler, St. Ignatius
		St. Joseph- 22	St. Edward- 0		Bob Bobrowski, St. Joseph
1970	Nov. 28	Benedictine- 38	St. Ignatius- 12	10,994	(MVP) James Johnson, Benedictine
		St. Edward- 21	St. Joseph- 14		Dave Mooney, Dan Viglione, St. Edward

First Charity Games were played on Saturday[1]
Highest Charity Game attendance[2]
First Junior Chamber of Commerce Most Valuable Player trophy awarded[3]

Charity Game was moved to Friday night[4]
First Charity Game played on Thanksgiving Day[5]
Most points scored in a city championship game[6]

November 27, 1943 / Cathedral Latin-18 / Lincoln High-12

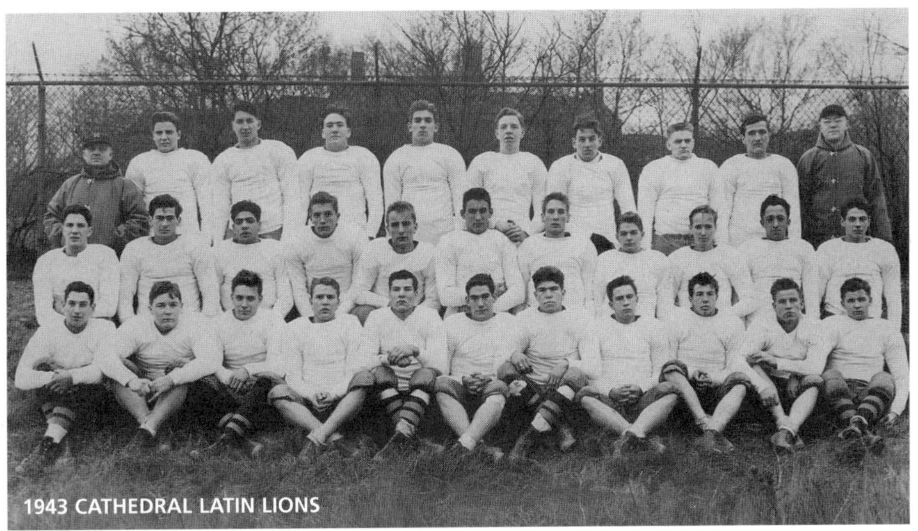

1943 CATHEDRAL LATIN LIONS

The Championship Game

The Lincoln High Presidents saw their undefeated streak stopped at 29 games by an 18-12 upset loss to Cathedral Latin who remained undefeated in six Charity Game appearances. Latin led 12-0 at the half, on 46-yard and 19-yard runs by HB Ray Rakar (first row, far right). Latin's game-winning points came when LT Bill McKeon intercepted a pass from Lincoln LH Don Bania and returned it 38 yards for a TD and an 18-6 Latin lead. Lincoln's two scores came on fourth quarter passes from FB Ray Koscianski to Bania and RE Harold Paul.

November 25, 1944 / Cathedral Latin-33 / Lincoln High-0

The Championship Game

Coach Herb Eisele's powerful Cathedral Latin Lions, led by veterans LT Frank Gaul, RE Bob Malaga, LE Dave Lally, Cliff Oliver and RT Bill McKeon, beat coach Howard Filiere's Lincoln Presidents 33-0 in the 14th Charity Game, continuing their unbeaten streak in city championship competition. Latin held the Presidents, playing in their fourth straight title game, without a first down until the fourth quarter, and held Paul Maximuk (72 below), Lincoln's highly regarded fullback, to only four yards on four carries. QB John Washko, who replaced injured QB Ted Urbanowicz, led Lincoln rushers with 18 yards on four carries. Cathedral Latin gained 306 yards on offense, all on the ground, with LH Bill Feldkircher

1944 CATHEDRAL LATIN LIONS

gaining 52 yards on five carries, and Oliver, Latin's unstoppable 150-pound fullback, rushing 23 times for 176 yards. Oliver scored four of Cathedral Latin's five TDs, one on an interception. Extra point conversations were added by end George Raggets and Malaga, who scored Latin's first TD by running in a punt blocked by McKeon at Lincoln's six yard line. The win gave Cathedral Latin its seventh victory in eight Charity Game appearances. Among the stars for Lincoln were Joe Zielinski, who suffered a broken left leg, Andy Duch and team captain Al Kowalczyk.

1944 LINCOLN PRESIDENTS

1945
ST. IGNATIUS
WILDCATS

The Championship Game

The St. Ignatius Wildcats (8-1-0), of coach Lenny Brickman (upper left), playing in their first city championship game, battled coach Herb Eisele's undefeated Cathedral Latin Lions (8-0-1), in the 15th annual Charity Game. The Lions, seeking their third straight city title, entered the game with a 19-0 season opening win over the Wildcats. St. Ignatius led in almost every category except the score, losing to Latin, 13-7. The Wildcats recorded 12 first downs to Latin's two; 10 rushing first downs to Latin's one; 129 net yards rushing to Latin's 25 and 171 yards in total offense to 109 yards by the Lions. St. Ignatius scored the game's first points in the second quarter when LH Tom Lobe (45), ran three yards for the TD and RH Bob Kilfoyle (21), kicked the extra point. Latin also scored in the second quarter on a 41-yard pass from QB Joe Amato to 6-3 senior LE Len Lapka. RG George Raggets' extra point attempt was blocked, giving St. Ignatius a 7-6 halftime lead. Latin scored their game-winning points in the last seven minutes after Bob Matoney returned a Lobe fumble to the St. Ignatius 20-yard line. After moving the ball to the 14-yard line, substitute Lion QB George Werling passed on fourth down to Lapka, who made a sensational leaping catch over St. Ignatius defender Dave Burkhart to score the winning points. Raggets converted the extra point to give the Lions a 13-7 win. The victory extended Cathedral Latin's unbeaten streak to 24 games over a three-year period.

November 23, 1946 / Cathedral Latin-35 / Holy Name-6

1946
CATHEDRAL
LATIN LIONS

The Championship Game

On Saturday, November 23, 1946, the largest turnout in championship game history, 70,955, paid from 45¢ for student tickets, to $3.60 for reserved seats, to watch the Cathedral Latin Lions of coach Herb Eisele (upper left), battle coach Joe Gavin's Holy Name Green Wave in the 16th Charity Game. After playing Holy Name to a scoreless tie only a month before at the Stadium, Cathedral Latin beat the Green Wave 35-6 on the frozen Stadium turf, extending the school's unbeaten streak to 34 games over a four-year period. Led by the bruising running of senior FB Emery Csizma (77), who gained 167 yards, RH Jerry Beckrest (99), LH George Werling (88), and HB Earl Gentile (75), the Lions gained 296 yards on the ground and scored four of their five TDs by the run. Csizma, Gentile, Werling and QB Bill Petersen (66), all rushed for scores against a Holy Name defense that had allowed only one rushing TD all season. Cathedral Latin's other TD came on a 10-yard pass from Petersen to end Tom Behm (51), for their third score. Sure-footed Latin kicker George Raggets (33), added five extra points. The lone Holy Name touchdown came on a third-quarter pass from QB Tony Ferrante to LE Dick Ziebro.

1947
CATHEDRAL
LATIN LIONS

The Championship Game

The 17th annual Charity Game pitted the returning champion Cathedral Latin Lions, beaten only once and tied twice in their last 44 games, against the James F. Rhodes Rams of coach Andy Moran (second row left, below), who were playing in their first Charity Game contest. Leading the Lions as head coach was Augie Bossu (upper right), in his first year at Cathedral Latin. The Lions continued their unbeaten streak in city championship play by defeating the Rams, 12-0, behind the running of RH Joe Pilla (77), LH Joe Raggets (71), and FB Earl Gentile (75). The Lions gained 140 yards rushing to only 52 net rushing yards for Rhodes, rolling up seven of their nine first downs on the ground. On defense, the Latin Lions shut down Rams QB Bill Putich (45), holding the All-Scholastic passer to only 44 net yards and three first downs passing. Cathedral Latin defenders also intercepted five Rhodes passes. Three Putich passes were picked off by Cathedral Latin's Jerry Mullin (84), with two turned into scores on quarterback sneaks by Latin QB Bill Petersen (66). RH Art Martin (44), the Rams' leading scorer, was held to only 26 yards on 14 carries by the Latin defense. Following the game, a most valuable player was named for the first time in Charity Game history. The Junior Chamber of Commerce Trophy went to senior guard Marty Kiousis (33), who starred for Cathedral Latin on both offense and defense. Runner-up was Rams RE Dick Velotta (63). The win gave Cathedral Latin its ninth win in ten Charity Game appearances. In 1936, the Lions played Cleveland Heights to a scoreless tie.

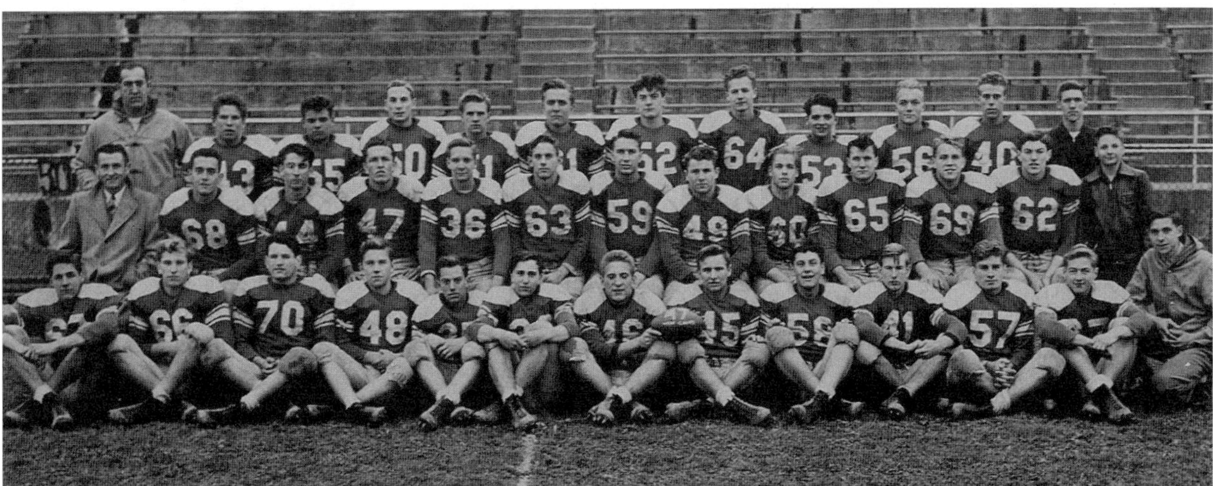

1947 JAMES F. RHODES RAMS

1948 BENEDICTINE BENGALS

The Championship Game

Making their first title game appearance, the East Senate-winning Benedictine Bengals of coach Joe Rufus (second row above left), after knocking the Cathedral Latin Lions out of championship play for the first time since 1942, faced the South High Flyers (6-0), of coach Gene Wolanski (top row right, below), in the 18th Charity Game. South was vying for the title for the first time since losing to John Adams nine years earlier. Led by game MVP John Turk (33), and QB John Golembieski (24), who passed for 70 yards and ran for 16 more, South battled Benedictine to a 0-0 tie over the first 47 minutes of play. With seconds remaining and the ball on the South 22-yard line, Benedictine QB Gil Verderber (60), after faking a hand-off to RH Ed Belin (88), dropped back to pass from the South 40 yard line, but found his primary receivers Eddie Stakolich (59), and Ray Borovich (58), covered. Verderber threw instead to Bengals FB Jim McNeely (70), who made a leaping catch in the end zone to pull in the winning TD. Belin added the extra point to cement the victory. After the game, Rufus remarked, "They outplayed us in the first half. They've got a good line. In fact the line play on both sides was terrific. Guard Chuck Noll (32), played a great game for us. So did Belin and Verderber and tackle Ed Powell (44). Oh, they all played a great game." Bengals LH Jim Liberatore (99), led all rushers with 77 yards on 32 carries. HB Wally Polcyn (37), led the Flyers with 43 yards on eight carries.

1948 SOUTH FLYERS

1949
ST. IGNATIUS
WILDCATS

The Championship Game

Playing in their first city championship game, the East Tech Artisans of coach Paul Anderson (third row right, below), were in search of their first undefeated season since 1930 when they faced the St. Ignatius Wildcats of coach Fred George (third row left, above), in the 19th annual Charity Game. St. Ignatius picked up its first points when FB Paul Brubeck (12), who led all rushers with 48 yards on 18 carries, scored on a one-yard, first quarter run. John Gill (47), kicked the extra point for a 7-0 lead. Artisan QB Ed Bilinovich (20), who led all passers with 10 completions for 103 yards, drove East Tech to the St. Ignatius four-yard line late in the first half, but failed to score when HB Ray Mickshaw (35), was stopped by the Wildcats on fourth down at the two-inch line. St. Ignatius scored for the final time in the fourth quarter when end Larry Dolan (top right), threw a 42-yard TD pass to QB Don McLaughlin (16). The 13-0 victory gave St. Ignatius its first city championship title, becoming the second West Side school to capture the scholastic crown since Lincoln High beat Collinwood, 26-0, in 1942.

1949 EAST TECH ARTISANS

(Editor's note: The Cleveland News referred to East Tech as the Artisans in its November 17, 1949 newspaper, but called East Tech the Scarabs on November 18th. The Cleveland Press referred to East Tech as the Scarabs, but The Plain Dealer called East Tech the Artisans in articles published before and after the Charity Game. I chose the Artisans, the nickname used by the Charity Game sponsors.)

(Left) Collinwood FB Dom Grassie eludes Frank Guzik of Rhodes for a 10-yard gain in the first quarter after taking the handoff from QB Dom Pannitto (48). A 36-yard run by Grassie in the early minutes of the game set up a three-yard run by HB Joe Trivisonno for Collinwood's first touchdown.

The Championship Game

Hoping to become the third West Side school to win the city scholastic football title, the undefeated and untied Rhodes High Rams of coach Andy Moran faced coach Frank Lauterbur's Collinwood Railroaders in the 21st Charity Game. After Collinwood HB Joe Trivisonno scored the first of two TDs, FB Bob Kurtz (84), caught the kickoff and flipped the ball to HB John Budko (75), who who raced 74 yards for the Rams' first score. Rams end Frank Guzik (85), scored the school's next TD on a 40-yard pass from QB Don Kasner (second row, fifth from left), to give Rhodes a 14-7 lead. Early in the fourth quarter, a wild lateral from Collinwood QB Dom Pannitto to FB Dom Grassie was recovered by Rhodes at the Collinwood five yard line. Rams HB Tony Rocco (61), ran the ball in to give Rhodes a 21-7 lead. Rocco also kicked the Rams' three extra points. Trivisonno, who gained 137 yards rushing, scored his second TD in the final minutes, closing the final score to 21-14. The Rhodes High Rams captured their first city title with the win.

1951 JAMES F. RHODES RAMS

The Championship Game

After battling the St. Ignatius Wildcats to a 14-14 tie in the 1950 title game, the Benedictine Bengals faced St. Ignatius again in the 22nd annual Charity Game. Benedictine beat the Wildcats of first-year coach John Wirtz, 26-18, to win the school's second city title in five years. Bengal TDs were scored by FB Jerry Bush (2), who ran for 214 yards on 22 carries, QB George Schmidt and RB Bob Konkoly. St. Ignatius QB Tom Forrestal, who beat Bush for MVP honors, completed 13 passes for 186 yards, including TD passes to Dan Stringer and Terry Conway. Stringer scored the final Wildcat TD on a one-yard plunge in the second half.

(Above left) Victorious Benedictine High head coach Joe Rufus is carried off the field after the game. **(Above)** Benedictine's Jerry Bush throws a perfect block to take out Jim Lavelle (80), as Bob Konkoly (75), eludes Wildcat defenders Jerry Porter (17), Norm Prosser (66), and Joe Mawby (16), for an 18-yard gain. Bush scored the game's first TD on the next play. Konkoly, who rushed 15 times for 141 yards, caught the TD pass that led to the 14-14 tie in the 1950 title game. Bush and Konkoly combined for 355 yards rushing.

1955 BENEDICTINE BENGALS

The Championship Game

Head coach Augie Bossu (far left standing, above), was in his first year as the school's head football coach when his undefeated Benedictine Bengals met the St. Ignatius Wildcats of coach John Wirtz (third row right, below), in the 25th annual Charity Game, the first title classic held on Thanksgiving Day. Led by QB Mel Smolik (55), and senior HB Tom Rini (77), who rushed for 99 yards on 13 carries, Benedictine amassed a total of 407 yards on offense, with 363 coming on the ground. Paced by Rini, who scored three times, the Bengals won 47-6, racking up a Charity Game record seven TDs. HB Ray Hudiak (66), scored on a four-yard run in the second period to give Benedictine a 13-0 lead. In the second half, FB Fred Yarris (90), who gained 89 yards on seven carries, raced 61 yards for six points after Chuck Reynolds (44), set up the score by recovering a St. Ignatius fumble at the Benedictine 44-yard line. Sophomore HB Gary Hansley (70), who ran four times for 103 yards, scored on a 74-yard run to give Benedictine a 40-6 lead. Minutes later, sophomore HB George Sefcik (95), scored the Bengals' final TD on a 14-yard run. Sefcik also kicked four extra points. St. Ignatius, held without a first down in the first half, scored in the third quarter when QB Jack O'Brien (fourth row, second from right), connected with end Tom O'Malley (13), on a 71-yard pass play. The win gave Benedictine High its fourth undefeated season and the first of three straight scholastic football titles.

**1955
ST.
IGNATIUS
WILDCATS**

November 28, 1957 / Benedictine-27 / St. Ignatius-3

The Championship Game

The Cleveland Press sports page headline read, "Bengals City's Best Ever," after head coach Augie Bossu's Benedictine Bengals, ranked No. 1 in the state by The Associated Press, beat the St. Ignatius Wildcats, 27-3, in the 27th Charity Game. St. Ignatius scored first on Chuck Baloga's 20-yard, first quarter field goal to lead, 3-0, at halftime. In the second half, it was all Benedictine, as the Bengals rallied to score 20 points in the first eleven minutes of the third period on 14-yard and one-yard runs by senior HB Gary Hansley and a one-yard run by senior HB George Sefcik. Hansley, the game MVP, rushed for 81 yards on 19 carries. Benedictine scored again in the fourth quarter as Hansley raced three yards for his third TD of the game. The win gave Benedictine High, the first district team to play with numbers on their helmets, their fifth perfect season and third straight city championship.

(Above) Benedictine HB Gary Hansley (50), scores the second of his three TDs on a one-yard plunge with help from team-mates Ray Baumbick (24), and Stan Sczurek (31). Among the St. Ignatius defenders trying to stop Hansley are Mike Reitz (79), and Fred Oblak (95). It was the Wildcats' third straight loss to the Bengals in city championship play. The undefeated Benedictine Bengals became the first local school to finish on top of both the final United Press Board of Coaches statewide scholastic football poll and The Associated Press state high school football poll.

November 27, 1958 / Cathedral Latin-12 / St. Ignatius-6

The Championship Game

Coach Fred George's undefeated Cathedral Latin Lions captured the school's 12th city title in 26 years with a 12-6 win over coach John Wirtz's St. Ignatius Wildcats. The Wildcats' tenacious defense held Cathedral Latin HB Leo Caito to less than a yard a carry, but FB Carl Pikus picked up much of Caito's load, averaging seven yards a carry. Pikus also punted four times, averaging 42.2 yards per punt. Cathedral Latin's two scores came on a 38-yard screen pass from QB Norb Rascher to Jim Barrett in the second quarter and a one-yard run by Caito in the fourth period. Caito's game-winning score came after a bad snap on a Wildcat punt gave Latin the ball on the St. Ignatius 20-yard line. Pikus ran 19 yards to the one-yard line, setting up Caito, who took it over for the score. The lone St. Ignatius touchdown came in the third period when E Jim Caloferas raced 38 yards for the score after intercepting a Rascher screen pass.

(Above) St. Ignatius HB Mike Hegan is hauled down on the frigid Stadium turf after picking up short yardage. Latin tackle Wayne Urban leaps over Wildcat FB Ken Lutke as Tom Wasdovich (58), the game MVP, and St. Ignatius co-captain Tim Gautner (80), watch in the background. Hegan, the game's busiest rusher, gained 42 yards on 14 attempts. Wasdovich, Latin's 230-pound All-Senate senior tackle, played much of the game with an injured shoulder.

The Championship Game

Coach Sam Ruvolo's Cathedral Latin Lions, unbeaten in 12 previous city title battles, faced coach Carl Falivene's Holy Name Green Wave (9-0-1) in the 31st annual Plain Dealer City Championship game. With 5-6, 150-pound tailback Frank Solich leading the way, Holy Name beat the Lions, 12-7, handing Latin its first loss in Charity Game play. Solich scored both Green Wave TDs on an eight-yard run in the first period and a 50-yard dash with less than seven minutes left in the game. Solich, who rushed for 184 yards, also made a game-saving tackle with Don Konopka to stop a fourth and one sweep by Latin's Rick Myslenski at the Holy Name 12-yard line. The win gave the Green Wave their first high school football championship after four tries.

(Right) The Green Wave celebrate after the win. The play of Solich (No. 12, front and center with ball), was called one of the title game's single greatest performances.

The Championship Game

Played before 37,673, the largest Stadium gathering to watch the Plain Dealer City Championship Game since 1953, coach Augie Bossu's underdog Benedictine Bengals upset the unbeaten and 5th-ranked St. Ignatius Wildcats, 30-16. Before the half ended, the Wildcats lost the services of starting QB Brian Dowling (3 of 8, 48 yards), who left with a broken collar bone. Helping lead the Bengals to victory were HB John Sanders, who rushed for 122 yards on 17 carries; captain Bob Zelina at FB, who scored on a one-yard run; HB Greg Betts, who scored on a 43-yard pass from QB Joe Palagyi; and end Jim Yacknow, the game MVP, who scored on a 46-yard pass from junior HB Greg Marn, who surprised the Wildcats with his passing. St. Ignatius scored on TDs by HB Don Ross and end Tom Furlong. After the win, Bossu told reporters that the game had been dedicated to Eddie Beskid, a star athlete who died in a farm accident during the summer.

(Above) Benedictine HB Greg Marn (99), launches a second-quarter pass from his own 15 yard line. In pursuit are St. Ignatius defenders E Tom Furlong (96), and G Mike Ginley (99). Marn completed three of four passes for 97 yards. Marn also ran for 93 yards and scored a Bengal TD on a three-yard run. HB Don Ross gained 144 yards on 18 carries for St. Ignatius.

The Championship Game

After a loss to Benedictine High in the 1963 Charity Game, a determined St. Ignatius squad returned to battle coach Augie Bossu's Benedictine Bengals on November 26, 1964 in the eighth championship meeting between the two schools. St. Ignatius captured the school's 29th victory in the last 30 games, beating the Bengals in convincing fashion, 48-6. Two-time All-Scholastic QB Brian Dowling, credited with calling 95% of the team's plays on offense, led the Wildcats by tossing four TD passes and scoring twice on 71-yard and two-yard runs. HB Jim Grace caught two Dowling TD passes, the others going to HB Dan Milligan and E Tom Drabik. A three-yard run by Grace and six PATs by Rick Rose accounted for the other St. Ignatius points. Dowling completed 14 of 21 passes, including eight in the first half, for 180 yards. Benedictine HB Greg Marn, who carried 15 times for 48 yards and completed four of nine passes for 72 yards, scored the Bengals' only TD on a three-yard run in the fourth quarter. The St. Ignatius team later presented an autographed game ball to the widow of popular Wildcats line coach Ab Strosnider, who passed away less than a month before the title match. The St. Ignatius players wore black arm-bands in memory of their coach. Wirtz reportedly told his players, "If the going gets tough, just look the arm bands and remember what they represent."

(Above) Jubilant St. Ignatius players celebrate after beating the Bengals. In the center is head coach John Wirtz who said, "This is by far the best football team I've ever coached." Game MVP, QB Brian Dowling, is No. 15 lower right.

(Left) St. Ignatius coach John Wirtz is carried off the field after the game. Players left to right are Jim Bunsey (20), Phil Murphy (58), Mike Duffin (38), and Rick Rose (11).

(Above) Benedictine HB Glen Novak (95), scores his second touchdown of the game on a one-yard, fourth-quarter run with South defenders E Jim Ciesla (67), and LB Mickey Gallegos (27), in pursuit. The TD gave the Bengals a 27-0 lead. Benedictine scored its final points on a two-point conversion pass from teammate Bill Scanlon to Novak. Tickets for the championship ran 60¢ (students), $1 (upper reserved sold only in advance), $1.50, $2.50 and $3.50.

The Championship Game

Coach Augie Bossu's Benedictine Bengals, ranked 7th in the state, were making their 13th championship game appearance when they faced coach John Gentile's South Flyers in the 35th annual Plain Dealer City Championship game. Led by the rushing tandem of halfbacks Glen Novak (15 carries, 95 yards), and junior Larry Zelina (14 carries, 101 yards), who each scored twice, Benedictine jumped to a 14-0 lead at halftime, scoring two TDs in the last three minutes of the second quarter. The Bengals added 15 points in the second half to win, 29-8. Bengals QB Jim Betts passed for 75 yards, completing 4 of 7, including a 49-yard pass to Zelina and two passes for 19 yards to Novak. The Benedictine defense held sophomore QB Don Lampka to 111 yards passing (7 of 19), and shut down the Flyers' running game, allowing South only 54 yards on 23 attempts. South's lone TD came in the final minute on a four-yard run by FB Mickey Gallegos, set up by a bomb from Lampka to Jeff Kaczmarek. A two-point conversion pass from Lampka to E Jim Ciesla scored South's final points. After the game, Bossu called his 1965 squad one of the best, with more team depth than his 1957 state champions. The victory gave the Bengals their seventh city scholastic football title and their 10th win in the last eleven outings. Benedictine returned to the city championship game in 1966, beating South, 32-6, before 35,327 at the Stadium. Zelina carried 19 times for 152 yards.

(Right) HB Larry Zelina, the Charity Game MVP, ended the 1965 season as the top scholastic scorer in Ohio with 210 points and 30 touchdowns. The following year, Zelina became the only player to win the city championship Most Valuable Player award twice. Among the guests watching Zelina play in the 1965 Charity Game was Ohio State University head football coach Woody Hayes. Zelina later played football for Hayes at Ohio State.

HB Larry Zelina

PHOTOGRAPH CREDITS

The Cleveland Press newspaper operated as an afternoon daily in various formats from Nov. 2, 1878 to June 17, 1982. The photographs found in this book salute the work done by these former Cleveland Press photographers.

Frank Aleksandrowicz
Fred Bottomer
Timothy Culek
Van Dillard
Byron Filkins
Walter Kneal
Clayton Knipper
Ron Kuntz
Bud Nash
Bill Nehez
Larry Nighswander
Bernie Noble
Frank Reed
Ted R. Schneider, Jr.
Herman Seid
Paul Tepley
James Thomas
Bob Tomsic
Tony Tomsic
Paul Toppelstein
Louis Van Oeyen
Glenn Zahn

Information on specific photographs can be obtained by contacting Instant Concepts at (440) 891-1964.

March, 1956

Cleveland Press sports photographer Fred Bottomer chats with Cleveland Indians southpaw Herb Score as spring training begins at Hi Corbett Field in Tucson, Arizona.